STOCKTON ON TEES

(including Thornaby, Yarm, Norton & Billingham)

A COLOURFUL PAST

Days of long ago in South Durham and North Yorkshire

I would like to dedicate this book to the late Peter Brack who would have enjoyed this book so much
Lara, James, Seb & Florence and the ever smiling Carol Wilson

First Edition 2025

ISBN 978 1 7398194 4 6

The information in this book is true and complete to the best of our knowledge. All recommendations are made without any guarantee on the part of the Publisher, who also disclaims any liability incurred in connection with the use of specific details or content within this book.

printed in China

British Library Cataloguing-in-Publication Data
A catalogue record for this book is available from the British Library.

Published by Destinworld Publishing Ltd.
www.destinworld.com

FSC
MIX
Paper
FSC® C145202

CONTENTS:

Gathering outside the Black Bull, Yarm

A Technical Note

There are many methods available now to convert a black and white image to a colour image. Most of these provide an efficient way to do a task which only a few years ago would have been regarded as work for a digital art or graphic designer specialist.

However whilst many of these methods provide a 'passable' colour conversion for a more versatile and custom finished product, there is greater control and adaptation available if one of the specialist programs is used, for example Adobe Photoshop.

The images in this book have all been completed using Adobe Photoshop 2024. This allows manipulation of the content and in particular, restoration of sources including both images and text . **The developments of AI has had a marked effect on this process enabling breathtaking results.**

The process includes a number of stages:

i: conversion to black and white of the image as this allows easier examination

ii: basic cleaning of the image to remove any scratches or other damage that has been incurred over time. An image clean to the naked eye can be covered in scratches when it is closely examined using digital magnification.

iii: restoration of any missing areas is undertaken - if suitable. Nothing is added that wouldn't be there in the original image but it is possible to put back missing areas of an image perhaps working at individual pixel level. Where text is involved this may even include replacing individual letters.

iv: colour restored or colour conversion is undertaken once the image has been repaired or restored. This will often require considerable research to ensure that the correct color or the nearest match possible is found.

v: final stages include any adjustment to basic presentation for example clarity or dehazing, shadow and custom white spot check are among the many procedures that are able to be used here.

The above stages can take an hour or even several days to complete and often it may be necessary to begin the whole process again. The result can be very revealing of details ranging from 'much improved' to astounding.

Ultimately judgement will always be personal but whatever your thoughts we have the tools to produce enhanced images beyond our imagination and this can only add to our capability to understand our past.

Finally - I have tried to ensure that there are no errors in this work. Ultimately the work is my interpretation but like history this is always evolving so if there are any errors please let me know.

Leven Bridge 1946

Introduction

Welcome to a journey back in time, where the past becomes as vivid as the present. Recent technological advancements in image management have revolutionised the way we repair, restore, and enhance visual content. These innovations not only restore images and text but bring us closer to the reality of the times they depict. The key to this transformative journey is color restoration, offering a window into the world as seen by the photographers of yesteryear.

Image restoration and colorisation involve processes like repairing surface scratches, removing stains, replacing missing parts, and adding realistic color. Previously, these tasks were exploratory, challenging, and time-consuming. However, with the advent of advanced techniques, I was inspired in 2022 to create 'Middlesbrough: A Colorful Past' – a three-hundred-page collection of restored and colorised images, presenting the past as vividly as our grandparents experienced it.

The response to the book was extraordinary, transforming people's perceptions of local history and offering a new way to view the past. A two-week display in central Middlesbrough to celebrate the book, extended to three months due to popular demand. It attracted record numbers, including people brought specifically to see the display. It was admired as it toured around the region.

Encouraged by this reception, I decided to restore and present more of the work I had documented over the past four decades. This effort culminated in a companion volume, completing the historical coverage of the lower Tees Valley. With the latest advancements, particularly in Artificial Intelligence (AI), image management has surpassed the advances of 2022, enhancing both the range and precision of restoration techniques. A range of restoration techniques delivered with speed and accuracy. Armed with these new tools, I set out once more to revive the past, bringing history to life over three-hundred pages in a way that was unimaginable even in 2022.

'Stockton A Colourful Past' is the result. Your window to enjoying yesterday's world today, is ready to open.

Acknowledgements

This book covers a lifetime of research; my grateful thanks to all those individuals and organisations since 1977 have allowed me to access their material, given of their time and generally helped or supported my research. Inevitably over 47 years, some people are no longer with us, whilst other people have moved on to different roles now (so I can only refer to their role when they helped me).

A thank you to the late Len Whitehouse, Reverend W. Wright, Freda Bell-Moulang, George McDougall, Julian Philips, Kenneth Warne, Arthur, Arnold & Winifred Dent, Leslie Dixon, Adrian Ward-Jackson, Peter Brack, David Tyrell (Teesside Archives) Donald Blakely and Helen Hay.

From organisations I would like to thank Mark Rowland-Jones & Jo Faulkner at Stockton on Tees Borough Council Museums Service, Steve Wild at Stockton Reference Library, the now defunct Cleveland County Council Planning Department, Steve Hearn at the Ordnance Survey, Julian Harrop (Beamish Museum), all staff at Middlesbrough Reference Library especially Larry Bruce & Jenny Parker.

In particular, I cannot thank Samantha Clarke enough for always giving her help, time and encouragement over the past two years. There are many people from 1977 onwards at Teesside Archives – Janet Baker, Anne Thirsk, Stuart Pacitto, Anne Hill, Debbi Stalwarts, Kimberley Starkie, Corrie Dales and the excellent leader Ruth Hobbins. Similarly at the Dorman Museum thanks for so much help 35 years, thanks to Phil Philo, Louise Harrison, Gill Moore. My research at the Evening Gazette 1982-2017 – I owe thanks to Alan Sims, Paul Delplanque, Dave Robson, Joanne Welford, Chris Styles and all who looked after me so well during my years there. Thanks also to Scott Makin (BBC Tees) and John Foster, Bob Fisher, Diane Youdale & Neil Green (ex- BBC Tees). I thank the following for their incredible support: Trevor Miles (my first literary agent 40 years ago), Matilda Richards, Alan McKinnell, Colin Riley, Dave Summerfield, Glen Arno, Tommy Stafford , Simon Crabtree, Margaret McManus, Janice Foley, Dave Cannings, Dr Peter Fletcher. Finally special thanks to Andrew Stoves (material on the S&D Railway) & Craig Willis, Jonathan Groom, the late John Pollock (material on Thornaby Airfield). Craig and Andrew spent many hours patiently sharing their material with me. Other sources are my own collection. If I've missed anyone I apologise - please know I send my gratitude.

Finally the amazing Matt Falcus and Destinworld for allowing me not only write this book but to do all of the graphic design work too.

It was quite a journey.

Stockton Castle

The Boldon Book notes in 1183 that Stockton was one of several small settlements in the parish of Norton. There is also reference to a fortified manor house (close to the river to the south) for the use of the Bishop of Durham primarily for social and residential purposes. Modern excavations suggest a structure similar to this with four main towers probably linked by blocks containing residential facilities. King John stayed there in 1214 when he signed a charter for the burgesses at Newcastle. By 1376 it was known as Stockton Castle with further development taking place in the fifteenth century. Soldiers were garrisoned there in 1543 following the Pilgrimage of Grace and again in 1640 when Royalist forces were placed there. The castle remained a Royalist stronghold during the Civil War until it was taken by the Scots in 1644 under the Earl of Callendar, after the Battle of Marston Moor. In 1647 by Order of Parliament the building was destroyed except for the castle barn (later described as a 'castellated cowhouse'), which survived until its demolition on 29 June 1865.

Stockton... a town with history

Stockton is a town known by name at least, throughout the world because of its role in the history of railways. The famous High Street is another well known aspect of the town but how many people for example know Stockton once had a castle? Then there is John Walker and the invention of the 'friction light' - or matches to you and I! Or that Signor Paganini once performed here - as did Buddy Holly and the Beatles. Famous cricketer John Wisden once played here too and Stockton FC could once claim to be the best amateur football team in the land! The town of Stockton has a rich tapestry of events to celebrate as we look at 'a town with history'.

Stockton-on-Tees in the 18th Century

1724.—A map of Stockton was taken this year by Thos. Pattison. Various alterations have since been made in the names of streets, &c. Castle-gate has taken the place of Boat-house or Ferry lane (afterwards Cooke's wynd), and Ramsgate of Taggy lane; South and North-streets have yielded to Silver and Bishop-streets, and Douthwaite's buildings (afterwards the Ropery) are now named Paradise Row. The sites of the old Tolbooth and Market Cross are now occupied by the Town-house and Doric Column.

18th century Stockton......

The view opposite of Stockton in the eighteenth century looks towards the Bishop's Landing Place and area east of the High Street.

The eighteenth century was a time when there was evidence that the town was gaining economic confidence - certainly it was starting to prosper helped in particular by improved trade links with London and Northern Europe.

Establishing these links meant that ships carrying lead, wool and hides from North Yorkshire brought back imports of timber and other raw materials to be used in Cleveland's thriving linen industry in particular.

Other trade prospered too. Agricultural products including the fine quality wheat grown locally meant that in 1718 for example, seventy-five corn ships entered the port of London from Stockton - more than from Hartlepool and Sunderland combined.

This was a time of rebuilding and development within the town too including a new road linking Finkle Street and Castlegate built in 1706. Silver and Bishop Streets also date from this time. In 1730 the Customs Office, having already moved to the Red Lion Yard in Stockton from Hartlepool in 1696, found a more permanent home close by the river. The £150 building costs were funded by the Corporation.

The Town House, built in 1735, dominates the skyline along with the Parish Church.

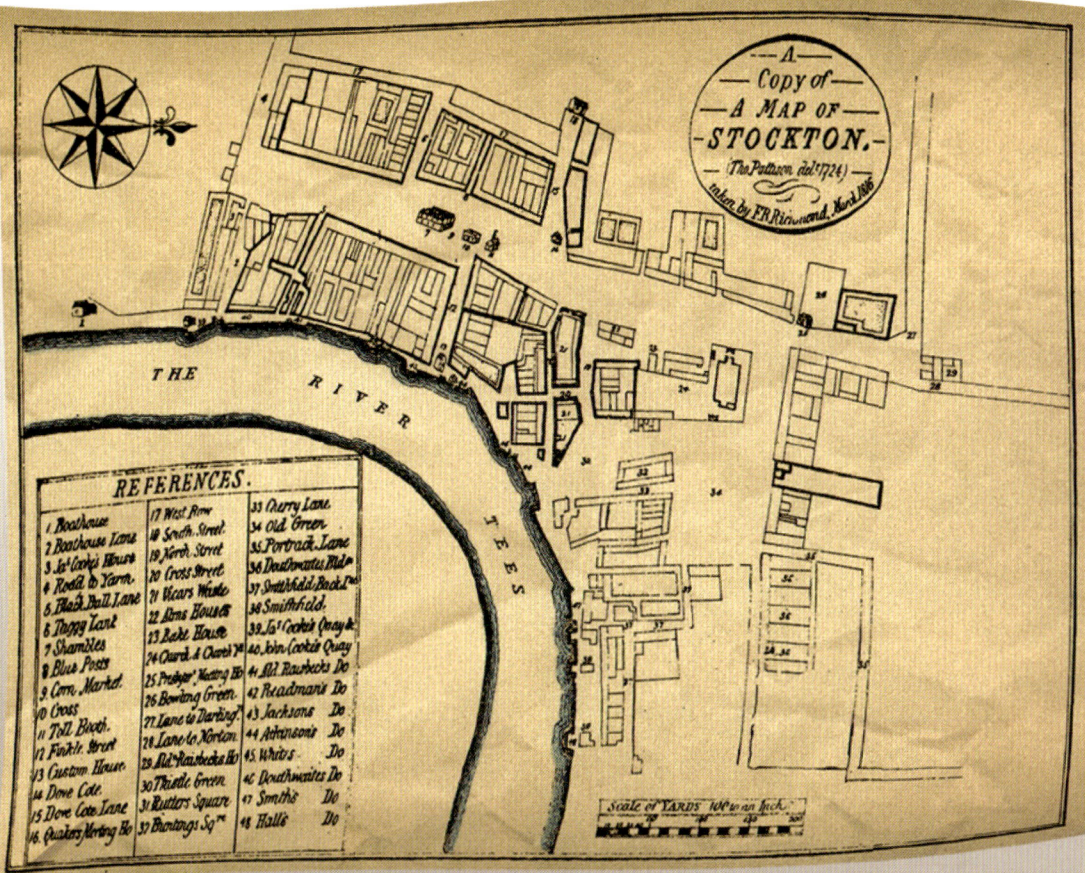

Thomas Pattison's plan of 1724 shows the full extent of Stockton at that time. West Row marked the western limit of the town. Travelling south meant using the ferry - the boathouse is clearly marked, or travelling via Park Row, Yarm Lane (close to the boundary at the end of the High Street) & then Yarm Bridge. The Tollbooth with its small shops leased by the Bishop of Durham stands in the High Street close to the old market cross. Finkle Street and the Custom House are part of the development close to the river. The medieval 'Dove Cote' stands at the entrance to 'Dove Cote Lane'. Old Green and the road east to Portrack via Portrack Lane are visible close to the Parish Church, as is Thistle Green.

Ralph Jackson...extraordinary diarist of ordinary eighteenth century life

THE DIARIES OF RALPH JACKSON

JOURNAL N
OCTOBER 1768 - AUGUST 1770

Ralph Jackson of Guisborough and later Normanby Hall, wrote a diary from 1749 to 1790. His daily entries provide a wonderful record of eighteenth-century life locally and further afield. Many entries feature the town of Stockton as records of business and social affairs provide a 'window' on life in the town at that time.

From Jackson's words it is evident that Stockton was growing in importance. The town's increasing status means there are regular visits attending to business affairs, visiting Stockton Market or the Hirings. There are details of many social occasions including the popular Stockton Race meetings, or just meeting citizens of the town.

Important events are also noted. The opening of the new bridge at Stockton (Journal N: Oct 1768 to Aug 1779: 5 October 1768) would impact greatly on the future of Stockton and Yarm too but it had however, a more personal relevance for Jackson in providing easier access to Stockton. He had written several times on problems getting to Stockton including 5 February 1757 when Jackson notes a conversation with John Johnson, the 'Stockton Carrier', who told Jackson that the frost at Stockton was so great that the horses 'went over the ice upon the Tees'.

The diaries provide a fascinating account of not only Jackson's life but his contemporaries too as he encountered a broad spectrum of people. These ranged from high profile Stockton citizens like George Sutton who was Mayor in 1759, 1760 and 1768 to ordinary tradesmen like shoemaker, Jas. Grey. On Wednesday 5 April 1769 Jackson writes that 'he called at Stockton... where I heard of the death of Wm Sutton Esq very suddenly yesterday morning, aged about 69'.

Noting social events provides a sense of society life in the town. On many occasions (e.g. May 1778) Jackson writes of attending an evening Assembly in Stockton and there are many other accounts of 'meeting to take tea' in the town or attending assemblies held there.

1771...A changing world... the new bridge at Stockton

One of the major developments that would later benefit Middlesbrough too, was the replacement of the ferry service at the site of the old castle in Stockton. An impressive five-arched stone bridge was built, saving six miles for travellers who no longer had to use the bridge at Yarm. Tolls financed the £8,000 building costs. Although it wasn't officially opened until 1771, so eager were the Trust to recoup their money, they opened the bridge early as noted by Ralph Jackson on 5 October 1768, when he writes that he 'rode along the New-bridg (sic) at Stockton, which has been passible (sic) for Horses & light Carriages for a month past...'

South East Durham 1820

Stockton 1825

The Iron Bridge at Yarm

Old Yarm Bridge
Egglescliffe Church

Expanding trade with London and Northern Europe brought demand for more ships, benefiting local ship building and other subsidiary industries, a development which filtered through into the regional economy.

The opening of Stockton Bridge in 1771, the creation of new turnpike roads and in 1825, the Stockton to Darlington Railway, improved land access to Stockton, crucial to the town's development.

Ironically the river and the difficult navigation from the sea to Stockton (sandbanks and two large meanders meant it could take up to a week), would severely limit Stockton's development as a port.

The land beyond Stockton to the sea was still largely undeveloped and isolated. Other local communities were generally small villages or hamlets unchanged across the years.

Principal landowners included the Church or wealthy individuals such as the Marquess of Londonderry at Wynyard.

*the extract is from Christopher Greenwood's map of Durham surveyed 1818-1819 & published 1820

All roads lead to Stockton

There were two roads heading from Stockton to Darlington: Old Darlington Lane (later Bishopton Lane) and Oxbridge Lane. They converged at Two Mile House heading towards Darlington.

This 19th century oil painting features the road approaching Stockton. In the distance a chimney from the Stockton Iron Works on West Row, built 1765, together with a windmill built in 1814 on Mill Lane (an extension of Dovecot Street) are visible on the horizon.

Wren's Factory c1912

The area east of High Street grew faster in the 18th century than the west side. By the 1820s, streets like Brunswick, Albion, Skinner, William, and Lodge were all constructed. This sketch of Brown's Bridge on Bishopton Lane, just a short distance away from town, shows how rural it was. There'd been a mill on Brown's Haugh since 1786, owned by William Smith until Tommy Wren bought it in 1832.

Brown's Bridge & Tommy Wren's Mill

The High Street.... Stockton

Stockton increasingly became a regional social and economic centre throughout the eighteenth century. The socio-economic centre of the town was the High Street with its mix of residential buildings as well as those used for commercial purpose.

The economic prosperity brought visible improvements - a new Parish Church was built in 1712 whilst the Corporation of Stockton ordered the paving of the streets in 1717.

The centuries old tollbooth was replaced by an elegant new Town House in 1735. This Parish Church and Town House are visible in this 1785 image, as featured in Brewster's book on Stockton.

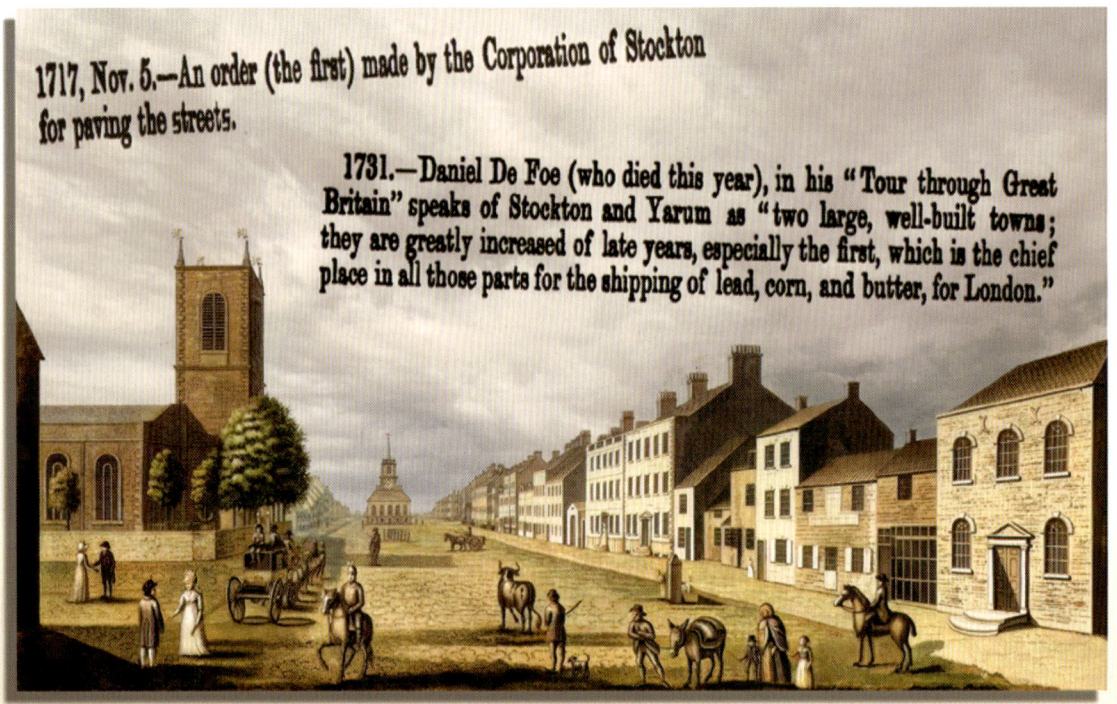

1717, Nov. 5.—An order (the first) made by the Corporation of Stockton for paving the streets.

1731.—Daniel De Foe (who died this year), in his "Tour through Great Britain" speaks of Stockton and Yarum as "two large, well-built towns; they are greatly increased of late years, especially the first, which is the chief place in all those parts for the shipping of lead, corn, and butter, for London."

The *Town-house*, or *Town Hall*, is a large, handsome, and commodious structure, forming a square, with four fronts, and ornamented with a light and beautiful spire. It stands in the centre of the High street

John Brewster MA (1753-1842) was an author and clergyman. In 1796 he wrote the 'Parochial History & Antiquities of Stockton upon Tees', an informative illustrated account of the town. A second & enlarged edition was published in 1829 whilst he was rector of Egglescliffe. Many of the images of Stockton at this time are based on those found in his work.

Another 18th century image shows the High Street viewed from the south. Before the bridge opened in 1769, travellers who were going south either used the ferry or entered Park Row and Yarm Lane from the end of the High Street. Many brick buildings seen here were part of the general rebuilding that took place in the post-Reformation period replacing many of the old wattle and daub structures that existed before.

The old and the new in 18th century Stockton

1735, March 9.—The Stockton Corporation made an order for erecting the Town-house. In this order, power is given to D. Douthwaite (Mayor), Wm. Sutton, and Henry Brown (aldermen), and Edmund Bunting and Wm. Barker, to take down the smith's shop, and build a dwelling-house for the serjeant, with convenient cellars, &c., and to make several convenient shops, and above them a large room for the entertainment of the mayor, aldermen, and burgesses

Hatfield's survey of 1384 suggests that the Mayor's House had once stood on this site; by the 17th century part of the building was being used as a tollbooth which author; historian John Brewster described it as 'a mean building, ascended by steps and built on open arches'. The tollbooth was replaced in 1735 by a new Town House (seen here from the north east) with four bow-fronted shops. An inn and cellars were added in 1744 followed by the addition of a piazza in 1768. The Town House, a mark of the town's progress, was a statement of local pride.

A single storey, flat-topped structure, the Covered Cross situated between the Shambles and the Tollbooth, providing shelter for market traders, was erected in 1709.

The impressive market cross with its 10 metre (33 feet) high Doric column dominates this view of the western side of the High Street. Built in 1768 at a cost of £45 by John Shout, it replaced the old Market Cross. Also visible is the Blue Posts Hotel, built in 1485 and then, one of the town's oldest buildings. It was said to have within its structure, a pair of Frosterley marble posts thought to be from Stockton Castle.

Stockton Parish Church

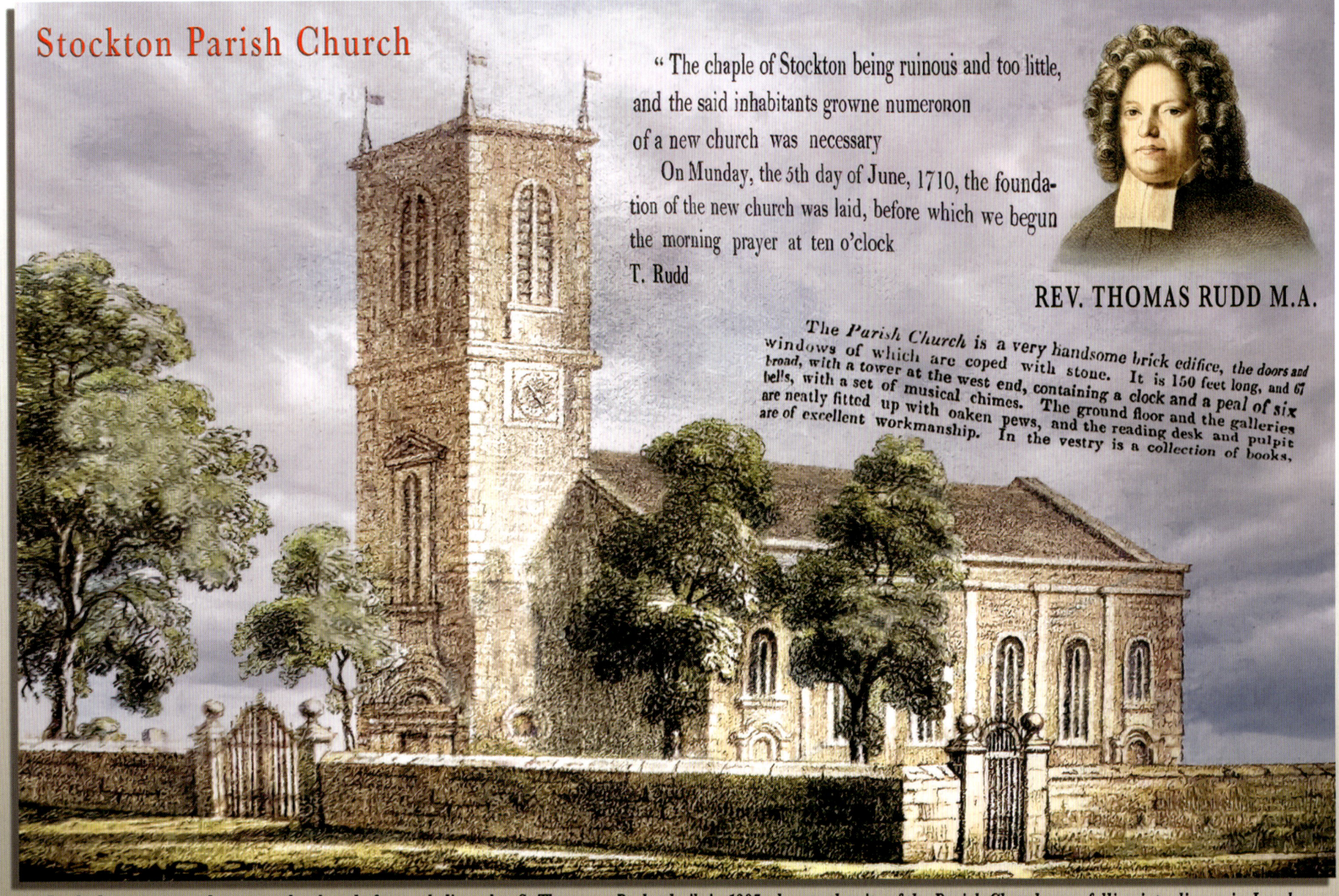

" The chaple of Stockton being ruinous and too little, and the said inhabitants growne numeronon of a new church was necessary

On Munday, the 5th day of June, 1710, the foundation of the new church was laid, before which we begun the morning prayer at ten o'clock

T. Rudd

REV. THOMAS RUDD M.A.

The *Parish Church* is a very handsome brick edifice, the doors and windows of which are coped with stone. It is 150 feet long, and 67 broad, with a tower at the west end, containing a clock and a peal of six bells, with a set of musical chimes. The ground floor and the galleries are neatly fitted up with oaken pews, and the reading desk and pulpit are of excellent workmanship. In the vestry is a collection of books,

By the late seventeenth century the chapel of ease, dedicated to St Thomas a Becket built in 1235, close to the site of the Parish Church, was falling into disrepair. Local feeling was that the general development of the town merited a new church, a proposal very much driven by the Rev. Thomas Rudd, who had arrived at the chapel in 1663. Building began in 1710 with the first sermon in the new church being preached by Rev. Thomas Rudd on 20 March 1712. The first Vicar at the new church was the Rev. George Gibson. Further development included a west gallery in 1719, a north gallery in 1748, the clock and chimes in 1759 and the south gallery in 1827.

The Square Stockton

East of the church is a spacious square, or green, surrounded on three sides by dwelling-houses ; the church-yard wall forming the fourth. The vicarage-house is situated at the north-west corner of this square. This piece of ground was enclosed about four and twenty years ago.... and beautifully planted with trees and shrubs, at the expense of several gentlemen of the town. It now constitutes a very distinguished ornament of the place.

When the Parish Church was built in 1712 a piece of wasteland was purchased for a new vicarage. As the vicarage was never built the land became a garden or 'Green'. It was renamed 'The Square' to avoid confusion with nearby Thistle Green. Surrounded by wooden railings and bushes The Square was described by Brewster as a very fashionable part of Stockton in the Georgian period. A theatre opened in nearby Green Dragon Yard in 1766. In this image c1829, Church Row is on the left, Paradise Row is in the distance and the road to Thistle Green is on the right.

The alms-house is now a handsome building, in the Gothic stile, which occupies a conspicuous situation on the east side of the High-street, near the church....erected A.D. 1816

The Alms-houses: legacy of George Brown

The demolition of the old Stockton Alms-houses (built in 1682) had started on 1 July 1816 to be replaced by the buildings shown here. The project was financed by a bequest in 1814 of £3000 from George Brown, a citizen and wealthy benefactor of the town.

The new Alms-houses, completed in November 1816 were located close to the Parish Church. Built in Gothic style there was an arched entrance with a committee room to the right and to the left, rooms for use as a dispensary.

The rest of the building, both on the ground floor and upper storey offered accommodation for up to thirty-six widows and their families.

A portrait of benefactor and philanthropist George Brown, could be found in the committee room hung above the chimney piece.

The House of Major John Jenkins

Major John Jenkins was a Welshman in Cromwell's army which arrived in Stockton towards the end of the Civil War.

After hostilities ended Major Jenkins remained in the town and had an elegant house built at the north end of the High Street on the lane which went to Norton.

When Major Jenkins died just before Christmas 1661, his will stipulated one shilling should be used to purchase white bread to given to the poor in the Parish Church every Sunday.

CHARITABLE BEQUESTS.

Major John Jenkins bequeathed 52 shillings per annum £. s. d.
for ever to the poor of Stockton, to be paid every sabbath-day
12d. in white bread. Will dated 1661 - - - 2 12 0

A large house at the north end of the town, near the division of the Norton and Redmarshall roads, fronting the street was the habitation of Major Jenkins,

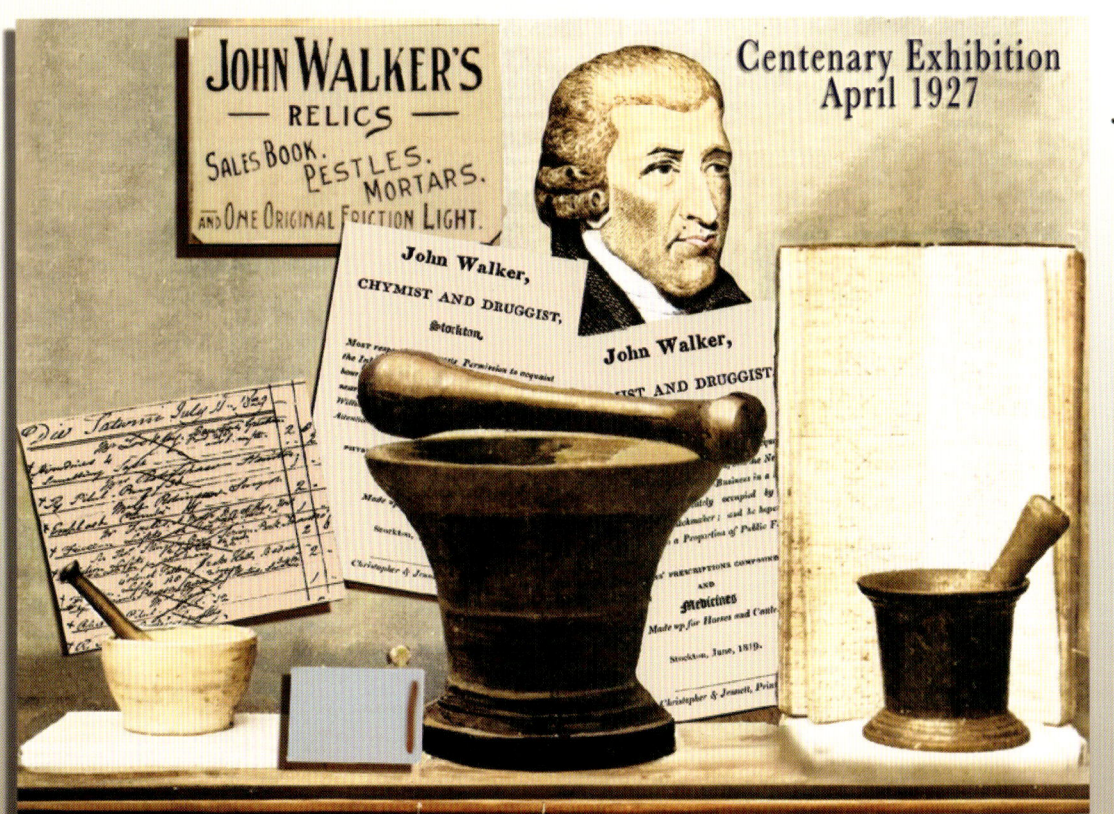

John Walker & his 'friction light'

John Walker, creator of the 'friction light,' refused to patent it despite encouragement from scientists like Michael Faraday. Walker grew up in Stockton at 104 High Street, apprenticed with a local surgeon, before pursuing further pharmaceutical training in London.

Returning to Stockton, he opened a 'Chemyst & Druggist' business at 59 High Street. There, he stumbled upon the discovery leading to his 'friction light.' Walker's daybook was written in Latin and he called the mixture 'sulphurata hyperoxygenata' to hide the formula.

He sold the first box of 100 friction lights in April 1827 but stopped production in 1829. Despite this, his invention thrived, benefiting companies like Bryant & May.

Walker continued as a Chemyst and Druggist until the business was sold when he retired in 1858. Walker died on May 1, 1859, at 78.

These artefacts are from a centenary exhibition at Walker's establishment in April 1927.

A NOTABLE CENTENARY.

ON THURSDAY, April 7th, 1827, John Walker, a surgeon, who carried on business as a pharmacist in a little shop in High-street, Stockton, took up his pen and made an entry in his day-book.

That historic memo was a record of the first sale of his newly-invented "Friction Lights," the forerunner of the multifarious means of ignition which exist to-day, and of a large and extensive industry which has now a capital amounting to many millions of pounds.

So notable a centenary cannot fail to arouse interest, and of the numerous historic incidents with which the borough is associated Stockton should feel as proud of this as any. It is a remarkable fact, however, that there is very little to which the townspeople can point as a symbol of so unique an achievement.

The famous entry which established Walker's distinction is inscribed in the book as follows:—

Die Saturni, April 7th, 1827. No 30. Mr Hixon.
Sulphurata Hyperoxygenata Frict. 100. 1.2.
Tin case 2d.

The Stockton representative of the "Tees-side Herald" discovered an interesting link with the great inventor, in the person of Miss A. Wilkinson, who resides at 7, Clarence-terrace, North-road. She is justifiably proud of being with her brother, who lives at Wallasey, the only descendants of John Walker. These two are respectively his grand niece and grand nephew.

Miss Wilkinson has very distinct and happy memories of the inventor. She was only five years of age when he died, but Walker had by that time imprinted a lasting impression upon her childish mind.

"He was a very clever man, and he was just as good as he was clever," she said. "He was never anything else but kind."

In April 1927, the centenary of John Walker's invention saw a subdued celebration. The Stockton & Tees-Side Herald newspaper printed a front-page article acknowledging the occasion, mirroring Walker's own modest approach to his work. A small exhibition was held at Walker's former business premises.

April 1927: Miss A Wilkinson lays flowers at the grave of John Walker at Norton Churchyard

John Walker's great niece Miss Anne Maria Wilkinson, recalled childhood memories of Walker teaching her Latin. She remembered him as 'a very kind man dismissive of his fame and who as a fully fledged doctor, refused to take money from poor for their medicines.'

Stockton 1828

By 1828, Stockton's economic growth was thriving. The map illustrates the presence of five coal staiths alongside the railway, accompanied by two shipyards and two sailcloth manufacturers. Notably, development was now extending beyond the established boundaries, particularly west of the High Street, marking a significant shift from the previous trend of housing infilling in populated areas. This expansion beyond the old limits hinted at future growth prospects.

The map also shows the location of Stockton Castle, with only the remnants of the old moat and a castellated outbuilding remaining.

The remains of Stockton Castle

During the 16th century, Stockton castle increased in size. It served as a garrison for soldiers in 1543 during the Pilgrimage of Grace and again in 1640 when Royalist forces occupied Stockton Castle.

Throughout the Civil War, it remained a Royalist stronghold until 1644, when Scottish forces, led by the Earl of Callendar, captured it following the Battle of Marston Moor.

Parliament subsequently ordered its demolition in 1647, sparing only the castle barn, later referred to as a 'castellated cowhouse,' which stood until its dismantlement on June 29, 1865.

Stockton High Street and Finkle Street

In the mid-1820s, Stockton experienced two notable days of lively public celebration.
First, on 27 September 1825 the formal inauguration of the Stockton to Darlington railway took place. Almost two years later on September 24, 1827, a visit from the heroic Duke of Wellington. His arrival was heralded by a nineteen-gun salute and the joyous pealing of church bells.

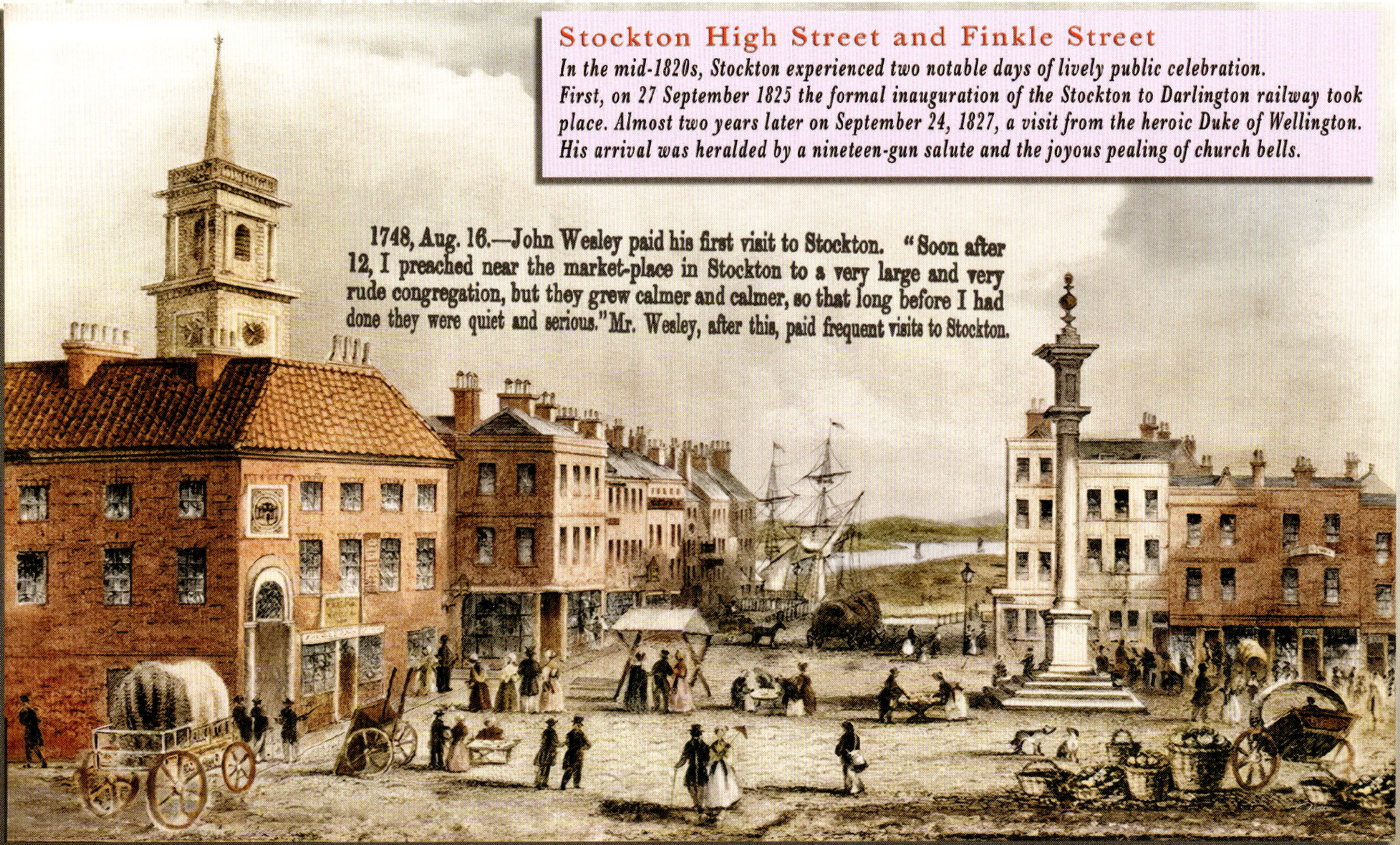

1748, Aug. 16.—John Wesley paid his first visit to Stockton. "Soon after 12, I preached near the market-place in Stockton to a very large and very rude congregation, but they grew calmer and calmer, so that long before I had done they were quiet and serious." Mr. Wesley, after this, paid frequent visits to Stockton.

A contemporary painting from that time captures the essence of the town: a vibrant market square, adorned with an elegant Town House and a stylish market cross, surrounded by splendid buildings. From the market place, the view extends down Finkle Street towards the River Tees, with the distant 'Janny Mills' Island visible

Should we build a canal or a railway?

A meeting in Darlington on 9 November 1767 decided to commission a survey for a canal linking the coalfields to Stockton. Robert Whitworth & George Dixon produced this plan for a 47 mile canal from Winston to Stockton with an estimated cost for construction of £64,000 - one of the reasons necessary support for the scheme never materialised.

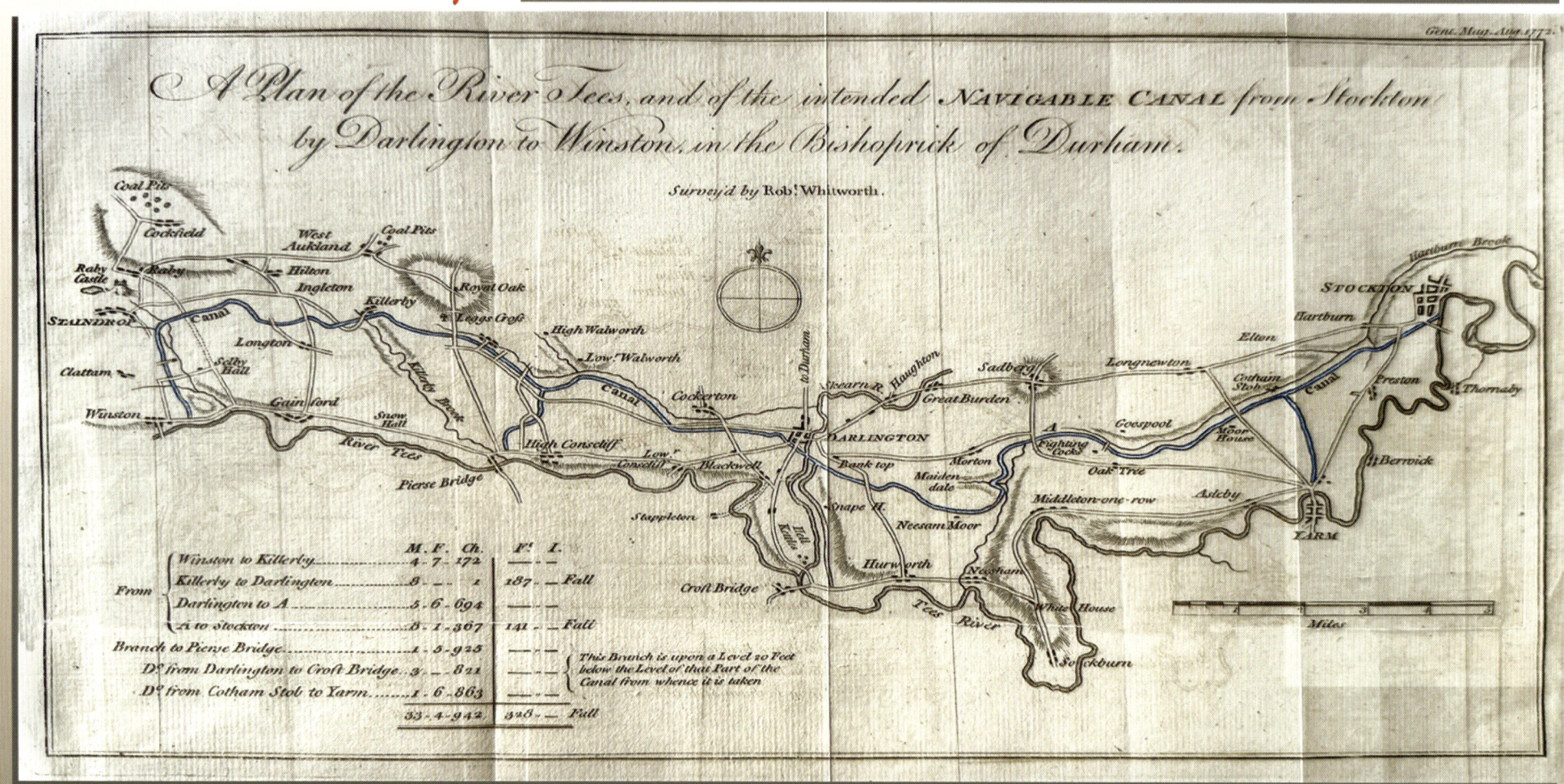

A Plan of the River Tees, and of the intended NAVIGABLE CANAL from Stockton by Darlington to Winston, in the Bishoprick of Durham.

Survey'd by Robt Whitworth.

From	M.F. Ch.	Ft I.	
Winston to Killerby	4 - 7 - 172		
Killerby to Darlington	8 - - 1	187	Fall
Darlington to A	5 - 6 - 694		
A to Stockton	8 - 1 - 367	141	Fall
Branch to Pierse Bridge	1 - 5 - 925		
Do from Darlington to Croft Bridge	3 - - 821		
Do from Cotham Stob to Yarm	1 - 6 - 863		
	33 - 4 - 942	328	Fall

This Branch is upon a Level to Feet below the Level of that Part of the Canal from whence it is taken

In the next fifty years there were further schemes & resolutions, including one made in 1810 at a dinner celebrating the cut in the Mandale Loop, by Leonard Raisbeck, Recorder of Stockton, that a committee should look at the 'practicability and advantage of a railway or canal (linking Stockton to the south Durham coalfield via Darlington) for the carriage of coal, lead etc'. In 1820 further support was evident at a meeting presided over by Thomas Meynell in Yarm; in 1821 a Bill to build the Stockton and Darlington Railway was finally passed and a Company formed. Two key figures came together - Edward Pease who led financial support and engineer George Stephenson, the man who would bring the venture to fruition. The first rail was laid at St. John's Well in Stockton on 23 May 1823 by Thomas Meynell. Construction followed; on 12 July 1825, S&D Directors announced the historic opening date of 27 September.

TUESDAY 27 SEPTEMBER 1825: THE OPENING OF THE STOCKTON AND DARLINGTON RAILWAY

S. & D.R.
IN THE COMMERCIAL ROOM OF THIS HOTEL, ON THE
12th Day of February, 1820
WAS HELD THE
PROMOTERS' MEETING
OF THE
Stockton & Darlington Railway.
THE FIRST PUBLIC RAILWAY IN THE WORLD.

THOMAS MEYNELL, ESQ. OF YARM, PRESIDENT

The room at the George & Dragon Inn Yarm where Thomas Meynell chaired a meeting in 1820 confirming support for the railway.

On Tuesday last, that great work, the Darlington and Stockton Railway was formally opened by the proprietors, for the use of the public. It is a single rail-way of 25 miles in length, and will open the London market to the collieries in the western part of the county of Durham, as well as facilitate the obtaining of fuel to the country along its line, and the northern parts of Yorkshire. The line of Railway extends from the collieries in a direction nearly from west to east from Witton Park and Etherly, near West Auckland, to Stockton upon Tees, with branches to Darlington, Yarm, &c. The engine arrived at Stockton in 3 hours and 7 minutes after leaving Darlington, including stops, the distance being nearly 12 miles, which is at the rate of four miles an hour; and upon the level part of the Railway, the number of passengers in the waggons were counted about 550, and several more clung to the carriages on each side, so that the whole number could not be less than six hundred, which, with the other load, would amount to about eighty tons. Nothing could exceed the beauty and grandeur of the scene. Throughout the whole distance, the fields and lanes were covered with elegantly dressed females, and all descriptions of spectators. In contemplating the events of the day, either in a national point of view, or as the efforts of a company of individuals furnishing a speedy, efficacious, and certain means of traffic to a wide and extended district, it alike excites the deepest interest and admiration; and the immense train of carriages covered with people, forming a load of from 80 to 90 tons, gliding as it were smoothly and majestically along the Railway through files of spectators, at such an astonishing rate of speed, left an impression on those who witnessed it that never will be forgot.

Newcastle Courant... 1 October 1825

THE YARM BRANCH CONNECTION

FIRST WATER TANK ERECTED AT YARM TO STORE WATER FOR LOCOS

RELICS OF YARM STATION PLATFORM

FIRST COAL DEPOT AT YARM

THE NEW INN WHERE THE COAL DEPOT OPENING TOOK PLACE

The branchline to Yarm opened on 17 October 1825 as a horse drawn service until 1833. When steam replaced horses it was decided that steam locos would only call at Yarm Station. The station closed on 16 June 1862 and the line was finally abandoned in 1871.

See page 211 for more...

THE STOCKTON & DARLINGTON RAILWAY COMPANY
Hereby give Notice,

THAT the FORMAL OPENING of their RAILWAY will take place on the 27th instant, as announced in the public Papers.—The Proprietors will assemble at the Permanent Steam Engine, situated below BRUSSELTON TOWER, about nine Miles West of DARLINGTON, at 8 o'clock, and, after examining their extensive inclined Planes there, will start from the Foot of the BRUSSELTON descending Plane, at 9 o'clock, in the following Order:—

1. THE COMPANY'S LOCOMOTIVE ENGINE.
2. THE ENGINE'S TENDER, with Water and Coals.
3. SIX WAGGONS, laden with Coal, Merchandise, &c.
4. THE COMMITTEE, and other Proprietors, in the COACH belonging to the Company.
5. SIX WAGGONS, with Seats reserved for STRANGERS.
6. FOURTEEN WAGGONS, for the Conveyance of Workmen and others.
☞ The WHOLE of the above to proceed to STOCKTON.
7. SIX WAGGONS, laden with Coals, to leave the Procession at the DARLINGTON BRANCH.
8. SIX WAGGONS, drawn by Horses, for Workmen and others.
9. Ditto Ditto.
10. Ditto Ditto.
11. Ditto Ditto.

The COMPANY'S WORKMEN to leave the Procession at DARLINGTON, and dine at that Place at one o'clock; excepting those to whom Tickets are specially given for YARM, and for whom Conveyances will be provided, on their Arrival at STOCKTON.

TICKETS will be given to the Workmen who are to dine at DARLINGTON, specifying the Houses of Entertainment.

The PROPRIETORS, and such of the NOBILITY and GENTRY as may honour them with their Company, will DINE precisely at THREE o'clock, at the TOWN-HALL, STOCKTON.—Such of the Party as may incline to return to DARLINGTON that Evening, will find Conveyances in waiting for their Accommodation, to start from the COMPANY'S WHARF there precisely at SEVEN o'clock.

The COMPANY take this Opportunity of enjoining on all their WORK-PEOPLE that Attention to Sobriety and Decorum which they have hitherto had the Pleasure of observing.

The COMMITTEE give this PUBLIC NOTICE, that all Persons who shall ride upon, or by the side of, the RAILWAY, on Horseback, will incur the Penalties imposed by the Acts of Parliament passed relative to this RAILWAY.

Any Individuals desirous of seeing the Train of Waggons descending the inclined Plane from Etherly, may have an Opportunity of so doing, as the Engine at the Head of it, at Mr. HALE'S AUCKLAND and later than Half past Seven o'clock.

RAILWAY-OFFICE, Sept. 19th, 1825.
ATKINSON'S Office, High-Row, Darlington.

19 September 1825 - notice of the forthcoming opening of the Stockton and Darlington Railway line.

St John's Crossing where the first rails were laid & the buildings where the first tickets were sold

THE S&D AT STOCKTON

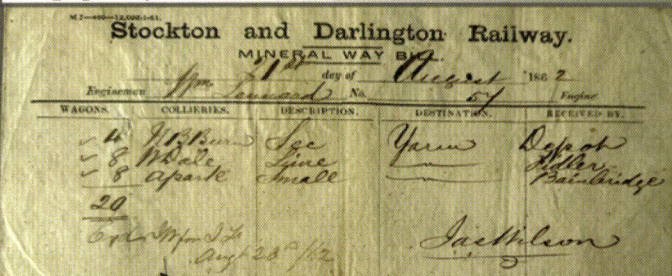

Stockton and Darlington Railway.
MINERAL WAY BILL

A Way Bill for a delivery received by the Depot Manager at Yarm made using the Yarm Branchline in 1862.

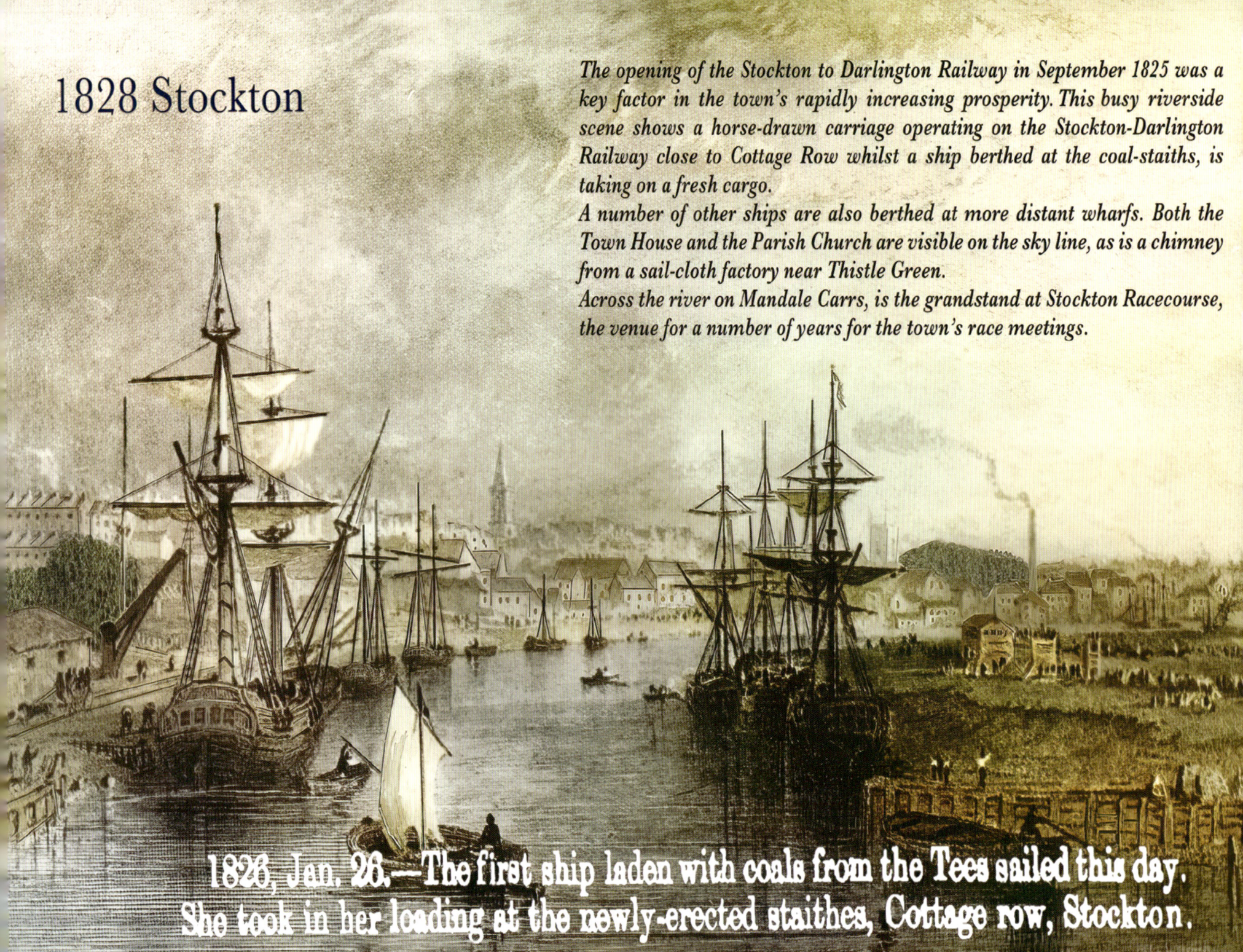

1828 Stockton

The opening of the Stockton to Darlington Railway in September 1825 was a key factor in the town's rapidly increasing prosperity. This busy riverside scene shows a horse-drawn carriage operating on the Stockton-Darlington Railway close to Cottage Row whilst a ship berthed at the coal-staiths, is taking on a fresh cargo.

A number of other ships are also berthed at more distant wharfs. Both the Town House and the Parish Church are visible on the sky line, as is a chimney from a sail-cloth factory near Thistle Green.

Across the river on Mandale Carrs, is the grandstand at Stockton Racecourse, the venue for a number of years for the town's race meetings.

1826, Jan. 26.—The first ship laden with coals from the Tees sailed this day. She took in her loading at the newly-erected staithes, Cottage row, Stockton.

From coal to people... those early years

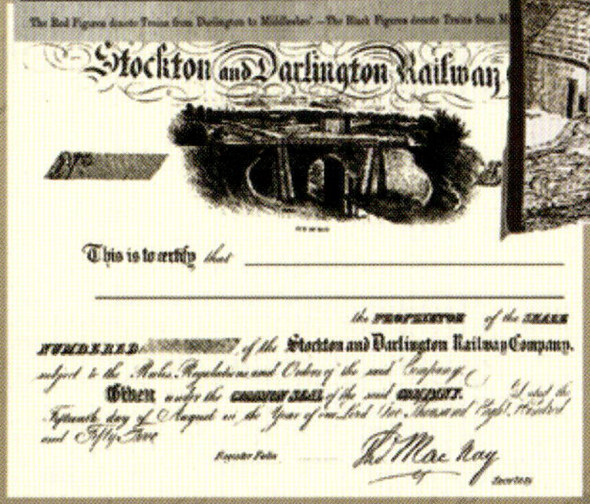

Stockton & Darlington Railway.

The Company's COACH

CALLED THE

EXPERIMENT,

Which commenced Travelling on MONDAY, the 10th of OCTOBER, 1825, will continue to run from Stockton to Darlington, and from Stockton to Darlington every Day, (Sunday's excepted) setting off from the DEPOT at each place, at the times specified as under, (viz.):—

ON MONDAY,

From Stockton at half-past 7 in the Morning, and will reach Darlington about half-past 9; the Coach will set off from the latter place on its return at 3 in the Afternoon, and reach Stockton about 5.

TUESDAY,

From Stockton at 3 in the Afternoon, and will reach Darlington about 5.

On the following Days, viz.:—

WEDNESDAY, THURSDAY & FRIDAY,

From Darlington at half-past 7 in the Morning, and will reach Stockton about half-past 9; the Coach will set off from the latter place on its return at 3 in the Afternoon, and reach Darlington about 5.

SATURDAY,

From Darlington at 1 in the Afternoon, and will reach Stockton about 3.

Passengers to pay 1s. each, and will be allowed a Package not exceeding 14lb. all above that weight to pay at the rate of 9d. per Stone extra. Carriage of small Parcels 3d. each. The Company will not be accountable for Parcels of above £5. Value, unless paid for as such.

Mr. RICHARD PICKERSGILL at his Office in Commercial Street, Darlington; and Mr TULLY at Stockton, will for the present receive any Parcels and Book Passengers.

RAPID, SAFE, AND CHEAP TRAVELLING
By the Elegant NEW RAILWAY COACH,

THE UNION,

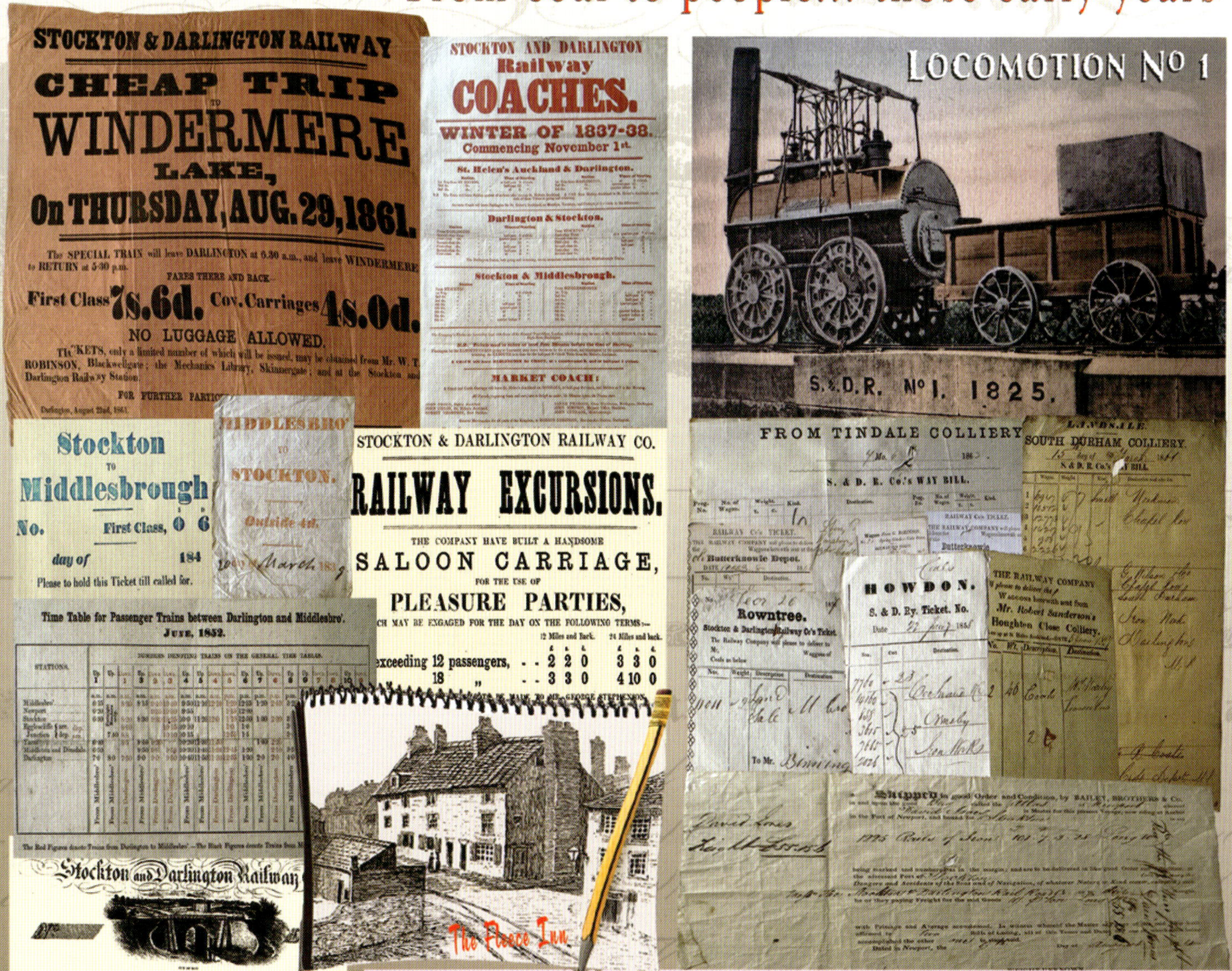

Which will COMMENCE RUNNING the STOCKTON and DARLINGTON RAILWAY, on MONDAY the 16th day of October, 1826,

And will call at Yarm, and pass within a mile of Middleton Spa, on its way from Stockton to Darlington, and vice versa. FARES, Inside 1¼d.—Outside, 1d. per Mile. Parcels in proportion.

No gratuities expected by the Guard or Coachman.

N.B. The Proprietors will not be accountable for any Parcel of more than £5. value, unless entered and paid for accordingly. The UNION will run from the Black Lion Hotel and Inn Yard, Stockton, to the New Inn, Yarm, and to the Black Swan Inn, near the Croft Branch, Darlington; at each of which Inns passengers and parcels are booked, and the times of starting may be ascertained, as also at the Union Inn, Yarm, and Ticket Inn, Darlington.

On the 19th and 16th of October, the Fair Days at Yarm, the Union will leave Darlington at six in the morning for Yarm, and will leave Yarm for Darlington again as six in the evening; in the intermediate time, each day, it will ply constantly between Stockton and Darlington, leaving each place every half hour.

STOCKTON & DARLINGTON RAILWAY

CHEAP TRIP TO WINDERMERE LAKE,

On THURSDAY, AUG. 29, 1861.

The SPECIAL TRAIN will leave DARLINGTON at 6.30 a.m., and leave WINDERMERE to RETURN at 5.00 p.m.

FARES THERE AND BACK.

First Class 7s.6d. Cov. Carriages 4s.0d.

NO LUGGAGE ALLOWED.

TICKETS, only a limited number of which will be issued, may be obtained from Mr. W. T. ROBINSON, Blackwellgate; the Mechanics Library, Skinnergate; and at the Stockton and Darlington Railway Station.

FOR FURTHER PARTICULARS...

Darlington, August 22nd, 1861.

STOCKTON AND DARLINGTON Railway COACHES.

WINTER OF 1837-38.
Commencing November 1st.

St. Helen's Auckland & Darlington.

Darlington & Stockton.

Stockton & Middlesbrough.

MARKET COACH.

LOCOMOTION Nº 1

S.&D.R. Nº 1. 1825.

FROM TINDALE COLLIERY

Stockton to Middlesbrough
No. ___ First Class, 0 6
day of ___ 184_
Please to hold this Ticket till called for.

MIDDLESBRO' to STOCKTON. Outside 4d.

STOCKTON & DARLINGTON RAILWAY CO.

RAILWAY EXCURSIONS.

THE COMPANY HAVE BUILT A HANDSOME SALOON CARRIAGE, FOR THE USE OF PLEASURE PARTIES,

WHICH MAY BE ENGAGED FOR THE DAY ON THE FOLLOWING TERMS:—

Time Table for Passenger Trains between Darlington and Middlesbro' JUNE, 1852.

Stockton and Darlington Railway

The Fleece Inn

It was quickly realised that carrying passengers could be profitable and very quickly a timetable was put in place to carry people. The first coach used was called 'Experiment', heralding a new era in public transport.

The Fleece Inn, Stockton where passengers boarded coaches - as well as tickets, timetables, a Share Certificate and Way Bills from S&D early years. The Company soon faced intense competition as the line was extended to Middlesbrough in 1830 and the opening of the Clarence Railway in 1833 created other loading points on the River Tees. Locomotion No 1 pulled the train on the first journey in 1825.

1875...CELEBRATING FIFTY YEARS

North Eastern Railway.

FIFTIETH ANNIVERSARY
OF THE OPENING OF THE
STOCKTON & DARLINGTON
RAILWAY.
27th September, 1875.

MENU

POTAGES.

PROGRAMME OF MUSIC

To be Performed during Dinner
BY
THE BAND OF THE GRENADIER GUARDS.

CONDUCTOR — MR. DAN. GODFREY.

NATIONAL AIRS, &c.

North-Eastern Railway Company
Fiftieth Anniversary of the opening of
The Stockton and Darlington Railway
27th September 1875

LADY'S TICKET

Admit Mrs.

To Gallery at the Banquet

No. 10

NORTH·EASTERN·RAILWAY·COMPY·
FIFTIETH·ANNIVERSARY
·of·the·Opening·of·the·
·STOCKTON·&·DARLINGTON·
·RAILWAY·
·27th·September·1875·

·MENU·
and
·PROGRAMME·OF·MUSIC·

NORTH EASTERN RAILWAY.

FIFTIETH ANNIVERSARY OF THE OPENING OF
THE STOCKTON & DARLINGTON RAILWAY.

BANQUET,
MONDAY, SEPTEMBER 27th, 1875.

TOAST LIST.

A Banquet in Darlington to celebrate the 75th anniversary

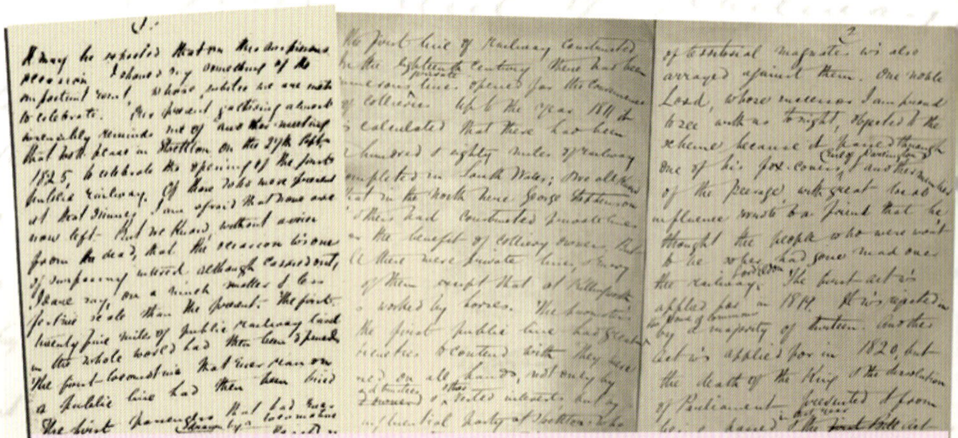

Henry Pease's notes from the speech he made at the 75th celebration

THE RAILWAY JUBILEE AT DARLINGTON.

GEORGE STEPHENSON.

EDWARD PEASE.

FRANCIS MEWBURN.

STATUE OF JOSEPH PEASE.

JOSEPH PEASE.

THE FIRST LOCOMOTIVE ENGINE.

THE ROCKET.

THE ROYAL GEORGE.

A Unique Procession of Rail History

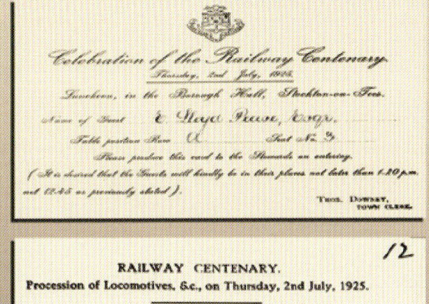

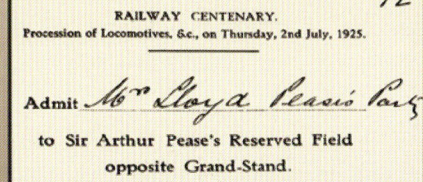

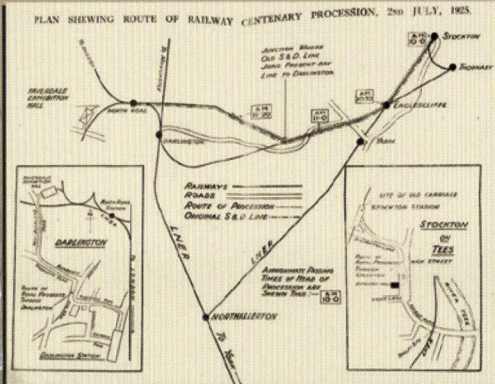

2 July 1925..A Railway Centenary

The Duke & Duchess of York arrive at Stockton station. The Duke later unveiled a commemorative tablet at St Johns Crossing to mark the very first booking office.

The unique centenary procession included Locomotion arriving at Stockton, pulling a replica of the very first train. Large crowds attended the centenary celebrations.

THE TEES AT STOCKTON: A CENTRE OF INDUSTRY

Reproduced from 1915 Twenty-Five inch series, with the kind permission of the Ordnance Survey

This map extract of the riverside area in Stockton and Thornaby brings location detail to the images in the next few pages.

A number of mooring stages (some used by ferry boats as landings) and wharfs can be seen; ferry routes across the river were an important part of local life providing access to the main industries - shipbuilding and the iron and steel factories.

Three main shipyards are visible:

Thornaby Shipbuilding Yard (Craig Taylor was established here in 1884)

South Stockton Shipbuilding Yard (from 1854 the yard was Richardson Duck & Co.)

North Shore Ship Yard from which Pearse, Lockwood & Co. traded from 1854-1888 when it became the Ropner Shipbuilding Company trading from 1888 until going into voluntary liquidation in 1928. (Although Smiths Dock Middlesbrough used the yard as an overflow yard it finally closed in 1931.)

There were a range of other smaller shipbuilding concerns - before and after this time but the industry never again enjoyed it's earlier economic success.

Three of the larger iron companies can be seen too - the Teesdale Iron Works (later Head Wrightson), the Thornaby Iron Works (later Whitwell & Co.) and the Union Foundry (later Crosthwaite).

It is interesting to note how close residential properties are to industry – despite constant local pollution this was common during the industrial era when this would save any transport costs to work.

Stockton riverside....Thornaby Carrs

This vista is a fascinating view of Thornaby Carrs (or Mandale Carrs) and the North Shore shipbuilding yard on the other side of the river. Waterloo Mills, the large building behind the shipyard opened in 1780, to be used for refining crude imported sugar. Later it was one of several quayside buildings used by corn merchants as a granary and warehouse. Close to Waterloo Mills is Thistle Green whilst the Parish Church is just visible in the distance. Two schooners are moored on the river; an unnamed schooner is moored next to a steamship whilst the vessel in front is named the 'Young Hudson'. Stockton race meetings were held on Thornaby Carrs from 1724 to 1816.

A river at work

This view c1906, taken from Victoria Bridge looks towards the array of quays and industrial buildings at Stockton riverside. In the fore-ground, a boat is moored at the quayside of the North of England Pure Oil Cake Company, opened in 1869. Linseed and cotton seed were processed here as part of the manufacture of cattle feeds .

The variety of ships using on the river can be seen here - including barges, sailing ships and iron vessels. Hubback's Quay lies in the distance, with the Ship Launch public house visible close by.

1832, May 1.—Stockton made a warehousing port for sugar, coffee, &c. These, with the privileges before granted, made it a bonded port for all articles of general merchandise allowed to be warehoused except tobacco.

Ships moored at the Corporation Quayside (left) are a reminder of busier days on the river at Stockton. Behind the ships are the warehouses that offered a valuable storage facility - as advertised by Stockton Corporation (right).

In the distance houses seem to tumble down towards the riverside at Hub-backs Quay – this area up to Thistle Green with its crowded yards created during the infilling of the nineteenth century, was heavily criticised as being unsuitable to live in by the Ranger Report in 1850.

Stockton-on-Tees Corporation Wharf, Grain & Bonded Warehouses.

GRAIN STORAGE FOR 50,000 QRS. ON FLOORS IN SILOS. GRAIN ELEVATORS WORKING UP TO 50 TONS PER HOUR. STEAM CRANES FROM 3 TO 20 TONS CAPACITY.

No Cartage or Haulage, as the Railway Wagons are put alongside the ship or warehouse.

Bunkering Facilities.—Vessels can take bunker coal aboard when receiving or delivering cargoes.

Moored at Stockton

November 1866

The Duncan brothers' paddle steamer River Queen moored at the landing stage at Black Lion Yard at the rear of the Black Lion Hotel. The Duncan family operated a regular service from here up to Newport - with fierce competition from their rivals the Dixons. Before the Newport to Thornaby road was built the boats provided an important transport link.

This image from c1870 shows an unamed sailing ship taking on a fresh cargo whilst moored at Corporation Quay. In the background is the Baltic Tavern, one of several public houses close to the quayside

Stockton remained a reasonably busy port well into the twentieth century. One of the busiest areas was Corporation Quay shown here c1906. The ship, Manoela Victoriano is at its mooring with Finkle Street leading to the High Street visible behind.

One of Stockton's best known quayside buildings, the Custom House Hotel, is visible as also are the warehouse premises of Raimes and Co., oil and paint merchants.

The Raimes family, well known in Stockton, lived at Hartburn Lodge, a substantial property in East Hartburn.

Awaiting the ferry at Stockton

Crossing the River Tees at Stockton using the ferry, could often be a precarious experience. This view looking upriver, shows the end of Finkle Street (mid-left) the quayside cranes and storage buildings beyond. On the riverbank at Stockton there are steps going down to the river whilst a paddle steamer is close to the landing stage on the Thornaby side of the river and the stocks at the Craig Taylor shipyard. A crowd of people are stood on Corporation Quay, which with the Waterloo Mills building, dominates mid-picture.

Kelly's Ferry...known to all

Kelly's Ferry is best remembered for ferrying workers from Stockton to the iron foundries and shipyards at Thornaby. Operating daily from an inlet close to Thistle Green across to the end of Trafalgar Street at Thornaby, it was a vital transport link for workers.

Two landing stages were used at Stockton (one for low and one for high tide) but a long set of steps served both tides at Thornaby.

A brush was used to clean away odorous silt left by the receding water but it was not unknown for a hurrying worker to slip and fall in the river!

The crossing was often described as 'nerve-racking' as boats carried up to sixty men bringing the water level to just below the edge of the boat. As industry at Thornaby declined so too did the need for the ferry.

Travelling further afield.....

This image circa early 1890's shows 'Old Glory', one of the steam-powered paddle boats that operated on the route from Middlesbrough to Stockton. At this time there was still no bridging point below Stockton so ferry services sailing downriver to the landing at Newport, Middlesbrough were well used.

Shipbuilding at Stockton

The post 1850 period were busy years for the shipyards in Stockton. These extracts, 10 September 1891, are from an order with Richardson Duck & Co shipyard for the steel ship 'The Highfields'. The Richardson Duck shipyard, which had opened in 1854, built twenty-four vessels in the period 1891-1892 with eight also being built at Craig Taylor's yard on the same river.

The numerous vessels built by Messrs. Richardson & Duck have been distributed all over the world, and, in general, they are looked upon as models of naval architecture.

CRAIG, TAYLOR & CO., LTD.
Telegraphic Address—"Craytaylor, Stockton-on-Tees."   Telephone No. 636 (Three Lines).
Oil, Passenger, and Cargo Steamers of all Description.
Yard fully equipped with all the latest ELECTRIC, HYDRAULIC & PNEUMATIC PLANT.
SHIPBUILDERS, ENGINEERS, and REPAIRERS.
PUBLIC Graving Dock 376 feet long   Builders of longitudinally framed vessels (ISHERWOOD SYSTEM)   THORNABY SHIPBUILDING YARD   **STOCKTON-ON-TEES.**

No. 399
RICHARDSON, DUCK & Co.,
SHIPBUILDERS,
STOCKTON-ON-TEES.
10 Sept. 1891
Specification of Steel SAILING SHIP to be built for Messrs. Liverpool

THE ROPNER SHIPBUILDING & REPAIRING CO. (Stockton) LTD.
PASSENGER, CARGO & OIL STEAMERS, STEAM HOPPERS, Etc.
Telegrams: "ROPNER."   **STOCKTON-ON-TEES.**   Telephone: Nos. 609 & 610.

ESTABLISHED 1854.
RICHARDSON, DUCK & CO.
LIMITED
Shipbuilders,
STOCKTON-ON-TEES.
* * * *
:: Builders of ::
FIRST-CLASS PASSENGER CARGO AND OIL STEAMERS
SELF-TRIMMING COLLIERS
STEEL LIGHTERS
ETC.
On Admiralty List.   Over 680 Vessels already Built.

23 July 1888: crwods gather to see a launch, ship name unknown

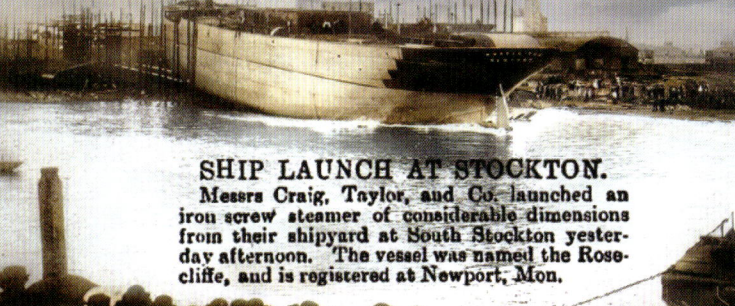

23 July 1888: The 'Rosecliffe' is launched

SHIP LAUNCH AT STOCKTON.

Messrs Craig, Taylor, and Co. launched an iron screw steamer of considerable dimensions from their shipyard at South Stockton yesterday afternoon. The vessel was named the Rosecliffe, and is registered at Newport, Mon.

10 August 1903: The launch of the 'Kilsyth'

Launchday at Craig Taylor's Shipyard

The first iron ship building yard on the banks of the Tees commenced in 1852, on the south shore, opposite to the Clarence staithes, at Stockton, by the Stockton Iron Shipbuilding Company, and the first vessel launched from their yard was the "Advance."

The launch of a ship from a shipyard at Stockton and Thornaby always attracted big crowds as shown here in the three launches from the Craig Taylor Shipyard. Ships would usually then be fitted out prior to their making their initial voyage.

On the 23rd July there was launched from the shipbuilding-yard of Messrs. Craig, Taylor and Co., Stockton-on-Tees, a screw steamer, the ROSECLIFFE, of the following dimensions: Length 281 feet 3 inches, breadth 40 feet, depth 20 feet 11 inches. The vessel has been built with a long-raised quarter-deck bridge extending to and including foremast and forewinch, short well, and topgallant forecastle.

CRAIG, TAYLOR & CO., LTD.
Shipbuilders, Engineers and Repairers.

Thornaby Shipbuilding Yard. STOCKTON-ON-TEES.

LAUNCH AT THORNABY

Yesterday Messrs Craig, Taylor and Co. launched from their shipbuilding yard, Thornaby-on-Tees, a steel screw steamer of the following dimensions, viz., 316ft. by 44ft. by 22ft. 6ft The ceremony of naming the vessel Kilsyth was performed by Miss Hunter, of Wentworth, Gosforth.

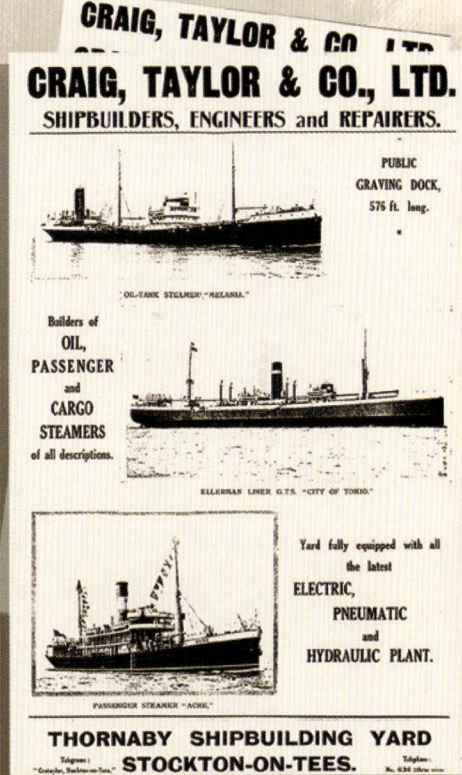

CRAIG, TAYLOR & CO., LTD.
SHIPBUILDERS, ENGINEERS and REPAIRERS.

PUBLIC GRAVING DOCK, 576 ft. long.

Builders of OIL, PASSENGER and CARGO STEAMERS of all descriptions.

Yard fully equipped with all the latest ELECTRIC, PNEUMATIC and HYDRAULIC PLANT.

THORNABY SHIPBUILDING YARD STOCKTON-ON-TEES.

IRON WORKS AT THORNABY

This image (possibly from the Cleveland Flour Mills Building c1930) is dominated by a group of chimneys at Whitwell & Co. with Head Wrightson's on the left, Thornaby Iron Works and Teesdale Engineering Works respectively, had become established on these sites by the mid-nineteenth century, part of the vast number of iron works opening at this time along the south bank of the Tees. In 1879 Whitwells had five blast furnaces operating here; by 1897 the company had over 1,000 employees and an annual output of over 125,000 tons of pig iron. In the foreground is Trafalgar Street with a line of washing hanging out to dry across Albert Street with Prince Street and Railway Street also visible.

Head, Wrightson & Co., Limited

UNIONIST BANQUET TO THOS. WRIGHTSON, ESQ. M.P. AT STOCKTON.

In 1890 Thomas Wrightson, now very much an important local figure was living in Norton Hall, a centre of political ideas.

STOCKTON FORGE,
STOCKTON-ON-TEES.
TELEPHONE Nº 666.

EGGLESCLIFFE FOUNDRY
STOCKTON-ON-TEES.

LONDON OFFICE.
5, VICTORIA STREET
WESTMINSTER S.W.1

HEAD, WRIGHTSON & CO. LIMITED.

Registered Office

TEESDALE IRON WORKS,

THORNABY ON TEES.

TELEPHONE Nº 587 (4 LINES)
CODES:
LIEBERS, WESTERN UNION
SCATT, TYE A.B.C. 5ª EDITION
TELEGRAMS.
"TEESDALE, VIC, LONDON
"TEESDALE, STOCKTON ON TEE"

PARIS OFFICE.
6 BOULEVARD DES CAPUCINES

SOUTH AFRICAN OFFICE:
P.O. BOX 1034,
JOHANNESBURG.

CANADIAN AGENTS
MACKAY BROTHERS
14 ROSS BLOCK,
SYDNEY,
NOVA SCOTIA.

S. A. WILLIAMS,
847, BEATTY STREET,
VANCOUVER, B.C.

Head Wrightson railway wagons line the riverside in this view of the iron works at Thornaby 1906.

Thomas Wrightson seen here in 1899, had been elected in 1892 as Stockton's first Conservative MP, a seat he held until 1895.

Down by the riverside... a legacy of industrial days

THE CUSTOM HOUSE HOTEL

A prominent feature close to the quayside at the lower end of Finkle Street incline, was the Custom House Hotel, which opened in 1730. In the foreground are the railway lines that ran along the quayside from St John's Crossing to Corporation Quay.

1730.—The Custom-house at Stockton, which was removed to Finkle-street in 1696, was rebuilt, near the same spot, by the Corporation, at an expense of about £150; and a lease was granted for 21 years, at the annual rent of £16.

This map extract shows the quayside and nearby residential area around Thistle Green including Housewife Lane and Cherry Lane. Large scale demolition of this area took place in the 1920s during the big slum clean-up. Note too Cleveland Row, where John Walker lived as a boy. Two popular public houses, the Ship Launch Inn & the Baltic Tavern, and local landmark, Waterloo Mills, a huge building used as a granary, all stand on the quayside. Ferries regularly crossed the river here taking workers to Thornaby Shipbuilding Yard (Craig Taylor Shipyard from 1884) and South Stockton Shipyard (later Richardson Duck & Co.).

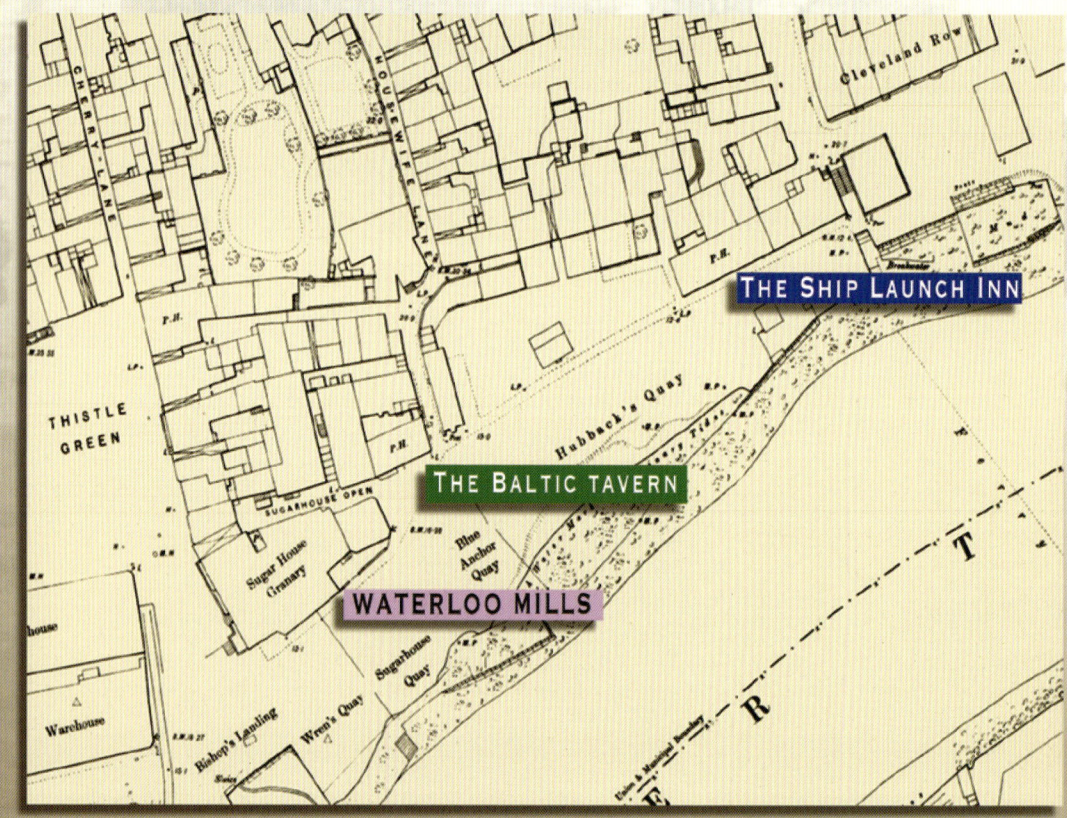

THE SHIP LAUNCH INN

THE BALTIC TAVERN

WATERLOO MILLS

(Reproduced from 1893 Large Town Plan series, with the kind permission of the Ordnance Survey)

Once known as the 'Blue Anchor Tavern', the 'Baltic Tavern' was one of several public houses in this area. Drawing many customers from those who lived and worked in the riverside area these public houses would have been crowded lively places during the years when industry was at its peak in Stockton. The incline to Thistle Green, by the side of the inn, was known as 'Sugar House Open' a reference to the eighteenth century sugar import trade.

THE BALTIC TAVERN

The advertisement boards on the side of the granary building confirms the date of this image as 1927, as this was when Syd Chaplin was starring in 'The Missing Link' at the local Globe Theatre.

WATERLOO MILLS

Adjacent to the Baltic Tavern was Waterloo Mills. A sugar refinery built in 1780 it faced onto the Wrens, Sugarhouse and Blue Anchor Quays, a link with the import of unrefined sugar from the Colonies and the Baltic. It was later used as a warehouse and granary.

The building is seen here in the final days before demolition in 1929. The slight incline at the side of the building went up to Thistle Green which was also being cleared at this time. The loss of this building was a reflection of the decline of the riverside area with the closure of industrial concerns driving the downward economic cycle.

THE SHIP LAUNCH INN

Only a short walk along the riverbank from the Baltic Tavern was the 'Ship Launch Inn' seen here in 1928 when it too was part of the ongoing mass slum clearance. A group of men seem to be marking the loss of the inn.

Beyond the inn are the terraced houses of Cleveland Row, built in the eighteenth century, whilst the ferry landing steps at the end of Smithfield are still in place. To the rear of the Ship Launch Inn was Dixon's Yard, one of many in this area with unacceptable living conditions including little or no sanitation.

STOCKTON QUAYSIDE c1930

The slump in the 1920's and 1930's brought economic decline to industries alongside the quayside area. Shipbuilding was hard hit with Richardson Duck and Craig Taylor both closing their yards. The iron and steel companies such as Head Wrightson only survived through financial help. In this image the premises of Thomas H. Purdey, Engineer, the Custom House Hotel and Finkle Street look on to the quayside at Corporation Wharf.

Coming into town... Bridge Road

The southern end of the High Street where the site of the old castle was located, was closed off by the Castle Park gates. However, when the new bridge opened in 1769, a rough track to St. John's Well was adopted to provide a route to the town. Although the link was named Bridge Road, it was locally dubbed 'The New Walk'. In 1787 it was described as a very popular scenic country walk, decked with trees, pretty hedges, seating spots, and a white fence. However in 1856 general development began, including widening the road and building houses - see the ad from 1864 for houses in Tower Street. This view towards the High Street c1865, shows the Castle Brewery on the right with the Court Offices built in 1865, opposite.

The site where the Hotel Metropole would be built is still rough ground with old fencing visible.

The Hotel Metropole on the corner of Park Terrace South and Bridge Road, and adjacent Court Offices, dominate this scene. A very popular venue (especially during Stockton Race meetings), the Metropole hosted many social and business events including a meeting convened by Stockton MP & future Prime Minister, Harold Macmillan in 1938.

Opposite is Edward Scott's newsagents on the corner of Tower Street. Leather merchant, Mrs Maria Bell's nameboard and the board for Van Houten's Cocoa are also visible. The newspaper board, 'Mr Balfour's trenchant attack on the Budget' dates this image to 1909.

TO BE SOLD, BY PRIVATE CONTRACT, SIX NEWLY-ERECTED DWELLING-HOUSES, situate in Tower-street, Castle Field, Stockton. The Houses contain six Rooms each, with large back-ground, and every other convenience attached.
For further particulars apply to JOHN BOWES, Castlegate, Stockton.

STOCKTON RACES.
The nearest Hotel to Racecourse.
HOTEL METROPOLE,
STOCKTON.
LUNCHEONS 11 30 a.m. to 2 p.
DINNERS .. .... 6 p.m to 8 p.
Finest food procurable.
Ales, Wines and Spirits in perfect cond

STOCKTON M.P. SEEKS NEW A.R.P. IDEAS
Mr Harold Macmillan, M.P. for Stockton, last night entertained to dinner at the Hotel Metropole, Stockton, the A.R.P. leaders of Stockton with a view to getting opinions for co-ordinating A.R.P. services of the town and the country.
The Mayor of Stockton (Councillor J. E. Wilyman) and leading Corporation officials were among those present.
Mr. Macmillan told a "Chronicle" representative that the idea of the function was to get together all those interested in such a vital service and to have a frank discussion.
He hoped to obtain new ideas which he could submit to the Government.

TEESSIDE SCOTSMEN DINE TOGETHER. — There was a notable gathering at the Hotel Metropole, Stockton, on Thursday, when, under the auspices of the Teesside Caledonian Society, a re-union took place of Scotsmen on Teeside. Ald A. Cameron, J.P., of Stockton, presided, and was supported by Ald J. Forbes, J.P., Middlesbrough; Ald R. Roper, J.P., Stockton; Dr Cameron, Stockton; Messrs Alex Inglis, W. Ford, A. Livingstone, D. Craig, N. Cairns, E.T. M. Cowburn, and John Cameron, Stockton; and W. Robertson, Middlesbrough. A number of toasts were honoured, and during the evening a number of Scottish and other songs were rendered by Messrs W. Cairns and A. Strike, while Mr Inglis gave a much-appreciated recitation.

Castle Gate

A large house (thought to be partly built with stones from the adjacent castle ruins) with its narrow garden that once ran down to the river, stood on the corner of Castle Gate and Bridge Road. The ivy-clad building, converted into two properties, is seen here c1901 when Elizabeth Faber, a 68-year- old widow, lived adjacent to Castle Gate and 37-year-old music teacher and organist, Felix Cruse, his wife and 5-year-old daughter Joan lived in the adjoining property. Born in Stockton in 1837, Elizabeth, (her father Thomas Faber was an 'attorney in law'), had lived here most of her life. When she died in Norton, December 1919 a theatre had been built here.

Castle Theatre..

The two late seventeenth century cottages were demolished in 1907 to be replaced by the Castle Theatre. A foundation stone for the building was laid on 3 October 1907 by Mrs Richard Murray of Harrogate. Construction was completed in 1908 with Dorman Long supplying the steelwork.

The theatre opened on 31 July 1908 with a play called 'The Lady of Lyons'. Despite its elegant interior featuring a white marble staircase, spectacular entrance and famous names of the theatre world such as Ellen Terry appearing, the Castle Theatre wasn't a financial success.

In March 1912 owner John Imeson, was granted a picture licence; with a redesigned interior the theatre renamed the Empire. In 1961 it became a bingo hall until being demolished when the Swallow Hotel was built in the 1970's.

In September 1908 a large audience came to see famous actresss Ellen Terry at the Castle Theatre.

The background is a rare image of the interior and stage of the Castle Theatre

STOCKTON HIGH STREET

The southern end of the High Street with the Shambles and the Town Hall as its central focus. The electric trams typified by those shown here, came into operation in 1898 and ran from North Ormesby to Norton. There are glimpses of the many shops and trade premises that operated along the busy High Street whilst Dovecot Street and the Parish Church can be seen in the distance.

...familiar throughout the region

The vast maze of yards behind the frontages of the High Street and other streets are shown. Also West Row which runs parallel to the High Street ending at 'Park Row', a row of properties looking on to Holy Trinity Church and Castle Field, the site of Stockton Castle.

The DODSHON MEMORIAL DRINKING FOUNTAIN will be OPENED for the Use of the Public on MONDAY AFTERNOON NEXT, August the 26th, 1878, at half past Four o'clock.

The Fountain will be presented to the town, on behalf of the Memorial Committee, by J. DODDS, ESQ., M.P. And will be received, on the part of the town, by the Vice-chairman, THE MAYOR OF STOCKTON. The Mayor and Corporation will attend officially on the occasion. Stockton-on-Tees, August 21st, 1878.

ORDNANCE MAPS. JENNETT & CO. RESPECTFULLY inform the Public they have been appointed Agents at Stockton-on-Tees, for the Sale of the ORDNANCE MAPS, and will be glad to supply any Sheet or Division immediately on publication.

The PARISH of STOCKTON-ON-TEES is published on the scale 25⁄314 inches to a mile, nearly equivalent to One Square Inch to an Acre, 11 Sheets at 6d each ; Index 4 Sheets, 2s each.

The TOWN of STOCKTON-ON-TEES, on Scale 10 Feet to a Mile, 12 Sheets at 2s each.

May be had mounted in Case, on Rollers, Varnished, or bound as a Book to any pattern.

Copperplate, Engraving, and Printing and Lithography done in any style well and punctually.

The Shambles, rebuilt in 1728 and 1825 after debate about relocation.

Dodshon's Monument erected in memory of John Dodshon in 1878

A view of the High Street in 1938 from the Empire Theatre where the film 'Just Around The Corner' is being shown.

Reproduced from 1857 Twenty-Five inch series, with the kind permission of the Ordnance Survey

Market Day...

A variety of market stalls nestle between the Shambles and the Town Hall, drawing many people to the town and bringing custom to local public houses like the Ship Inn. One of the oldest establishments, the Blue Post Hotel and Blue Post Yard (one of many yards along the High Street) is close by. F. Collitt & Co., a well established wholesale hardware, pottery and stationery business enjoyed a prime location with premises at the Town Hall. The entry to Dovecot Street is marked by the 'Bovril' sign.

..brings the crowds

For over 700 years, Stockton Market has remained a cornerstone of community life. This bustling marketplace has served as a hub for local tradesmen, showcasing an array of goods.

The southern facade of the Town Hall proudly displays Stockton's coat-of-arms. Nestled amidst the vibrant stalls is the Market Cross, an imposing Doric column erected in 1768 at a cost of £45, supplanting an earlier deteriorating edifice. This new landmark swiftly became a meeting point, attracting gatherings that included many public speakers, further solidifying its central role within the town's communal life.

The market stalls selling freshly caught local fish produce have always been popular with shoppers at Stockton Market. These well known stalls even featured on a postcard printed by local Stockton publisher, Michael Heavisides.

THE HIRINGS

Despite many links with industry Stockton still served a widespread farming community with events such as Stockton Hirings being important dates in the agricultural calendar. The Hirings took place on two Wednesdays in May and two Wednesdays in November. Farmers employed workers for six months, sealing the agreement with a Hiring Penny.

WM. BLACKBURN & CO.

TAILORS & OUTFITTERS

BOYS CLOTHIERS

WM. BLACKBURN & CO.

TEMPERANCE HOTEL

HARRITT & CO.

THE HATTERS

Northern Review. MAY 10, 1890

SKETCHES AT STOCKTON HIRINGS.

From the mid-1850's the Hirings had become more than just an agricultural event as it became an opportunity to enjoy a wide range of entertainments - as illustrated here in May 1890.

BRING PROBLEMS TO TOWN!

The Hirings became a fair with roundabouts, shooting booths and other amusements accompanying the traditional hiring of farm workers. Many farm labourers had travelled long distances; this was a rare visit to town so they often remained for several days many taking up lodgings in houses in Ramsgate at the cost of fourpence a night. However increasingly rowdy behaviour meant that by 1889 concerns were being raised in the press. In 1907 the very future of the event was being discussed. Although the Hirings continued until the start of the Great War the decreasing need for agricultural workers saw it fade away as an event.

STOCKTON HIRINGS

PANDEMONIUM IN HIGH-STREET.

THE CARNIVALS MAY BE STOPPED.

CORPORATION BEGIN TO MOVE.

VIEWS OF LEADING TRADESMEN.

Stockton's ancient carnival is threatened with expulsion from the High-street.

A VITAL ISSUE.

To the outside world this question of abolishing the Hiring Carnivals may not appear to be of any importance, but to Stocktonians it is of vital interest. The other evening, at a meeting of the Town

Early 1900's - the Carnival which accompanied the Hirings leading to behaviour issues...

HIGH STREET - EAST SIDE

A diverse tapestry of Georgian architecture lines the East Side of the High Street. This evocative glimpse encompasses a range of establishments including Rossi's confectioner shop, Calvert's 'The Castle Hat Shop', Laws drapery shop, the Royal Hotel, Martin's the costumier, and Doggarts the drapers at 74 High Street. Two very popular regional bus companies, United and Durham District, operated local and regional services from this High Street location.

Two of Stockton's old 18th century coaching inns, the Vane Arms & Black Lion Hotel, were popular with passengers on stage coaches when calling at Stockton. The Black Lion is reputed to have been visited by Hollywood film star, Clark Gable, when he was stationed at a USAAF base in the region.

THE TOWN HALL - CENTRE OF CIVIC LIFE

The majestic Town Hall, the centre of civic life, stands proud as a water cart sprays the High Street. Close by is the Market Cross. Nattrass and Grainger's home furnishings shop can be seen on the corner of Finkle Street.

The Council Chambers in the Town Hall, shown here, were the centre of civic life witnessing many moments of local and national history....

Civic times...& a royal declaration

Northern Review. JULY 25, 1891.

THE PROCESSION STARTING FROM THE TOWN HALL.

Sir Horace Davey Q.C. M.P. ADDRESSING THE MEETING.

THE VERY LATEST

A SHEPHERD

SKETCHES AT THE
TRADES DEMONSTRATION AT STOCKTON.

Major events were announced at the Town Hall, including on 22 June 1911 the declaration of the Coronation of King George V, when huge crowds gathered to celebrate. Note the tram trying to proceed past Winpenny House.

HOSPITAL DEMONSTRATION AT STOCKTON.

The seventh annual demonstration of the Friendly and Trades' Societies of Stockton, in aid of the funds of the hospital of that town, was held on Sunday. The various Friendly and Trades' Societies assembled in the High street, and marched through the principal streets of the town with eight brass bands. They met the Mayor (Councillor R. H. Appleton) and Corporation at the Town Hall, and proceeded thence to the great Exchange Hall, where a large public meeting, presided over by Mr. W. Whitwell, J.P., treasurer of the Stockton Hospital, took place. The Mayor, Sir Horace Davey, Q.C., M.P., Mr. T. Wrighton, J.P., Major Ropner, J.P., Mr. C. Head, J.P., and other well-known townsmen were on the platform. The Chairman said they had recently spent a considerable amount over the hospital, viz., £14,584 2s. 1d. They had provided a very considerable extension in the shape of a new wing, into which their old patients were taken while they were improving the old wing. On the new wing they had spent £5,379 3s. 1d., providing...

The speech by Sir Horace Davey delivered at the Friendly Societies' Demonstration in aid of the Stockton Hospital was worthy of himself, as well as of the leading philanthropic agitation in the community. The borough member is a liberal contributor to the Hospital, and on Sunday he showed himself both governed and just in his recognition of the support given by the industrial classes. In his speech he took special note of the fact that nearly two thirds of the income of the Hospital is met by the voluntary contributions of the working men of the town. He added:—"That it only a most creditable thing to the members, but it must be most satisfactory to themselves or their relatives they going to know that in case of sickness or any distress; and they show that in protect among their order the spirit of independence.

The importance of the Town Hall in being part of events in local civic life was demonstrated on many occasions. In 1891 the seventh annual demostration of the Friendly & Trades Societies of Stockton having gathered in aid of raising funds for the town's hospital, met in the High Street from where they marched to the Town Hall where they met the Mayor, Councillor R.H. Appleton before proceeding to the Exchange Hall where a number of local dignitaries, including Sir Horace Davey Q.C. & M.P. for Stockton spoke of their support.

When you walk beyond the Town Hall..

This image from the early 1900's shows the northern end of the High Street, a scene dominated by the Victoria Buildings, a late ninetenth century development which replaced the old almshouses. The sixteen ocupants of the almshouses were moved to another building on the corner of Dixon Street and Dovecote Street. Beyond the Victoria Buildings are the Royal Oak Hotel and the Parish Church whilst hansom cabs await their next fare.

...the northern end of the High Street

Hansom cabs trot along next to the no. 45 tram whilst in the distance the awnings of Matthias Robinson's Coliseum - one of the town's most popular retail stores, can be seen with Bishopton Lane beyond the store.

The northern end of the High Street is for once, devoid of any traffic as only a horse and cart and a horse being walked along the cobbles attract any attention in the view towards Church Row and Bishopton Lane.

A fine view from the end of Dovecot Street, of the northern end of the High Street on Market Day - a crowd in the foreground suggests it could be Stockton Hirings. Most of the market stalls in this part of the High Steeet sold fresh fruit and vegetables.

Two trams come into town along Norton Road.

Yarm Road

Fashionable suburban development along Yarm Road in the late 1920's, part of the expansion of the town west of the High Street. Just beyond the houses on the left was the Queen Victoria School which opened 28 October 1905. Opposite is St Peter's Church, consecrated in 1881, which had a capacity for 600 people. In the distance is Yarm Road Methodist Church, built in 1903.

Yarm Lane & Bowesfield Lane

Yarm Lane seen from the Empire Theatre. The Grey Horse Hotel is opposite the Royal London Insurance Company with the spire of St George's Church in the distance. The traffic officer is ensuring all flows well on this day in the late 1920's.

A children's fancy dress procession moves along Yarm Lane from the High Street. The Union flag suggest this may be at the end of the Great War. Or is it the Cherry Fair? The Castle Hat Shop and Rossi's confectioner shop are visible in the distance.

One of the town's most popular public houses was 'Ye Olde Green Bushes Inn', a Bass House in Yarm Lane close to the junction with Brunswick Street. This building which offered accommodation, was redeveloped in later years.

In their early days, Stockton Cricket, Football & Rugby clubs all used the fields at the end of the lane close to Bowesfield Farm, as a venue.

Bowesfield Lane c1860, known then as Love Lane. A footpath from a stile at the end of West Row joined Love Lane close to a large pond. It's suggested that William Wordsworth walked here during visits to his wife's family.

Dovecot Street

In the early nineteenth century Dovecot Street led to Windmill Lane (later Mill Lane) linking the town with Dovecot Mill, built c1814 and shown here in the 1920's. The mill was a tall structure of at least six storeys and features a reefing gallery. Dovecot Mill had easy access to send or receive grain from ships berthed on the River Tees. The mill in Dovecot Street was finally demolished in the early 1930's.

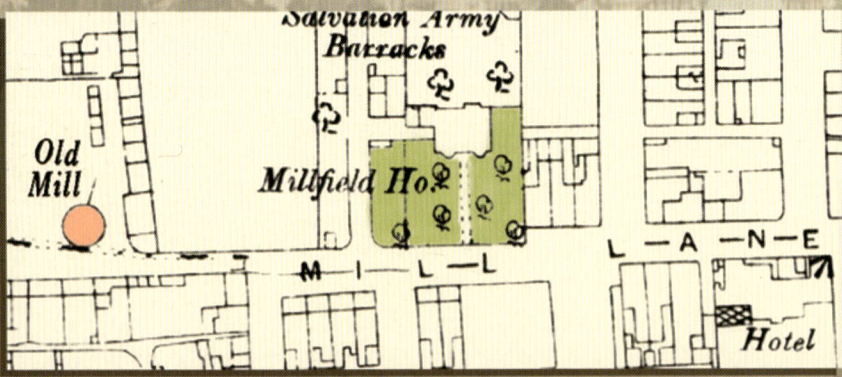

The old mill is shown here on this 1893 map, along with Millfield House, listed in a 1930 Directory as a Tax Office. (Reproduced with kind permission of Ordnance Survey).

Reproduced from 1895 Twenty-Five inch series, with the kind permission of the Ordnance Survey

A crowd of men and boys stand at the entrance to Dovecot Street c1909 with the Alma Hotel and Stockton Literary and Philosophical Institute dominating the background. With the Spread Eagle Hotel adjacent to the Alma, competition for trade must have been fierce.

View from Dovecot Street towards the High Street c1935

Dovecot Street was once called Ducket Lane, a name dating back to the time when it bordered ploughed narrow strips of land which stretched down to Yarm Lane. A dovecote at the entrance to the street had been converted to a house by 1639. Later called Dove Cote Lane the very short street ended at West Row – in 1724 a Quaker Meeting House stood there

The coming of E.S. Maxwell

THE GREATEST CLOTHING & OUTFITTING SALE

EVER HELD IN STOCKTON, STARTS

TO-MORROW, SATURDAY,

When the whole of JOHN PECKSTON'S HIGH-CLASS STOCK will be offered at Wonderful Reductions, having been bought by

E. S. MAXWELL,

(THE OUTFITTER of Newcastle-on-Tyne)

AT A LARGE DISCOUNT OFF COST PRICES.

SEE WINDOWS AND CATALOGUES.

We Show Below a Few of the Many Bargains to be Offered:	Peckston's Price	SALE PRICE
Men's Suits, Ready-to-wear, in Tweeds, Worsteds and Serges...	30/- to 35/6	19/11
Men's Overcoats in Tweeds, Rain-proof, Garbardine, etc. ...	21/6 to 45/	14/11 to 30/-
A lot of Youths' Black Suits, Long Trousers, Sizes 11 and 12	16/11 to 25/6	8/11 to 12/11
Boys' Brighton and Suffolk Suits, 3 Garments, in sound Tweeds	12/11 to 18/6	6/11 to 9/11
14 Girls' Reefer Coats ...	12/6 to 16/6	5/-
Little Boys' York Overcoats, Fine Serge, trimmed Red Cord	18/11 to 21/6	5/-
Boys' Portsmouth Overcoats, Fine Serge ...	13/11 to 15/6	7/11
Boys' Fancy Suits, Belted and 3-Garment Style ...	8/11 to 12/6	3/11 to 8/11
A lot of Oddments in Boys' and Girls' Pure Wool Jerseys ...	3/6 to 4/6	1/- & 1/6
Gent's Fancy Vests, Winter Weight, Beautiful Quality ...	10/6 to 18/6	4/11 to 5/11
100 Ladies' and Gent's Umbrellas	3/11 to 25/6	1/11 to 18/11
A lot of Gent's Fancy Print Shirts	2/6 to 5/6	1/- & 1/6
Gent's Silk Mufflers ...	6/6 to 10/6	3/11
Fancy Silk Handkerchiefs ...	1/11 to 3/11	1/- & 1/6
Gent's Ceylon and Wool Shirts (soiled) ...	1/11¼ to 2/11	1/- & 2/6
Gent's Felt Hats, a few to clear...	4/6 to 10/6	2/6
Boys' and Gent's Silk Hats ...	12/6 to 15/6	1/-
Gent's Tweed Hats ...	3/6 to 4/6	1/-
Ladies' Gloves, Beaver, Kid, and Suede ...	2/6 to 3/6	1/-
Dozens of Boys' and Men's Tweed Caps...	1/- to 3/6	2/d to 1/-

AND MANY HUNDREDS OF BARGAINS BESIDES IN EVERYTHING FOR BOYS', YOUTHS', AND GENTS' WEAR—COME AND SEE!

CENTRAL-BUILDINGS.

High-st., Stockton-on-Tees.

LAST TWO WEEKS OF THE GREATEST CLOTHING AND OUTFITTING SALE

Ever held in Stockton. The High-class Stock of JOHN PECKSTON having been bought at a large Discount off Cost Prices, is now being offered at WONDERFUL REDUCTIONS. Everything must go to make room for an entirely new stock.

BUY YOUR CHRISTMAS PRESENTS AT NEARLY HALF-PRICE.

	Peckston's Price	SALE PRICE
Gent's Overcoats in Blanket Tweeds, Rainproof Garbardines, etc.	30/- to 45/-	16/11 to 30/11
Gent's Tweed and Serge Suits ...	25/6 to 35/6	18/11 to 26/11
A few left, Ladies' and Gent's Umbrellas	10/6 to 15/6	3/11 to 7/11
Youths' Suits, Long Trousers ...	15/6 to 21/6	9/11 to 12/6
3-Garment Tweed Suits for Boys to 12 years ...	18/11 to 15/6	6/11 to 9/11
Little Boys' Fancy Suits and Tunic Style ...		3/11 & 5/11
A Lot of Boys' Fancy Overcoats ...	10/6 to 17/6	3/11 & 5/11
A few left, Gent's Fancy Vests, Heavyweight ...	12/6 to 15/6	3/11 & 6/11
Gent's Shirts, Flannel, Union, and Wool ...	2/11 to 6/11	1/11¼ to 3/6
A Lot of Men's Grandelle Shirts		1/11½ to 3/6
Men's Pyjamas, Lightweight ...	2/3 & 4/11½	1/9¼ & 1/6½

Buy your Underclothing at less than Cost Price. Useful Presents in Silk Handkerchiefs, Silk Mufflers, White lawn and Linen Handkerchiefs, Gloves, Ties, Fancy Scarfs, Trouser Presses, etc., all at Reduced Prices. Come and have a look at the Windows.

GET A SUIT OR OVERCOAT MADE NOW, AND YOU SAVE TWENTY-FIVE PER CENT.

E. S. MAXWELL,

THE OUTFITTER, CENTRAL BUILDINGS.

High St., Stockton-on-Tees.

The period before the Great War was a busy time for the retail trade with large new shops reflecting the expanding sales. One of the biggest takeovers in Stockton was when Newcastle retailer E.S.Maxwell bought out John Peckston who had been a 'complete outfitter' since 1885. Maxwell's purchase included the Central Buildings premises on the corner of Bishopton Lane and the High Street, known thereafter as 'Maxwell's Corner'.

MATTHIAS ROBINSON'S EMPORIUM

MATTHIAS ROBINSON

Matthias Robinson, born in Constable Burton 1849, was a draper who created a successful retail business in West Hartlepool in 1875. Robinson was ambitious and in May 1896, he purchased from George Young Blair (JP & a Director at Blair Engineering Co.), 149 & 150 High Street, Stockton which he transformed into Stockton's first department store, 'Robinson's Emporium'. Like well-known Middlesbrough retailers, Amos Hinton and John Newhouse, Matthias Robinson offered a complete 'shopping experience' - customers could shop for the latest fashions, buy household goods then socialise in the fashionable new cafe. The store, which opened 29 April 1896, was an immediate success.

Tragedy struck however on Saturday 16 December 1899, when a huge fire broke out just after midnight, destroying the store and causing extensive damage to neighbouring property. Despite this blow, Robinson continued the business from temporary premises and staff retained on full pay; most important he assured customers that all orders would be delivered!

An extensive press campaign was launched to reassure customers orders would be met whilst plans to rebuild were being made.

Matthias Robinson was a determined businessman. Two weeks after the fire, he erected a sizable wooden structure on nearby Wellington Street and resumed his business operations. The former site was swiftly cleared ready for the construction of an even larger department store known as 'Robinson's Coliseum'. Opening on 4 May 1901, the store set new standards. The North-Eastern Daily Gazette praised the 'magnificent new Coliseum' with its striking architectural classic style, describing in detail the 48 departments on three floors and the fashionable restaurant and cafe. One of the first multi-story steel framed buildings in the country, incorporating the latest technology, it included a generator to provide electric lighting. There was also a new pneumatic tube system that moved cash and receipts about the store. The top floors were where dressmakers and tailors worked whilst skilled cabinetmakers had their own workshops, all working in 'the best conditions.'

The phoenix had risen from the ashes.

...AND HIS COLISEUM

A familiar view to generations of shoppers in Stockton, Robinson's classic shop front dominated the northern end of the High Street.

DEATH OF MR M. ROBINSON

Ex-Mayor of Stockton's Fatal Illness

In 1925 Robinson's celebrated their Golden Jubilee year led by a 'Personal Message' from Matthias Robinson, exemplifying his lifelong belief that the customer came first. Four years later on 6 November 1929, Matthias Robinson died after a short illness aged 80 and is buried at Richmond. Robinson's & Sons continued until being bought by Debenhams in the 1960s.

Like many other retail giants, Robinson took a strong interest in local affairs becoming Mayor of Stockton in 1910, Coronation year. His retail business success continued as shown in the advertisement for Stockton's 'Coronation Shopping Week'. There was further expansion in 1914 when Robinson opened a store in Leeds.

In 1896 Robinson and his wife Margaret moved with their family from West Hartlepool to 'Landieu' a house in nearby Hartburn.

Bishopton Lane

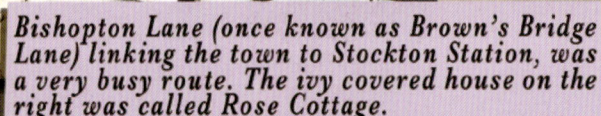

Bishopton Lane (once known as Brown's Bridge Lane) linking the town to Stockton Station, was a very busy route. The ivy covered house on the right was called Rose Cottage.

The junction of Bishopton Lane and Norton Road with John Peckston's store before it was bought by retailer E.S.Maxwell. The location was once an elegant garden adjacent to the house occupied by Major John Jenkins after the Civil War ended.

This 1920's view is looking towards town from outside the Queen's Hotel and the entrance to the station plaza area with Balaclava Street on the immediate left. Behind the fence and bushes is the incline on Bishopton Lane as it passes under the railway line. The Labour Exchange would be an all too familiar building to many people in Stockton at this time.

The convergence of Bishopton Lane and Durham Lane is seen here in an elegant corner building with it's memorable circular tower. Built in 1897 the building marked an area known as Newtown which as the name suggests was one of the early suburban areas of Stockton.

Extending to the west... Newtown

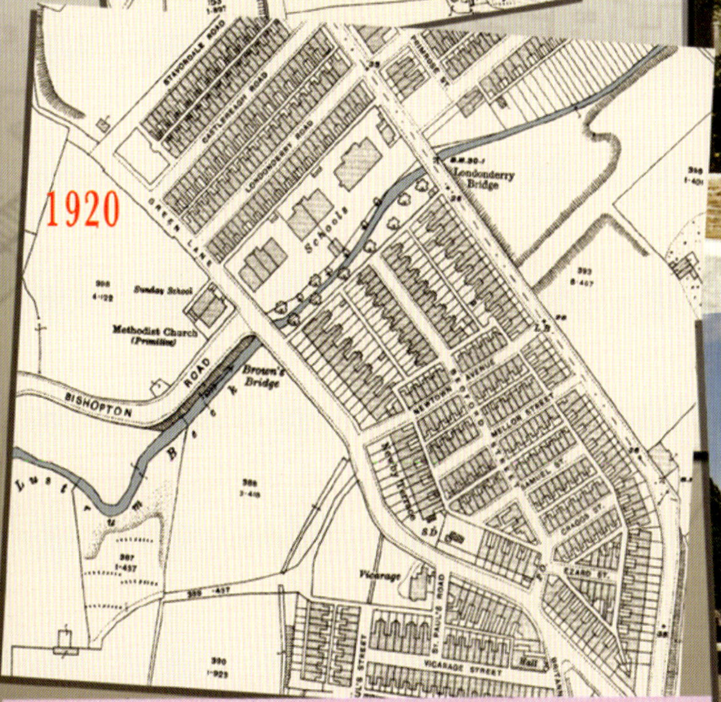

Brown's Bridge & Tommy Wren's Mill

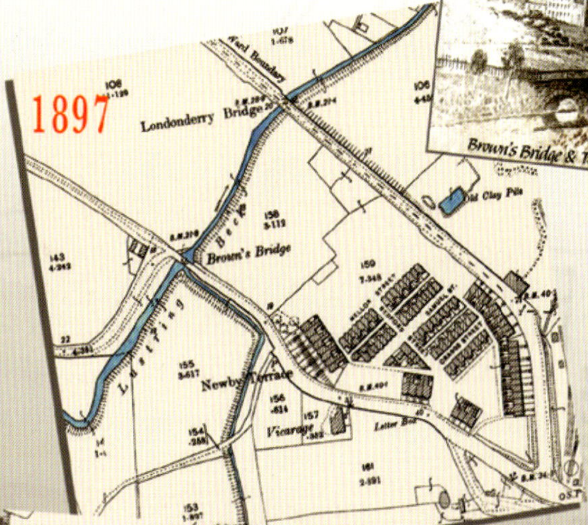

1897

1920

Development west of Stockton is shown here in these maps from 1897 and 1920. Brown's Bridge, a country lane in the sketch (top), is now increasingly surrounded by rows of tightly packed terraced houses.

Reproduced from 1897 & 1919 Twenty-Five inch series, with the kind permission of the Ordnance Survey

Vicarage Terrace, Newtown

This view of tree lined elegant late Victorian houses on Newby Terrace and St Paul's Vicarge in the distance contrasts with the terraced houses in the image of Vicarage Terrace. As the town expanded builders bought up pockets of land to provide housing for the emerging middle classes as suburbia was created. The once country lane is changing quickly.

The grandeur of Norton Road

This is Norton Road c1896. Immediately left is the entrance to Tennant Street, North Terrace, a fine row of Victorian properties then North Terrace Methodist Chapel built in 1866, followed by Eastman's butchers shop on the corner of Hume Street. Opposite is Oliver's Fruit & Confectioner's on the corner of Queen Street, Stockton Blue Coat School, Victoria Terrace and the tower of St Mary's Roman Catholic Church built in 1842 on the corner of Major Street.

and Durham Road

As Stockton expanded housing developed around the main routes from town including Durham Road. This view c1910, is taken from the Londonderry Bridge over the Lustrum Beck with Londonderry Road and Dundas Street also visible.

In the distance behind the hedgerows which line the road is the Fever Hospital. It opened in October 1890 when Stockton had to open a hospital for patients of a typhoid epidemic. This building was a controversial choice as critics considered it to be too close to Durham Road. Previously epidemic patients were placed in Middlesbrough but the epidemic reaching there too meant they could no longer take patients from Stockton.

The Fever Hospital November 1890

This view of Durham Road is looking towards the town across Londonderry Bridge which can be seen in the distance at the lower end of the slight incline of the road. The urban expansion beyond the town led to new communities with houses being built around many external routes including Durham Road. This was the era when local corner shops & post offices arrived to serve the new communities - one such shop can be seen here on the corner of Lambton Road. The images reflect a different age - a time when people walked more safely along roads as the phenomenon of heavy road traffic had yet to arrive.

Change is coming..

The 1920's was a time of change for Stockton as established industries had to adjust to a different economic climate. This aerial view, from 1933, provides an excellent view of the layout of Stockton during the later nineteenth century and early twentieth century.

The High Street is shown, along with other local landmarks such as the Parish Church, the Town Hall and at the top of the image, the Holy Trinity Church, Bridge Road and Victoria Bridge.

Change is evident though with demolition already ongoing in the Thistle Green area between the Parish Church and the river. Industries are retreating too with several shipyards closed.

STOCKTON RACECOURSE

THORNABY

HEAD WRIGHTSON'S

CLEVELAND FLOUR MILL

VICTORIA BRIDGE

CRAIG TAYLOR SHIPYARD (CLOSED)

BRIDGE ROAD

EMPIRE

HOLY TRINITY CHURCH

TOWN HALL

THISTLE GREEN

HIGH STREET

BISHOPTON LANE

This view looking across the river shows that many of the riverside buildings beyond Corporation Quay have been demolished. The area adjacent to the quayside cranes includes Silver Street, Bishop Street and Calvert Street whilst beyond is Thistle Green cleared in the 1920's. In the foreground are the rooftops of buildings on the north side of Finkle Street.

Across the river the remaining industrial buildings from the iron works are visible. The distant spire of Portrack's St James Church (which was opposite Stockton workhouse) can be seen.

Church Row & Stockton Cattle Market

LEFT: This aerial view c1930 shows the north end of the High Street and Church Row. The Georgian elegance of The Square had given way to the need for a dedicated site for Stockton Cattle Market in the mid-1870's. The completion of the demolition of buildings on Thistle Green in the 1920's is visible as the site has been cleared.

LOWER IMAGES: The opening of Stockton Cattle Market brought the need to herd livestock to the site. Sheep can be seen on Church Row (now Church Road) whilst sheep are also being held in The Square behind the Parish Church - as noted in the article from 1879. Stockton's links with agriculture remained until 1959 when the Cattle Market closed to be replaced by the new Stockton Library

CHRISTMAS SHOW

Fat Stock Awards at Stockton Market

Messrs T. Murray and Sons held their annual Christmas Fat Stock Show at the Stockton cattle market to-day. There were forward over 200 special cattle. The judges were Messrs A. Lewis, J. Stoddart and H. Snowdon, of Stockton, for fat cattle, and F. Jackson, North Ormesby and W. Wake, Stockton, for pigs.

The principal awards were:—

Fat Bullock ... Redcar; 2, J L
Dugdale, Cr...
Fat Heifers ...
Fat Cow ...
Fat Bull ...
Three For...
1, Hill, Stoc...
Bacon P...

CATALOGUE
Important Farming
STOCK SALE
6 Horses, Cattle,
Sheep and Poultry.
Implements of Husbandry,
etc.
On Friday, April 28, 1911
Mr. ROBERT HEDLEY

STOCKTON CATTLE MARKET.

Stockton Cattle Market is growing in importance amongst breeders and dealers in the North-Eastern district. The Auction Mart is an extremely popular institution. During the last two weeks the Christmas fat stock sales have large numbers of convenient...

STOCKTON CATTLE MARKET.

MR T. W. HORNBY will SELL BY AUCTION, in the above Market, on WEDNESDAY, the 26th day of January, 1887, at half-past Ten o'clock prompt, FOUR FAT HEIFERS, TWO FAT COWS, FOUR IN-CALVING HEIFERS close to profit. Other Cattle may be entered this Sale by applying to the Auctioneer, 6, Dovecot-street, Stockton-on-Tees. No charge for entry. Must be sold without reserve.

Note time of Sale : 10.30 a.m.

1887

1934

1914

Church Row

STOCKTON CATTLE MARKET.—At this market to-day (Wednesday) there was the largest show of fat beasts and all kinds of stock that has ever been seen in Stockton. During the early part of the day accommodation could not be found in the market enclosures, and scores of animals were standing in the street behind the Old Church and in The Square, while many hundreds of sheep were grouped in the High-street. It is usual for large quantities of cattle to be sent to market at this season on account of the grass being done, and this year the necessity of realizing money has no doubt ... to swell the market.

1879

OLD STOCKTON
Constable's Yard

View 1 (see map on p73)

Those hidden away yards & courts

Behind the elegant buildings along Stockton High Street there were many examples of the infamous 'infilling' resulting in the area behind these properties being crammed with narrow, dark, passageways lined with wholly inadequate housing which was home to many people, families of young and old.

In an area bounded by Finkle Street and Castle Gate (north and south) and by the High Street and quayside (west and east), George Yard, Sleigh Yard, Black Lion Yard, Clarence Court, William IV Yard, Dalton's Yard, Black Bull Yard, were all part of the enclosed pockets of slum housing.

A look at the census records cites evidence of living conditions in this area. The 1911 census records one family of eight children living along with their widower father in 4 rooms in Mason's Court - one of many examples of domestic hardship.

Mason's Court (see image left) is an example of the poor housing conditions faced by many of Stockton's inhabitants. Yards and Courts with narrow cobbled pathways, primitive sanitary arrangments with either a pump or standpump shared by all the families providing a sole water supply. Public health was commonly a major problem with outbreaks of disease often rife as epidemics spread quickly in these communities.

The image shows the challenges people faced each day. Stockton like many other industrial towns, had many of these pockets of desperate housing areas hidden away in many cases from the view of a public, who nevertheless knew they were there.

Yet Mason's Court was not the poorest housing area......

Cherry Lane ran from Thistle Green to The Square. A dark narrow cobbled street packed with terraced houses it was typical of this area. This 1927 image shows the area awaiting demolition - note the Trespass Notice on the wall.

CHERRY LANE 1927

View 2 (see map on p73)

THISTLE GREEN

View 3 — Burton House — Cherry Lane — Thistle Green

The clearing of Thistle Green took place in the Spring of 1928. Whilst the demolition was necessary it is poignant to see this once elegant square being pulled down. Burton House, once the Tees Conservancy Commissioners and Tees Navigation Company offices, was the final building to go.

APRIL 1928

The progress of the demolition was regularly featured in local newspapers as these images show. Burton House remained a recognisable feature as the buildings around it were torn down.

APRIL 1928

MAY 1928

Burton House — Cherry Lane — View 4 — Thistle Green — to Bishop's Landing & Quayside

Map extract reproduced from 1895 Twenty-Five inch series, with the kind permission of the Ordnance Survey

HOUSEWIFE LANE

1849, Oct. 24.—Wm. Ranger, Esq., Superintendent Inspector of the General Board of Health, on this and following days, held sittings at Darlington to enquire into its sanitary condition. He commenced a similar enquiry at Stockton, Oct. 31st, and Hartlepool, Nov. 7th. His remarks at the close of each enquiry shewed the necessity of attention to drainage, the supply of water, ventilation of streets and dwellings, &c., recommending also, in each case, application of the provisions of the Public Health Act 1848.

The privies are situated within three feet of the houses, the contents of which have to be carried through the living rooms, much to the discomfort of occupants.

JULY 1893: REPORT TO STOCKTON URBAN SANITARY AUTHORITY

1850, July 15.—A public meeting held at Stockton to consider Mr. Ranger's "Report to the General Board of Health on a preliminary inquiry into the sewerage, drainage, and supply of water, and the sanitary condition of the Inhabitants of Stockton-on-Tees."

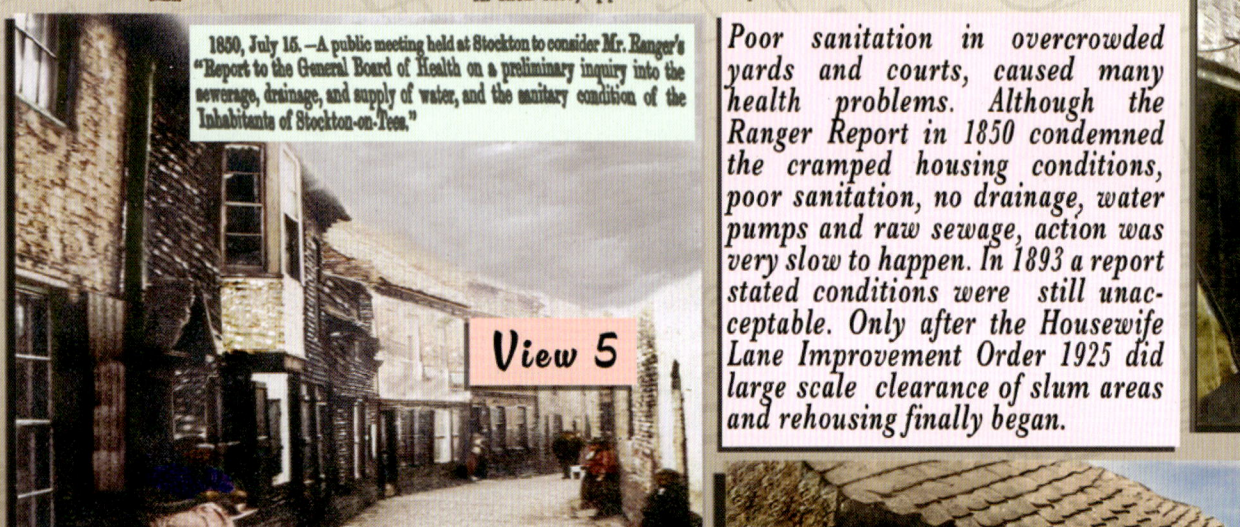

View 5

Poor sanitation in overcrowded yards and courts, caused many health problems. Although the Ranger Report in 1850 condemned the cramped housing conditions, poor sanitation, no drainage, water pumps and raw sewage, action was very slow to happen. In 1893 a report stated conditions were still unacceptable. Only after the Housewife Lane Improvement Order 1925 did large scale clearance of slum areas and rehousing finally began.

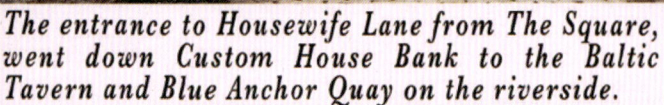

The entrance to Housewife Lane from The Square, went down Custom House Bank to the Baltic Tavern and Blue Anchor Quay on the riverside.

Stockton & Tees-Side Herald
SATURDAY. JULY 18, 1925.

STOCKTON'S £111,000 SLUM DEMOLITION SCHEME

BLACK SPOT THAT NEEDS CLEARING.

Eighty Families Living in Single Rooms.

HEALTH MINISTRY INQUIRY.

REVELATIONS OF HOUSE PROFITEERING AT STOCKTON.

Slum-demolition schemes estimated to cost £111,500 formed the subject of a special Ministry of Health Inquiry at Stockton this week.

The Corporation aim at demolishing all that unsightly property in the Housewife-lane area, the project being intended to clear out about four-and-a-half acres of slum-dwellings.

The considerable area thus released having been condemned as unfit for human habitation, will be suitable for new sites for industries.

As a pointer of the terrible overcrowding prevalent, a witness at the inquiry stated that no fewer than 80 families dwelling within the proposed demolition site are living in single rooms. In 75 houses there were 150 families.

Demolition of housing in Housewife Lane in 1928

1892

"HAVE YOU A TICKET SIR"

CHILDRENS BREAKFASTS
Primitive Methodists
Schools

"STEP THIS WAY."

SOME OF THE APPLICANTS

GIVING OUT SOUP

BREAD AT POLICE STATION.

HALFPENNY BREAKFASTS AT SOUTH STOCKTON MR ERRINGTON

AMONG THE DISTRESS AT STOCKTON.

There were areas of great poverty in Victorian Stockton as shown in this local newspaper page. Councils struggled to keep people fed and soup kitchens and the provision of free meals were commonly held.

1920'S - DEMOLISHING OLD STOCKTON

Four and a half acres of slum dwellings in the Thistle Green area were condemned as unfit for human habitation with evidence of massive overcrowding with density of housing double that of other areas in town. A total of 846 people lived here with 83 families living in single rooms and 23 families in two rooms. Not surprisingly the death rate in the Housewife Lane & Thistle Green was more than double that of the rest of the town. There was a lot of sub-letting too - one tenant (who paid his landlord £26 rent per annum) made £107.90p per year from sub-letting! The Council rehoused many families in new houses at Mount Pleasant and Blue Hall Estate. But in 1933 critics, including Stockton MoH, Dr George McGonigle, argued high rents for the new houses (46p - only 24p previously) meant that many residents remained impoverished despite livng in new homes.

MAY 1933

WHERE THE POOR STARVE TO PAY RENT

SOME ASPECTS OF STOCKTON'S SLUM PROBLEM

THE guarantee of cheap rents on new housing estates is essential if slum clearance schemes are to be successful.

This is emphasised in the case of Stockton, where, in any action under the Ministry of Health's Circular 1331, full consideration must be given to the fixing of rents within the means of the poorest of the working classes.

Thanks to the Government subsidy, low building costs, and cheap money, Stockton Corporation should now have

RENTS TOO HIGH

In 1932 the average rent on the Mount Pleasant estate was 9s 3½d. In the Riverside area for the same period it was 4s 10½d.

As the result of unemployment, the

"From a hygienic and environmental point of view, Mount Pleasant estate appears to be everything that modern sanitary science can demand," states Dr. McGonigle, who looks to rents and family budgets for an explanation of the remarkable divergence in the death rates of the two localities.

pays the landlord 20s per week and receives 45s per week from sub-tenants."

Questioned with regard to what should be done with cleared sites, Alderman Allison said that they certainly should not be left derelict as the Thistle Green site had been so far. The Corporation should utilise them as beautiful open spaces or recreation grounds for children, or modern houses should be built upon them at no more than 12 or 16 to the acre.

My tour of Stockton's poorer quarters revealed nothing that could be described as "shocking" or "appalling." Yet there are large

STOCKTON WORKHOUSE

The *Workhouse*, situated at the corner of the street to which it gives name, is the receptacle for the paupers of the parish

1730.—In the Stockton Corporation accounts this year is the following payment:—"To Mr. Pewterer, for his trouble of writing to the Bishop to obtain leave to dig brick and build a Workhouse

STOCKTON UNION.

THE BOARD of GUARDIANS of this UNION intend at their MEETING on SATURDAY the 14th day of July instant, at 12 o'clock at noon, to proceed to the appointment of a MASTER and MATRON (Man and Wife), for the STOCKTON WORKHOUSE. The Master will be required to act as Relieving Officer and Registrar of Births and Deaths for the Stockton District, comprising the following Townships, viz.:—Stockton, East Hartburn, Preston, Norton, and Thornaby.

WILLIAM BEST, Clerk. Stockton, 4th July, 1849.

A workhouse was established in Stockton in 1730; an entry in the Corporation accounts records a payment to Mr Pewterer 'for the trouble of writing to the Bishop to obtain leave to dig brick and build a Workhouse'. Located on the corner of Workhouse Street and Bishop Street the building was taken over by the Stockton Poor Law Union when it was formed in 1837 (representing 41 constituent parishes). With a limited capacity of 40 inmates, poor conditions with few facilities, plans were made to move to a larger building with capacity for up to 260 inmates.

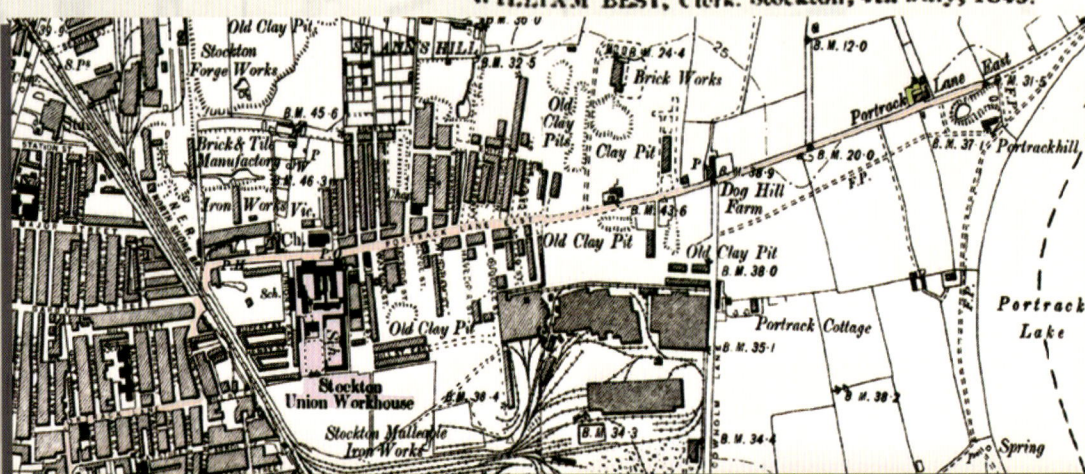

Reproduced from 1895 Twenty-Five inch series, with the kind permission of the Ordnance Survey

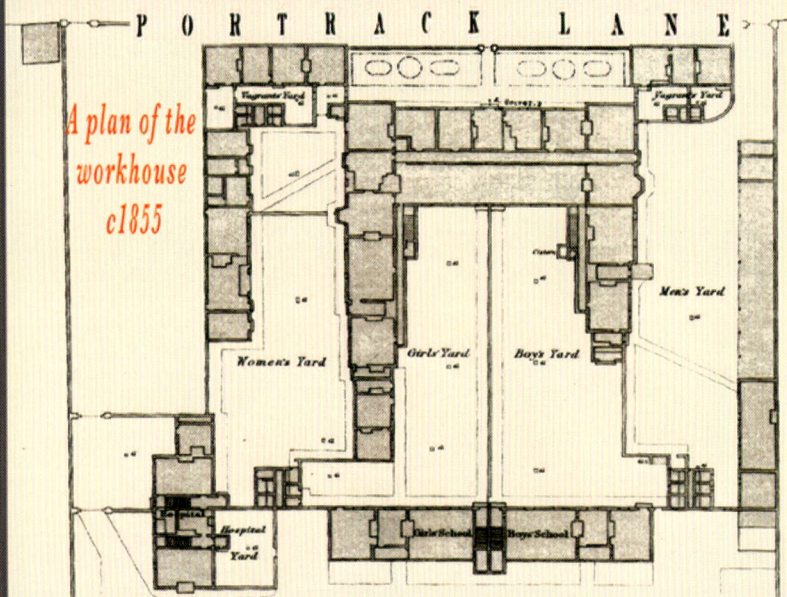

A plan of the workhouse c1855

The new workhouse was built on a nine acre site on Portrack Lane with Richard Langdale appointed as the new Master of the Workhouse on 14 July 1849. Workhouse inmates were moved from Bishop Street to Portrack on 19 April 1851. The plan of the workhouse includes a hospital - gender segregation is typical of the time. The Workhouse was soon extended with a large new infirmary for male patients in 1868. In 1930 the building became a Public Assistance Institution, then in 1948 it became Portrack Geriatric Hospital - renamed St Anne's Hospital in 1972, before being finally being demolished in the late 1970's.

1851, April 19.—The poor of the Stockton Union removed from the old workhouse in Bishop street to the New Union Poor House lately erected in Portrack Lane. [The old workhouse was sold in the following year for £600.]

The workhouse faced onto Portrack Lane. This view shows the entrance hall, and the Master's Quarters as well as the Porter's Lodge and Grocery Store

Union Workhouse, Bishop street, will accommodate 40, average 20,

Help for the needy: the Quayside Mission

Large crowds gathered to see the Quayside Mission Hall and Rescue Home open on 1 March 1906. Costing £600 to build, there was still a mortgage of £300 outstanding as well as £150 used for furnishing. This cost highlighted the need for ongoing donations for support. Located on the south side of The Square close to the entrance to Housewife Lane, the Mission offered accommodation to men who had nowhere else to go. Costing sixpence for one night it provided a much needed service for men who would otherwise be sleeping on the streets. It also offered hot meals to children - especially important when tough economic times hit the town - particularly in the 1920's when the old industries were either laying men off or closing down completely. There were also facilities for the rescue of girls who required help.

STOCKTON QUAYSIDE MISSION.

OPENING OF THE RESCUE HOME AND LODGING-HOUSE.

The Stockton Quayside Mission social scheme was successfully brought into force on Thursday. Since the commencement of the movement for social and moral reform initiated by the authorities of the Mission, a great deal of interest has been aroused on Tees-side by the effort, and there was a large attendance of the general public to witness the opening of the temporary rescue home for girls, and lodging accommodation for workmen. The reform comes under two divisions—namely, weekly boarders and casuals. The latter class is to be catered for in the near future by the erection of a large commodious building at the rear of the Mission Hall, with special facilities and conditions to accommodate upwards of 200 persons. The weekly boarders' quarters, which show a distinct advance for comfort and cleanliness on anything at present available in the town, have been fitted up similar to the Rowton House principle, in the main building. A few of the advantages available to the boarders in this department are:—Each man has a separate private cubicle, fitted with a comfortable bed, with clean bed clothing each week, the use of a private locker for his clothing, etc., the use of the public dining-room, bath and lavatories, the washing and repairing of his clothing, and the use of crockery and cutlery necessary for his requirements. These will only cost him 3s. 6d per week inclusive. The cubicles will be let by the week only. A good garden space at the back being for purposes of recreation. The room is a comfortably furnished apartment, under the control and care of the caretaker and his wife, and for the temporary isolation of girls, and will be for use, free of to all sects and creeds, subject to an order from either a magistrate or minister of the town. The latter department will be especially welcome to the philanthropic bodies in the town, as for years past there has been a great need for a place where rescued girls could be housed for such time as they could be removed to a healthier atmosphere. The Mission Committee have inevitably entailed great cost and provision for these, much needed, but they are sure to receive the sympathetic and practical support of all who have a knowledge of the deadly influence of lodging-house life in our great

Stockton Quayside Mission

Important Developments in Connection with Rescue Work

Those persons who work in the slums of our towns cannot fail to have noticed the conditions of the lodging-house life. The poor unfortunates who drag out their existence day by day in these dwellings have, as a rule, nothing to hope for. Struggle, struggle, week in and week out, the majority half-starved, sunk deep in degradation, with no purpose beyond the gaining of a few coppers for their food and shelter. These waifs and strays eke out their miserable existence, and in the majority of cases are callous of their condition—to the end that in innumerable instances is intimated by a newspaper paragraph which informs the public of the sudden death of an inmate of a lodging-house. Such a state of affairs is painful to those who have the wellbeing of their fellows at heart, so that a warm welcome will be extended the earnest local effort at social and moral reform started by the Stockton

QUAYSIDE MISSION

For the past eleven years, this has ministered in word and deed to the wants and necessities of the unfortunate people of the slums of Stockton. The thing aggressive in character, proved active in consequence, and the workers in connection therewith realising the limitations of their powers in handling the cases constantly coming under their care in an efficient manner, appealed to the people of the town to provide means for the carrying out of a great scheme of social reform, the needs of the case, its object being wide and inclusive:—

Temporary rescue home for fallen girls,

Better lodging-house accommodation for working men;

Mission hall and Sunday school for

A room at the Mission

Portrack Grange: a place of history

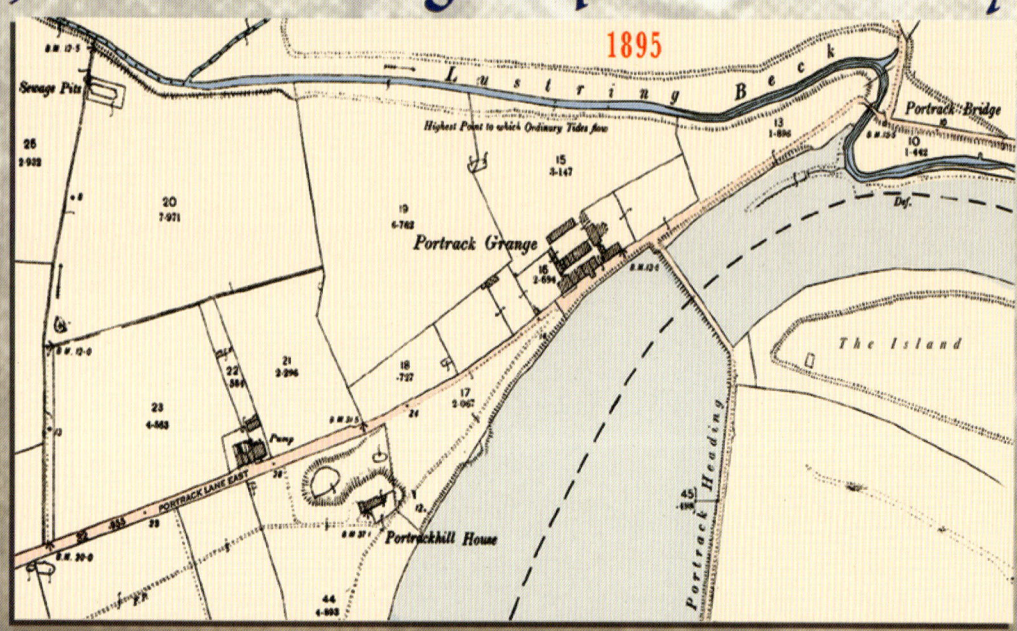

1895

Reproduced from 1895 Twenty-Five inch series, with the kind permission of the Ordnance Survey

Portrack Grange cottages - once a large farmhouse; the front facing window and blocked side window of the 'Angel Room' are in the end property.

Before 1900 Portrack Lane was undeveloped beyond the terraced houses occupied by men working at the local iron works, St James Church, and Stockton Union Workhouse. The ancient route (once called Holm Lane) led to Portrack Grange, & an old packhorse bridge over the Lustring Beck to join a pathway from Holm House Farm to the ferry at Newport. Before the Tees was straightened in 1831, Portrack Grange was close to the river on the Portrack loop. Strong currents caused silt to form large sandbanks making navigation difficult, often causing ships to ground. Struggling to sail around the bend of the river, ships hired men to drag or 'rack' the ships round to 'Port-rack' quay to transfer cargo to smaller craft and flat bottom barges for transport to Stockton. Despite these issues trade at Stockton increased – Thomas Richmond records in 1786 an oil house at Portrack serving Stockton ships involved in the Greenland oil trade whilst 'in the winter many vessels were laid up for the winter (and) delivered their cargoes' (Brewster 1829). A tavern at Portrack Grange (once known locally as 'The Flaming Stump') was popular with ship crews newly arrived or awaiting favourable conditions to sail. It is also thought smugglers hid contraband at the inn before taking it across the fields to Holm House Farm for storage there.

The back of Portrack Grange is visible here in May 1938 as structural alterations are carried out - the old inn is far right.

..& the elegance of the 'Angel Room'

The tavern at Portrack Grange is believed to be the first place at which a Freemasons' Lodge was held when the Lodge of Philanthropy, largely composed of master mariners, was removed from London to Stockton. A wooden ship brought the furniture from London, landing at Portrack at the Queen's Head tavern. The tavern had a very elegant room with a separate entrance called the Angel Room the room. It was named after a stucco frieze with a pattern of foliage and cherubs along its walls. Two cherubs are holding oval frames - one containing a silhouette of a woman's face, opposite a matching design with a head of a man in an oval frame. On the other opposite walls there is a cherub warming his hands by a fire and another cherub sitting astride a corncucopia. Several theories have been suggested about the origin of such delicate artistry; for example William Kent (1684-1748) designer of the Coronation coach and the Shakespeare Monument in Westminster Abbey or John Carr of York as his designs have featured cherub motifs and scrolled acanthus leaves similar to those found in the Angel Room at Portrack.

Mary Nattress wrote a very informative article on Portrack Grange and the Angel Room discussing the origin of the artwork as well as the Queen's Head Tavern at Portrack. A detailed examination in 1955, of the inn building, is included. (CTLHS Bulletin 20 Spring 1973)

Time finally caught up with this wonderful work of art however. In 1954 an article in the Stockton Express highlighted a doubtful future for Portrack Grange Cottages, despite their historic significance. Plans for use of the land for light industry were discussed from 1956 to 1963 before finally in 1964 outline planning permission was given for demolition and clearance of the buildings along Portrack Lane.

Stockton Parish Church

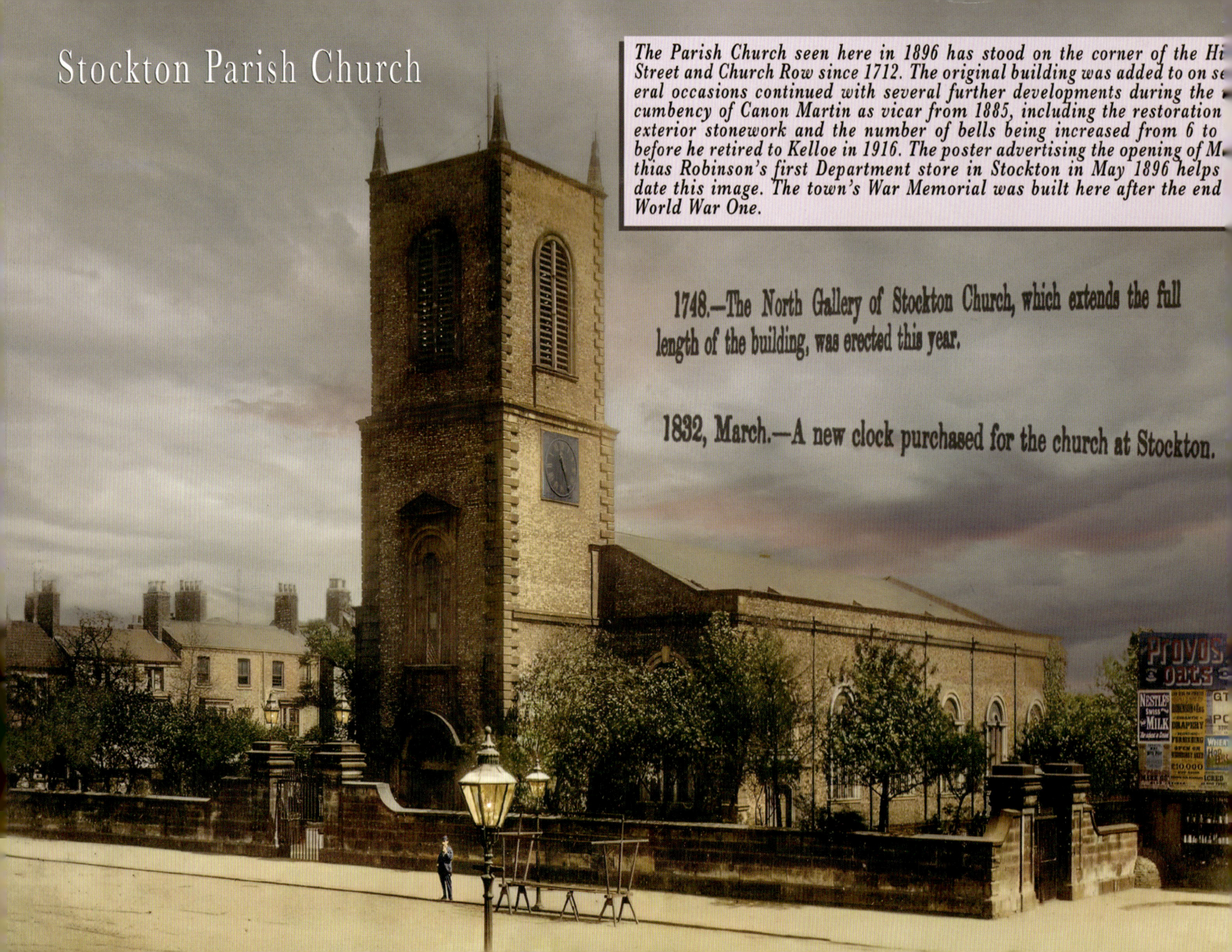

The Parish Church seen here in 1896 has stood on the corner of the Hi
Street and Church Row since 1712. The original building was added to on se
eral occasions continued with several further developments during the
cumbency of Canon Martin as vicar from 1885, including the restoration
exterior stonework and the number of bells being increased from 6 to
before he retired to Kelloe in 1916. The poster advertising the opening of M
thias Robinson's first Department store in Stockton in May 1896 helps
date this image. The town's War Memorial was built here after the end
World War One.

1748.—The North Gallery of Stockton Church, which extends the full
length of the building, was erected this year.

1832, March.—A new clock purchased for the church at Stockton.

The interior of Stockton Parish Church

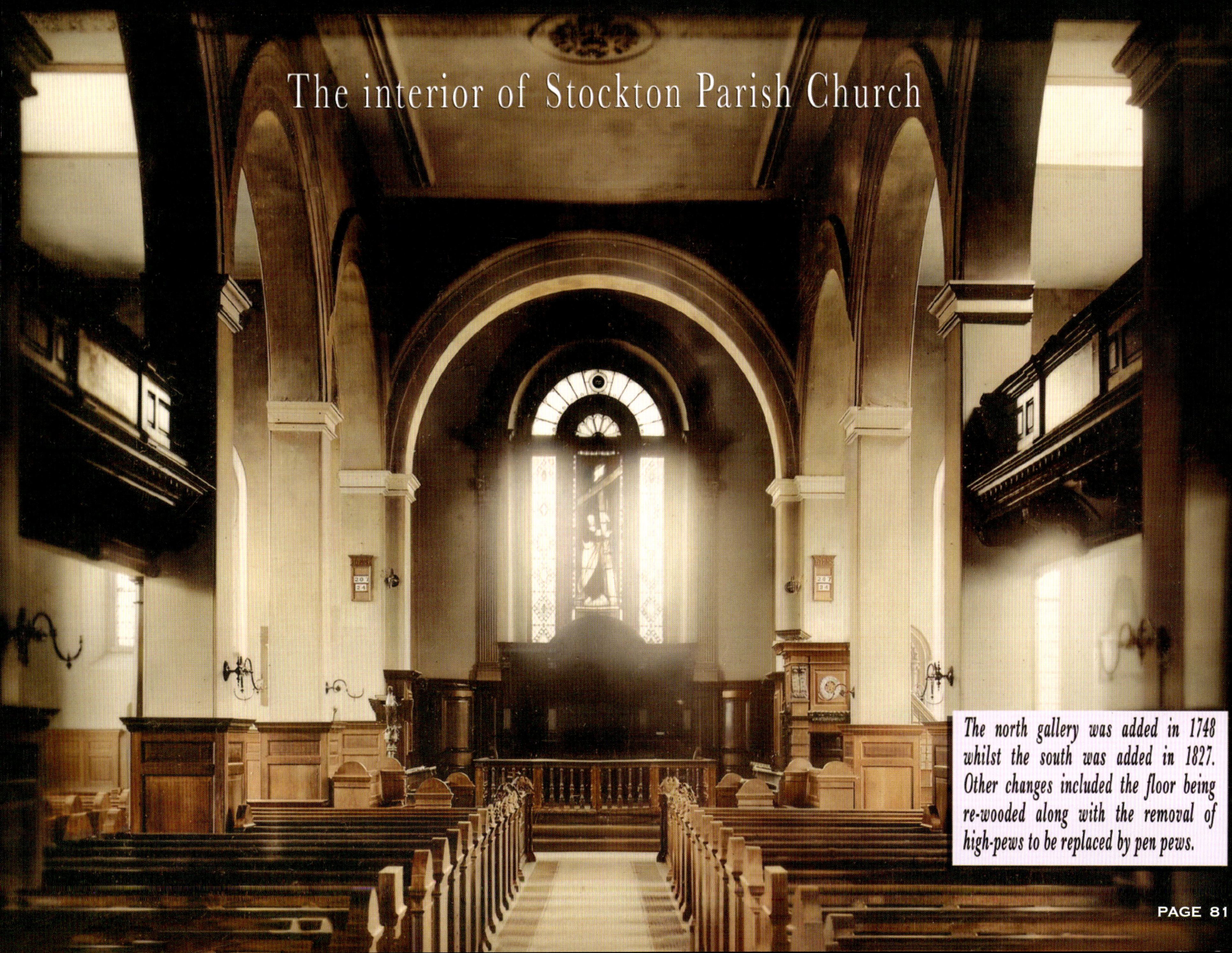

The north gallery was added in 1748 whilst the south was added in 1827. Other changes included the floor being re-wooded along with the removal of high-pews to be replaced by pen pews.

STOCKTON.

The trade of the port of Stockton is practically tied up, and in the course of 24 hours there will be a state of complete stagnation unless the situation suddenly changes. One of the ships of the regular Continental traffic in the absence of a general...

STOCKTON'S FOOD SUPPLIES.

STRONG DENUNCIATION OF TRADERS' UNREASONABLE PRICES

There is a most unreasonable and unjustifiable and un... invaded by people de... within eight hours and hundreds of customers disappointed. The North-Eastern Daily tradesmen will keep cool and not get the position will right food supplies, par... cent action of the... action calculated to which was reported at Board of Guardians that the prices of Board were £7 10s which was described as...

If these prices were here is no reason for merchants.

NORTH-EASTERN DAILY GAZETTE.
WEDNESDAY, AUGUST 5, 1914.

ENGLAND DECLARES WAR ON GERMANY

OFFICIAL.
NEWS OF FLEET IN ACTION

EXPECTED ANY MOMENT.

NEWS RECEIVED UP TO 1 P.M.

THE RED CROSS SOCIETY.

BRANCH FORMED AT STOCKTON.
MOVEMENT TAKEN UP WITH ENTHUSIASM.

A crowded town's meeting was held in the Empire Theatre, Stockton, last night, when a local branch was formed of the Red Cross Society with Surgeon Blandford as president.

The meeting was convened by Ald. R. Stephenson, and supported by the Mayoress, Sir Frank J. W. Blandford, the Town Clerk Cathy J.P.S, Mrs J. Sa...

THE WAR!

The NORTH-EASTERN DAILY GAZETTE have made special arrangements for receiving the latest telegrams of the hostilities now taking place between AUSTRIA AND SERVIA.

For all To-day's WAR NEWS GET TO-NIGHT'S FINAL EDITION of the NORTH-EASTERN DAILY GAZETTE.

WAR AND TRADE

Tees-Side Industries Will Go On. 🇬🇧

FINE PATRIOTISM

OF THE EMPLOYERS OF THE DISTRICT.

"EVERY EFFORT TO KEEP WORKS GOING."

POSITION REVIEWED

TEES-SIDE AN...
OVER-SEA TR...

STOCKTON PATRIOTS.

Civilian Training Corps
F...

PATRIOTIC C.L.B.
STOCKTON UNITS VOLUNTEER IN A BODY.

The following letter was addressed on August 7th by Field Marshall Lord Grenfell, Commandant of the Church Brigade, to the Secretary of the War London:

... desire of the Church Lads' ... over 17 years of age—I have honour to place the whole organization the service of His Majesty's Govern...

... officers commanding various units ... ordered to report themselves to ... Territorial Associations for any ... at may be required of them.—I am very truly, GRENFELL, Field Marshal...

STOCKTON CIVILIANS' TRAINING CORPS

R. Tyson Hodgson, J.P. presided largely attended meeting at the Vane ..., Stockton, last night, when it ... inaugurate a branch of...

SOLDIERS' WIVES' PLIGHT.

GREAT DISTRESS AT STOCKTON.
A RELIEF COMMITTEE FORMED.

A SPLENDID SPIRIT IN STOCKTON.

Volunteer Detachment of the Red Cross Society.

Stockton has not a volunteer detachment of the Red Cross Society, but steps were taken last night to form one, and at a crowded meeting of ladies and gentlemen held in the lecture hall of the Y.M.C.A.

The meeting was called by Mr. Louis I. Prinsky on behalf of the Literary and Philosophical Institute, but the opinion was expressed that the meeting was not sufficiently representative and the more...

Deserters Rejoin Colours at Stockton.
HORSES COMMANDEERED

More horses, carts and wagons belonging to the local tradesmen and others were commandeered at Stockton yesterday by the military authorities. The work is being attended to by Territorial officers and the local officer in charge is Lieut. Robson, son of Coun. Isaac Robson, who is attached to the local Territorials.

Altogether about 100 horses and 50 carts, wagons and flushing vans have been requisitioned and many of them were sent away yesterday. It is understood they are to be used in connection with home defence purposes.

The banks re-opened at Stockton yesterday and though they were kept very busy during the morning there was only what was expected after the additional bank holiday. All demands for gold for wages and other necessary purposes were readily...

Sergeant Edward Cooper V.C. returns home to Portrack

Born in Stockton 4th May 1896, Edward Cooper who was working for the Co-Op selling fruit when war broke out in 1914, joined the Kings Royal Rifle Corps. On 16 August 1917 Sergeant Edward Cooper was awarded the V.C. at the Third Battle of Ypres for his act of bravery during an attack on a blockhouse which captured enemy men and saved the lives of many of his colleagues. Sergeant Cooper only discovered news of his award returning home on leave. A huge crowd at Stockton Station cheered him home to 12 Barrett Street, Portrack. After the war Edward Cooper returned to Stockton becoming an honorary freeman a few weeks before his death in 1985.

STOCKTON MAN WINS V.C.

CO-OP WORKER'S VALOUR
THE STOCKTON V.C.

Stockton is proud of its V.C. It is claimed that in no part of the country has any particular locality responded more loyally to the call of the King than has the district of Portrack, Stockton, where there are whole streets of households represented in either the Army or Navy—more particularly the Navy—and it is, therefore, most fitting that this high distinction should come to that part of the town.

Sergt. Cooper, V.C., is a son of Mr and Mrs W. E. Cooper, of 12 Barrett street. Mr Cooper is a labourer, employed at the Malleable Ironworks, and has two other sons and five daughters.

SPECIAL EFFORT AT THORNABY.

At Thornaby, a special committee consisting of members of the Town Council and prominent citizens has been appointed...

TRAINING OF CITIZENS.
Proposal to Form a League at Stockton.

TOCKTON WAR MEMORIAL.

Sir.—The War Memorial Committee
...... anxious for the atten-

STOCKTON'S WAR MEMORIAL.

Bishop of Durham on the Message of the Martyrs.

STOCKTON'S WAR MEMORIAL

Unveiling By The Earl Of Durham.

War Memorial 31 May 1923...Stockton pays tribute to the fallen...

mally dedicated by the
in the presence of over
memorial consists of
stone, erectd, at a cost
outh-west corner of the
acing the High Street.
was attended by the
and Thornaby, mem-
tion, representatives of
ud friendly societies.
ren of the borough.
am, in unveiling the
y would reverence the
mbol of splendid ser-
d of courageous hope

op's Address.

tion having been per-
of Durham said it was
representative of the
se, to place their civic
rotection and blessing
owadays the results of
ointing, and they asked
men who had fallen

On 31 May 1923 a crowd of 20,000 including local civic dignitaries, soldiers and many school children watched as Stockton's War Memorial to 1,223 men who died during World War One was unveiled by the Earl of Durham and formally dedicated by the Bishop of Durham. The Portland stone memorial was erected, at a cost of £7,500, in the south-west corner of the parish churchyard.

Unveiling B

The Earl of Dur
afternoon, Stockton
which has been ere
street, at a cost, incl
of adjoining propert
service of dedicati
by the Bishop of Du

The Memorial Fu
£12,000, and the ba
in a scheme for pro
education of the chi

The Memorial, whi
old Parish Church, i
sides with a wrough
stone piers at the a
folding gates to the
space within being
flags and turf.

The monument itse
of Portland stone, and rests upon a re course over the
forced concrete foundation, is raised t: a moulded base course, and upon this is

PRICE 4d. EACH

BOROUGH OF ...
STOCKTON-ON-TEES

Peace
Celebrations.

July 13th & 19th, 1919.

Official Programme
of the
Celebrations and Sports.

... to a plain podium,
nze panel on its ....
ords: " The na....
scribed in the
laid up in the
e podium is cro....
ing, from which
t of the monum
s is practica
with detach....
ont of se
shaft is fin
and corn
d decorated
ds, while t
entation.
he shaft of
onze panel
with ornar
arms of St
a wreath
following
" To t
tockton-o
ar, 1914-1
th a ma
and R
s death
haft is o
wn carved in stone
above the blocking

STOCKTON'S WAR MEMORIAL.

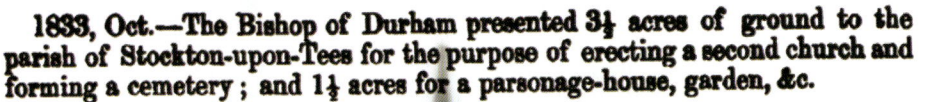

1833, Oct.—The Bishop of Durham presented 3¼ acres of ground to the parish of Stockton-upon-Tees for the purpose of erecting a second church and forming a cemetery; and 1½ acres for a parsonage-house, garden, &c.

1833, Nov. 2.—A meeting of the inhabitants of Stockton was held, at which subscriptions were commenced for the erection of a church or chapel, and for inclosing the ground recently given by the Bishop of Durham for a cemetery. A numerous committee was at the same time appointed to collect subscriptions.

Holy Trinity Church

Holy Trinity Church, which opened on 13 May 1838, was built on Black Lion Farm once part of Castle Park, land which had been farmed since the Restoration. The entrance to the farm track which crossed the site was reached from Yarm Lane. In the early years there were still haystacks and a large pond in the vicinity of the church. William Wordsworth the poet, is thought to have walked across this land when staying with his wife Mary's family in Stockton in the early 1800's. This image from 1896, shows the fine architectural style of the building.

St George's Presbyterian Church in 1896, on the corner of Yarm Lane and Lawson Street. The street lamp (with a boy leaning on it) stands on the corner of Bowesfield Lane.

St George's Church

St George's Church was built in 1876 with a capacity for 630 people. The south entrance is on to Yarm Lane whilst the school next to the church is partly visible. A tall tower behind the church is part of West End House, one of four houses which stood in substantial grounds.

North Terrace Methodist Chapel built in 1866, on the corner of Hume Street and Norton Road. The posters advertise Rev.C. Back from Darlington preaching on 24 September 1899.

North Terrace Methodist Chapel

John Wesley first visited Stockton on 10 August 1748, preaching in the Market Place 'to a large and rude congregation'. Wesley made several more visits recording his preaching was once badly disrupted by the Press Gang attempting to take two local men for a man-of war vessel.

St Mary's Catholic Church

There was a small Catholic population remaining in Stockton after the Reformation worshipping at a small chapel in Finkle Street until the 1840's when St Mary's was built. The church on Norton Road, designed by A. W. Pugin and built in Early English style, opened on 7 July 1842. Enlarged in 1870 at a cost of £3,000, 5am mass at the church is said to have been popular with Irish workers on their way to start the 6am day shift.

Lightfoot Grove Baptist Church

Located on the junction of Lightfoot Grove and Bowesfield Lane, Lightfoot Grove Baptist Church was opened at 3pm on 21 April 1904. With seating for 600, the architectural style, both inside and out, was 'an attempt to work in the spirit of the modern arts and craft movement'.

Stockton's Handsome Architecture. | Opening of New Baptist Church

NEW BAPTIST CHURCH OPENED AT STOCKTON

J.P. Pritchett of Darlington: church designer

The elegant spire of Yarm Road Methodist Church towers high into the sky. Built on the corner of Yarm Road and Grove Street, the church was designed by W.-J. Morley of Bradford, a prominent Wesleyan architect of the time. The church which had a capacity of 660, opened in October 1904.

St Paul's Church... interior

St Paul's Church was erected in 1885, in Wellington Street at a cost of £3,700. Designed by J.P. Pritchett of Darlington it was built of yellow and red brick, with stone facings in the Early English style and had a capacity of 380 people.

The Baptist Tabernacle on Wellington Street close to the High Street, opened on 11 June 1903. Designed by a Stockton architect, T.W.T Brown, the building cost £7,200, with local companies, including Head Wrightson & Co., being involved in the construction. Described as being elegant and spacious, the opening service was conducted by Rev. W.Y. Fullerton from Leicester after which there was tea in the school room.

Inside St James Church, Portrack

St James' Church was built on Portrack Lane in 1867-68 at a cost of £6,000. Seating 470, the church designed by J.P. Pritchett of Darlington was built of stone with Bath dressings in the Early Decorated style. The church was renovated in 1889 increasing the capacity to 670. The church was built opposite Stockton Workhouse, which became Portrack Hospital.

STOCKTON AND THORNABY HOSPITAL

Northern Echo 22 November 1876

When a 9 bed surgical hospital opened in Sugar House Lane near Thistle Green in 1862, became inadequate a Hospital Committee chaired by Marshall Fowler Esq. of Preston Hall purchased land on the west side of Bowesfield Lane for the new Stockton and Thornaby Hospital. The first patients entered the hospital in November 1876.

On 31 October 1875 large crowds lined the High Street to see a long procession of local dignitaries (including Joseph Dodds M.P.) and brass bands, led by the Mayor (G.M. Watson), proceed to Bowesfield Lane to the construction site to see a memorial stone laid by Mr Fowler. A sealed bottle was placed with the stone, containing the day's newspapers, coins & documents related to the hospital. To mark the occasion the hospital's architect, Eugene E. Clephan presented a silver mounted ivory mallet to Mr Fowler.

A Royal Day at Stockton and Thornaby Hospital

Queen's Nurses Home

Matron & Nurses

A commemorative booklet for the event

Princess Mary opened an extension in 1926, increasing beds to 133. After lunch at Preston Hall and cheered by crowds along Yarm Road and Bowesfield Lane, the Princess was welcomed at the hospital by Sir Frank Brown J.P. and many other local dignitaries. The ceremony included a service by the Vicar of Stockton and dedication by the Bishop of Durham before Princess Mary formally opened and then toured the new buildings. The day was concluded when she planted a tree in the hospital grounds.

The Hospital

Interior of Mens Ward

Hospital Day raising money

Queen's Nurses Home

The new wing

Arriving at the ceremony, Princess Mary & the Mayor of Stockton , Leonard Ropner.

To commemorate the day, Princes Mary plants a tree in the hospital grounds. Frank Downey, the Town Clerk of Stockton looks on as the crowd applaud. .

23 September 1926 HRH Princess Mary Opens Stockton and Thornaby Hospital Extension

The Higher Grade Schools

The Higher Grade Schools in Nelson Terrace were officially opened 18 January 1896. The ceremony, attended by many local dignitaries including the Mayors of Stockton (Ald. Walton) and Thornaby (Ald, Wm Whitwell J.P.), was preceded by a procession from the Borough Hall along the High Street. Guests gathered in the school hall as the Vicar of Stockton Henry Martin, led a service before the Rev. G.S. Ordish, Chairman of Stockton School Board formally opened the school. In turn an engraved silver key was presented by J.M. Bottomley architect of the building, to the Chairman.

The first floor had a senior central hall and science based classrooms whilst the second floor had classrooms for training pupil teachers and art subjects.

Along with several open fires in classrooms and staff room, there was an up-to-date heating system installed. The total cost including internal fittings was £19,000.

Mr Prest from Newcastle was appointed Headteacher. Two entrances for Girls (Junior & Senior) & the same for Boys gave access to the new four storey building. On the lower ground floor there was a gymnasium, a junior central hall, classrooms, with lecture rooms on the upper ground floor.

QUEEN VICTORIA HIGH SCHOOL FOR GIRLS

The foundation stone for the school had been laid on Thursday 14 July 1904. The first endowed school of its kind in Durham, most of the £10,000 cost was met by donations of £6,250 from Mayor of Stockton, Frank Brown and a grant of £3,750 from Durham County Council. An endowment fund of £5,000 had been set up to support the only school in the region established on a public basis for girls.

The Royal Visit to Stockton.
DETAILS OF THE VISIT.

Ever since it was first announced several months ago that a member of the Royal family had kindly consented to visit the town and open the schools which were recently presented, the public have been looking forward with most pleasurable anticipation to the happy event. It was not known until a day or two ago whether the Royal party would pass through the town and return direct from the school to Castle by motor, but is soon stated that the Princess would proceed via the main thoroughfares of Yarm-lane and High-street the interest in the visit became keener than ever. The Mayor is unable to give very little more than hours' request that tradesmen and should decorate their premises en route to the Station, but the short time they have any great effect on desire of the shopkeepers and private means to make the town look as attractive as the occasion demands

A Loyal Reception.
FLORAL TRIBUTES.

Miss Alice Brown, aged nine years, youngest daughter of the founder of the school, presented Princess Henry with handsome bouquets of orchids and white lilies; while Miss Freda Douglas, one of the eldest students presented a bouquet of pink roses to the Princess Ena.

ELABORATE DECORATIONS at the Town Hall and Borough Hall, the Tramway Company had the electric standards along the centre of High-street profusely covered with artistic bunting, and these, as night be imagined, played a very important part in the town's decorations. Shopkeepers, as already suggested, rose to the occasion in loyal style, and vied with the other in making the best display, with the result that some very pretty adornments were displayed. To add to the attractiveness of the open air surroundings it was Stockton's busy market-day, when the town gives prominent

THE CEREMONY.

The Chairman then presented Princess Henry with a gold and enamelled key as a memento of the interesting occasion, immediately after which her Royal Highness performed the ceremony in the words; "I declare this school open." (loud applause). The Right Rev. Dr. Hodges then offered dedicatory prayer, after which the founder of the school (Mr Frank Brown), founder of the Mayor of Stockton, and moved a vote of thanks to Princess Henry of Battenberg, on behalf of the town that day for having visited the school. He warmly observed that they were all aware of the deep interest the members of the Royal family had taken in institutions that had for their object the welfare and the alleviation of the suffering of His Majesty's subjects. H.R.H. they also knew, had been hourly engaged in the North of England during the past ten days.

A QUEEN VICTORIA MEMORIAL

Princess Henry of Battenberg, accompanied by Princess Victoria Eugénie, yesterday at Stockton-on-Tees opened the Queen Victoria High School for Girls, the gift of the mayor (Mr. Frank Brown) to the town, and which has been endowed by the inhabitants in commemoration of the long and glorious reign of Queen Victoria. Lord Londonderry attended the function, and said the educational facilities for girls had vastly enlarged during the past 30 years. The Princess and her daughter subsequently concluded their visit to Lord and Lady Barnard at Raby Castle, Durham county, and left for Beningbrough Hall, York, where they will be the guests of Capt. the Hon. W. F. Daunay.

Queen Victoria's youngest daughter, Princess Henry of Battenberg, accompanied by Princess Ena, were driven from Raby Castle where they had stayed overnight, arriving at the school amidst excited crowds of people. As they took their place in the assembly hall the National Anthem was played. Pupils, parents and members of the Old Girl Association joined the party of dignitaries to witness the ceremony. Greetings were shared and bouquets of orchids and white lillies & pink roses were presented by 8 yr old Alice Brown, daughter of the school founder. A gold enamelled key was presented to Princess Henry as the school was officially opened. A tour of the school followed before the Royal Party left in an open top carriage.

The day a Princess came to school in Stockton

The Royal guests greeted by large crowds in Yarm Road

The Marquess of Londonderry and Board of Governors greet the Princess arriving at the Queen Victoria School

Queen Victoria High School with Cranbourne Terrace to the right. After its auspicious opening the school merged with The Cleveland School in 1970 to form Teesside High. However the building was demolished in the early 1970's.

THE DRIVE TO THE STATION.

The ceremony ended, the Princess and party made a tour of inspection round the schools, and then partook of luncheon privately. Just before 2 p.m. Princess Henry and Princess Ena left the school by Yarm-lane and the High street, proceeded to Stockton Station, where they took train for the south. The party was heartily cheered as they passed through the streets and at the station, where a large number of people were gathered to obtain a glimpse of the Royal visitor.

After the opening was completed the Royal Party cheered by crowds drove in an open top carriage along the High Street to Stockton Station where they boarded their train.

Memories of schooldays in Stockton...

STOCKTON HIGH SCHOOL
Prize Distribution in the Masonic Hall.

PRESENTATION TO MRS EVERS.—The Industrial Schools at Portrack were finally closed on Friday, preparatory to the opening of the handsome new Board Schools erected in Bailey-street, also in Portrack. The occasion was very properly seized to express thanks to Mr and Mrs Evers, who have been engaged in the Ragged Board School for the long period of 22 years.

DEATH OF A STOCKTON SCHOOLMASTER.—Early this morning, Mr R. Evers, head master of the Bailey-street Board Schools, Stockton, died at his residence, Oxford-terrace, after a two days illness, though for some time past he has been in poor health. Mr Evers was the oldest schoolmaster in Stockton, having had charge of the Ragged Schools, which were taken over by the Board in 1874.

On 9 February 1874, Stockton School Board (elected November 1870) purchased the Ragged School on Portrack Lane for £1,500. A new school on Bailey Street which opened 9 June 1879, replaced the Ragged School, though Headmaster Mr R Evers was retained. He remained in post until his death in February 1890 when he was the town's oldest schoolmaster. Stockton's VC hero Edward Cooper attended Bailey Street School which remained open until being demolished in the early 1960's.

Alderman Hind Honoured.
Of all the public honours that Mr Hind had had conferred upon him that which was being conferred to-day by naming those schools after him was of the most importance, because of all the large varied interests in which he had been concerned not only in Stockton, but throughout Tees-side, they had all been of an educational character in one sense or another, and he was certain in his mind that Education Authorities of Stockton had done themselves a very great honour in naming the schools after such a grand old public servant. (Loud applause.)

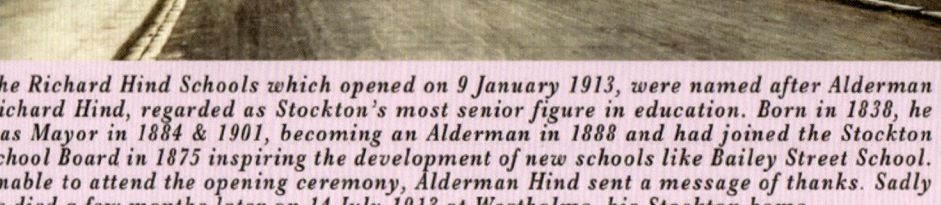

The Richard Hind Schools which opened on 9 January 1913, were named after Alderman Richard Hind, regarded as Stockton's most senior figure in education. Born in 1838, he was Mayor in 1884 & 1901, becoming an Alderman in 1888 and had joined the Stockton School Board in 1875 inspiring the development of new schools like Bailey Street School. Unable to attend the opening ceremony, Alderman Hind sent a message of thanks. Sadly he died a few months later on 14 July 1913 at Westholme, his Stockton home.

STOCKTON HIGH SCHOOL

They wrote about Stockton... the Heavisides

Henry Heavisides

THE ANNALS
OF
STOCKTON-ON-TEES;
WITH
Biographical Notices.

BY HENRY HEAVISIDES,
AUTHOR OF
"THE PLEASURES OF HOME," "THE MINSTRELSY OF BRITAIN,"
"COURTSHIP AND MATRIMONY," ETC.

"I'll view the manners of the town;
Peruse the traders, gaze upon the buildings,
And then return."
SHAKSPEAR.

STOCKTON-ON-TEES:
PRINTED BY H. HEAVISIDES AND SON.
1865.

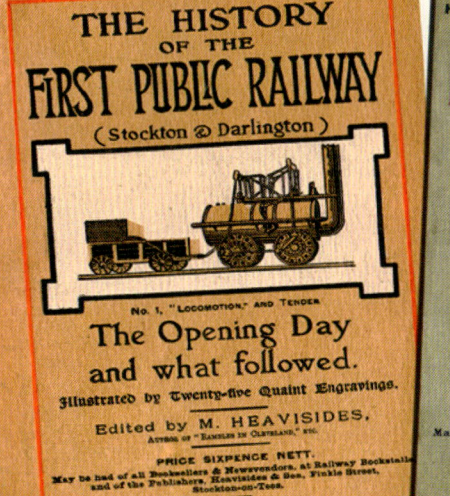

THE HISTORY OF THE FIRST PUBLIC RAILWAY
(Stockton & Darlington)

No. 1, "LOCOMOTION," AND TENDER

The Opening Day and what followed.
Illustrated by Twenty-five Quaint Engravings.

Edited by M. HEAVISIDES,
AUTHOR OF "RAMBLES IN CLEVELAND," ETC.

PRICE SIXPENCE NETT.
May be had of all Booksellers & Newsvendors, at Railway Bookstalls, and of the Publishers, Heavisides & Son, Stockton-on-Tees.

ALL RIGHTS RESERVED.

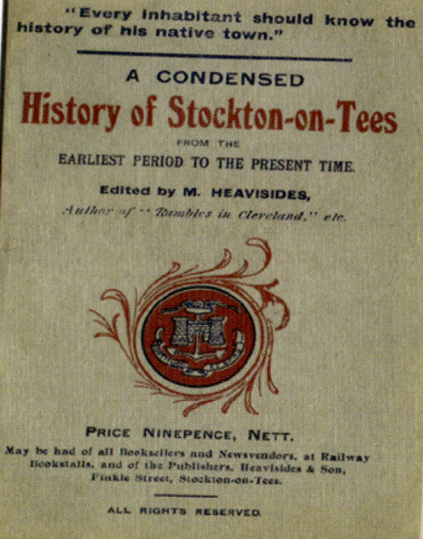

"Every inhabitant should know the history of his native town."

A CONDENSED History of Stockton-on-Tees
FROM THE
EARLIEST PERIOD TO THE PRESENT TIME.

Edited by M. HEAVISIDES,
Author of "Rambles in Cleveland," etc.

PRICE NINEPENCE, NETT.
May be had of all Booksellers and Newsvendors, at Railway Bookstalls, and of the Publishers, Heavisides & Son, Finkle Street, Stockton-on-Tees.

ALL RIGHTS RESERVED.

Four generations of a printing firm.

Michael Heavisides

It was in 1777 that Michael Heavisides, in the town of Darlington printed on a wooden press by the aid of pelt balls; in 1856 Heny Heavisides, his son, commenced business in Stockton and printed on an iron press using revolving rollers for inking; in 1870, Michael Heavisides, his son, continued the old business, using cylinder and platen machines, gas engine, stereotyping and other modern appliances; and in 1904, Frank Marsh Heavisides, his son, commenced his business career as a printer, with his father.

HEAVISIDES & SON,
4, Finkle Street, Stockton-on-Tees,

Entirely devote the whole of their attention to the production of Letterpress

PRINTING

From a small Handbill to the largest Poster. NOTHING comes wrong to them in the shape of printing.

The printing of fine Process Blocks a speciality.

A TRIAL RESPECTFULLY SOLICITED.

The business is under the immediate supervision of M. Heavisides.

HEAVISIDES & SON are the publishers of
"Rambles in Cleveland," - 6d., post free, 8½d.
"Rambles around Osmotherley" - 3d., " 4d.
"Rambles by the River Tees" - 9d., " 1/-

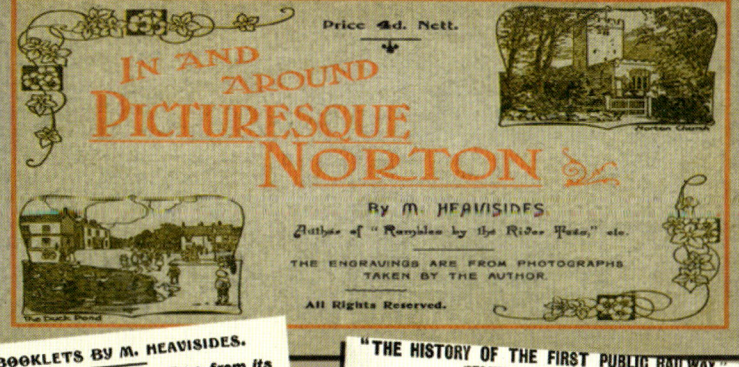

A HOLIDAY BOOK FOR THE PEOPLE!

RAMBLES BY THE RIVER TEES
FROM ITS RISE TO THE OCEAN.

BY M. HEAVISIDES,
AUTHOR OF "RAMBLES IN CLEVELAND," ETC.

69 High-class Photo Engravings.

PRICE 8d. NETT.

Price 4d. Nett.

IN AND AROUND PICTURESQUE NORTON

By M. HEAVISIDES,
Author of "Rambles by the River Tees," etc.

THE ENGRAVINGS ARE FROM PHOTOGRAPHS TAKEN BY THE AUTHOR.

All Rights Reserved.

BOOKLETS BY M. HEAVISIDES.
"*Rambles by the River Tees from its Rise to the Ocean.*"
With New and Attractive Pictorial Cover.
Reduced Price 8d. nett, post free 10d.
From the "Newcastle Weekly Chronicle," Aug. 5th, 1905.
"Mr. M. Heavisides, of Stockton, has placed all interested under a great obligation by the production of that useful work. - We endorse by the River Tees.' It is written in an agreeably chatty style, and story high-class photo-engravings, and the printing and general production of the guide is worthy of all praise.

"*Rambles in Cleveland and Peeps into the Dales.*"
Containing about 70 High-class Photo Engravings, mainly from Photographs taken by the Author, with Map.
Price 6d. nett; post free 8d.
The Yorkshire Weekly Post of Aug. 21st, 1909, says:—
"Rambles in Cleveland, and Peeps into the Dales on Foot, Cycle and Rail," by M. Heavisides, (Heavisides & Son, Stockton-on-Tees, 6d.) is a capital little guide-book for visitors to this famous part of Yorkshire. This is the third edition, revised and extended. It consists of more than a hundred pages, brightly written and uncommonly well illustrated."

"**THE HISTORY OF THE FIRST PUBLIC RAILWAY.**"
(STOCKTON & DARLINGTON.)
25 Quaint Illustrations.
Paper Covers, 6d., post free 6d.; Cloth Covers, 1/-, post free 1/2.
"*Rambles around Osmotherley,*"
Price 3d., post free 4d.
"*In and around Picturesque Norton,*"
Price 3d., post free 4d.
"**THE TRUE HISTORY OF THE LUCIFER MATCH,**"
Invented by JOHN WALKER, of Stockton-on-Tees;
Illustrated with Rare Engravings.
Price 2d., post free 3d.

MAY BE HAD FROM THE PUBLISHERS,
HEAVISIDES & SON, 6, Finkle Street, Stockton-on-Tees.

Your recommendation will be highly esteemed.

The Heavisides family were one of the leading printing firms in Stockton. Michael Heavisides had started printing in 1777 in Darlington. His son Henry later opened a printing business in Stockton in 1856 using an iron press and iron rollers for inking. Grandson Michael had in turn taken over the business in 1870 using the latest contemporary technology. Both Henry and his son were also authors; Henry Heavisides had written 'The Annals of Stockton' in 1865, whilst Michael wrote a number of publications about Stockton and the local area. At a time when leisure activities such as rambling and bicycle riding were increasingly fashionable, his guide books proved very popular. The print shop was located at 4 Finkle Street.

They wrote about Stockton too....Newspapers

Stockton Herald
SOUTH DURHAM AND CLEVELAND ADVERTISER.

NO. 1.   SATURDAY, JULY 10, 1858.   ONE PENNY.

1858

STOCKTON HERALD,
JULY 10th, 1858.
OUR OPENING ADDRESS.

Courteous Reader! Kind Friend-! Generous Public! We make our first appearance before you with no small diffidence.

We step forward at this particular time to risk both property and reputation, in endeavouring to do that for Stockton which no one else has ventured to do,—the issuing a weekly publication, creditable alike to the town and to the publisher.

We think the time has arrived when a good newspaper is required for Stockton and district.

THE STOCKTON HERALD
ESTABLISHED 1856.
Office—17, High Street, Stockton-on-Tees.

THE STOCKTON HERALD, SOUTH DURHAM AND CLEVELAND ADVERTISER, with which is incorporated the *Stockton Examiner*, is the oldest and most influential Weekly Paper in the district. It is read by all classes throughout the extensive mining and agricultural districts of South Durham and North Yorkshire, and is generally admitted to be the *best and cheapest medium* for every description of *advertising.*

EVERY DESCRIPTION OF
LETTER-PRESS PRINTING,
BOOKBINDING, &c.
Estimates given for all kinds of Printing, &c.

PUBLISHER – D. CRAIG,
STOCKTON HERALD OFFICE,
17, HIGH STREET,
STOCKTON-ON-TEES.

TO THE INHABITANTS OF STOCKTON AND NEIGHBOURHOOD.
T. GALLON,

NEWS AGENT, Bishop Street, (next door to Mr. Fenney's Toy Warehouse, supplies with promptitude all WEEKLY and MONTHLY JOURNALS, Current Numbers of WEEKLY PUBLICATIONS. Back Numbers procured to complete Sets. Current Numbers of METROPOLITAN and PROVINCIAL NEWSPAPERS. Agent for the ALLIANCE and RECORD Weekly News. STATIONERY in General. Agent for the STOCKTON HERALD. Licensed for the sale of TOBACCO and CIGARS; a supply of genuine and best quality always on hand.

Increased publication sales meant there was also a rise in the number of newsagent businesses. Directories in 1880 listed 14 seperate newsagent shops in central Stockton alone. As well as selling local newspapers they also sold newspapers from further afield as the development of the railway system meant that editions of many newspapers from other metropolitan centres could be bought on the same or next day.

The Stockton Examiner.
AND SOUTH DURHAM AND NORTH YORKSHIRE RECORD.

1878

Darlington and Stockton Times.
RIPON AND RICHMOND CHRONICLE

1911

The Stockton & Thornaby Herald
AND TEESIDE WEEKLY HERALD

1914

The Tees-Side Weekly Herald

The repeal of the newspaper tax 1855 and paper tax 1861 brought a dramatic rise in the number of newspapers. One new local title, the Stockton Herald, stated its objectives in the first edition on 14 July 1858 wanting to be 'creditable...to the town (Stockton)'. To attract a large readership (2,000 copies each week) the Herald sold at one penny, much cheaper than the national newspapers like The Times which cost three pence. Financing this required advertising and to encourage this, rates were reduced from four pence a line to two pence. The Herald proved to be a successful venture.

Stockton & Tees-Side Weekly Herald
LOCAL NEWS · LOCAL PICTURES

SATURDAY, AUGUST 1, 1931   PRICE ONE PENNY.

1931

Another Stockton based newspaper, the Stockton Examiner began in 1878, one of several publications to focus their attention on Stockton or feature the town in the title.

Newspapers of the region..

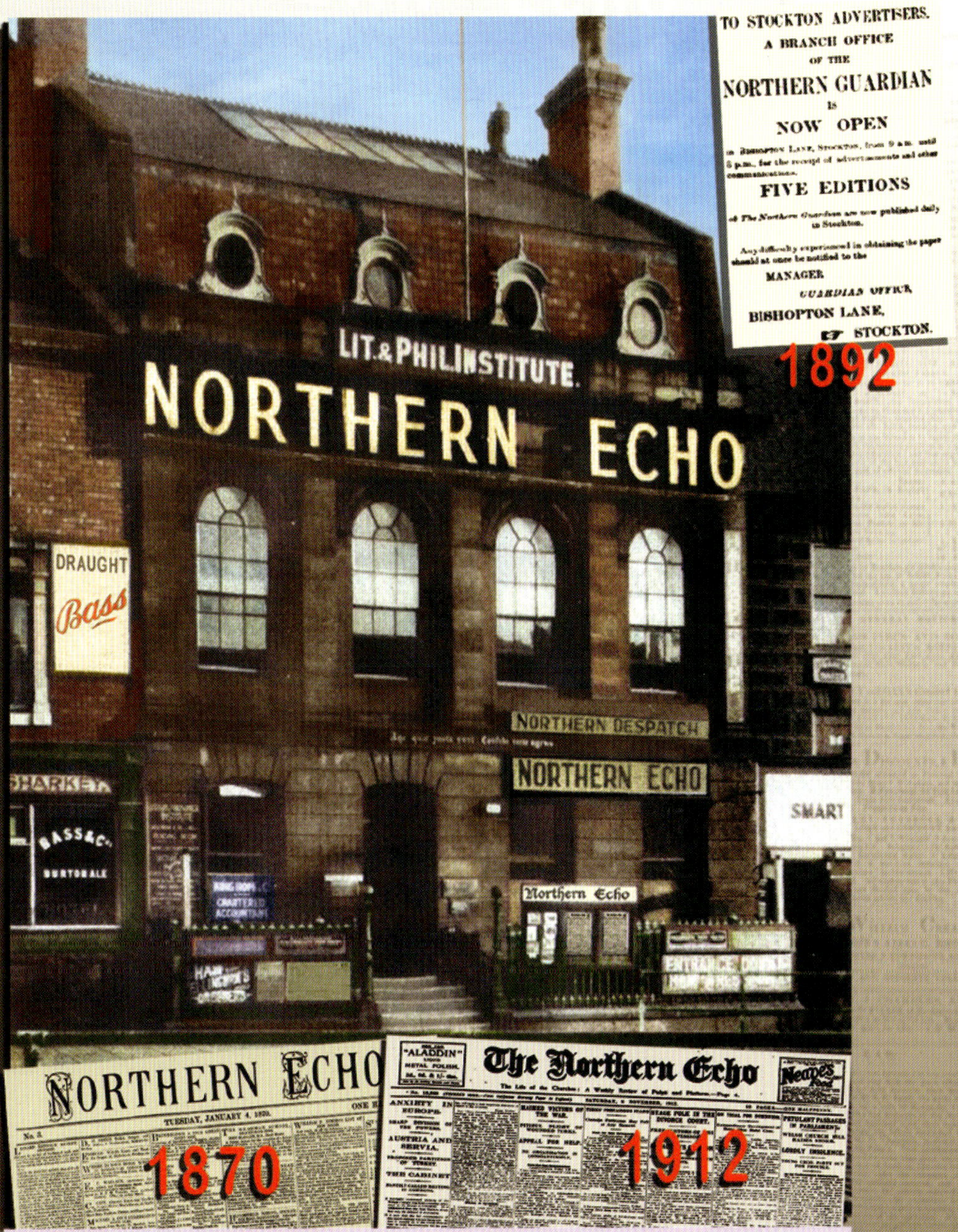

1892

1870

1880

1900

1909

1948

1900

1924

1870

1912

Newspapers from other towns often had local offices in Stockton - the Northern Echo office was in Dovecot Street alongside the Lit&Phil Institute

The Middlesbrough based Evening Gazette had an office for many years in Stockton High Street and featured many items related to the town over the years. The Saturday Sports Gazette also had many articles on sport in Stockton and like the daily newspaper, was very popular among people in Stockton.

THE NEW THEATRE ROYAL...DESTROYED BY FIRE

The New Theatre Royal, Yarm Lane opened in 1866 with a capacity for 1,650 people. Sir Henry Irving once played there. On 28 August 1906, the New Theatre Royal was destroyed by fire. A small group, standing outside the Garrick Hotel on the corner of West Row and Yarm Lane, gaze at the gutted shell of the building.
The buildings of the Holy Trinity School can be seen beyond the fire ruined theatre.

FIRE HAVOC.

Stockton Theatre Royal Burnt Out.

ABOUT £13,000 DAMAGE.

Dazzling Spectacle of Spark and Flame.

PIT LIKE A MOLTEN FURNACE

The Theatre Royal, Stockton, with large quantity of valuable scenery, was totally destroyed by fire during the late hours of Tuesday night and the early hours of Wednesday morning, the damage done being estimated at about £13,000. Our representative, who was on the scene from the time of the discovery of the outbreak until the fire was extinguished, says that the fire spread so rapidly and so quickly was the place a mass of smouldering ruins, that it was difficult to realise what had happened.

THE CROWDS AND THE SPECTACLE.

Cracking and creaking the huge fire continued, and people stood round the place in thousands admiring the brilliant spectacle, and expressing sympathy with those who might suffer loss by the wild destruction. A large number of policemen under Inspector Yeandle rendered valuable assistance to the Fire Brigades by keeping a clear course. At length, after about an hour's blaze, the praiseworthy and untiring efforts of the firemen were rewarded: the fire was mastered, and was now in hand, with less danger of spreading to the adjoining property. Every now and again the flames would shoot up, but only to be quelled by the water from more than a dozen powerful jets; and eventually by half an hour after midnight the fire was gradually killed until nothing in the shape of flames remained excepting a few pieces of smouldering wood in the elevation of the proscenium and in the pit. The theatre, which last night had a large audience, was now a very sorry sight, the only remains being three ghastly gables.

THE DAMAGE.

The damage to the theatre premises is estimated at between £10,000 and £12,000. In addition Mr Granville had a large quantity of valuable scenery and stock stored in the building, including the whole of the scenery, streets, and dresses for the "Forty Thieves" pantomime, which he was to produce at the Grand Theatre, Derby, this year. This is valued at £1,000, and was completely destroyed, not a single remnant of any of the property being left. The theatre and Mr Granville's scenery, etc., are largely covered by insurance.

The fire had started just after 11pm; with the evening's drama finishing at 10.20pm, manager Mr Berry had locked up soon after and was on his way home up Yarm Lane when he was stopped by someone with the news the theatre was on fire. Returning he saw it was ablaze - at 11.35 the main roof crashed down, at 11:45 the circle fell - firemen from Stockton and from Thornaby were at the scene. A dog was rescued from inside the building - there was fear of the fire spreading to the properties adjoining - a plumbers and a garage. Twenty vehicles were got out & taken to the Royal Hotel. Horses in the rear stables were turned out & taken down to the Grey Horse yard. A big crowd watched as the flames shot into the night sky until finally in the early hours, the blaze was contained.

THE THEATRE ROYAL IN BETTER TIMES

"BLUE BEARD" AT THEATRE ROYAL, STOCKTON.

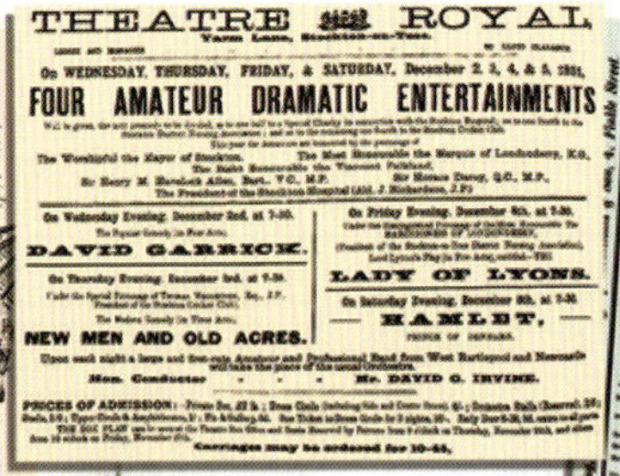

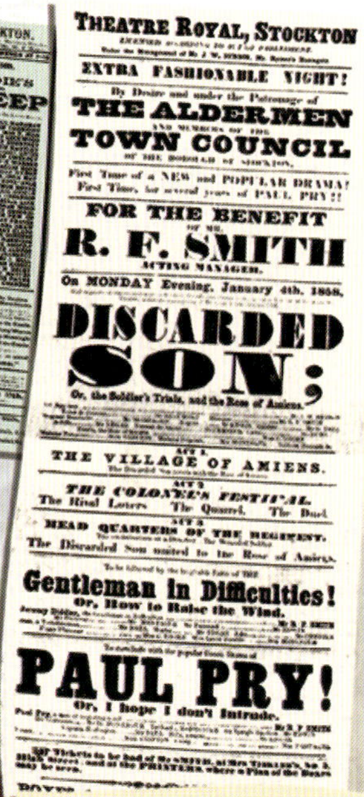

SKETCHES AT THE STOCKTON THEATRE.

THEATRE ROYAL. Yarm Lane, Stockton-on-Tees.

On WEDNESDAY, THURSDAY, FRIDAY, & SATURDAY, December 2, 3, 4, & 5, 1891.

FOUR AMATEUR DRAMATIC ENTERTAINMENTS

DAVID GARRICK

LADY OF LYONS

HAMLET.

NEW MEN AND OLD ACRES.

THEATRE ROYAL STOCKTON

MR. JAMES KIDDIE'S
Little BO-PEEP

THEATRE ROYAL, STOCKTON

EXTRA FASHIONABLE NIGHT!

THE ALDERMEN AND MEMBERS OF THE TOWN COUNCIL

FOR THE BENEFIT OF R. F. SMITH

On MONDAY Evening, January 6th, 1868.

DISCARDED SON;

Or, the Soldier's Trials, and the Rose of Amiens

THE VILLAGE OF AMIENS.

Gentleman in Difficulties!
Or, How to Raise the Wind.

PAUL PRY!
Or, I hope I don't Intrude.

THEATRE ROYAL, STOCKTON-ON-TEES.

THE BROTHERS STODDART.

On THURSDAY Evening, October 8th, 1863,

WARLOCK
OF THE GLEN!
OR, AULD LANG SYNE.

THE GHOST
THE GHOST!

LOOK OUT FOR
THE MAN IN THE IRON MASK!

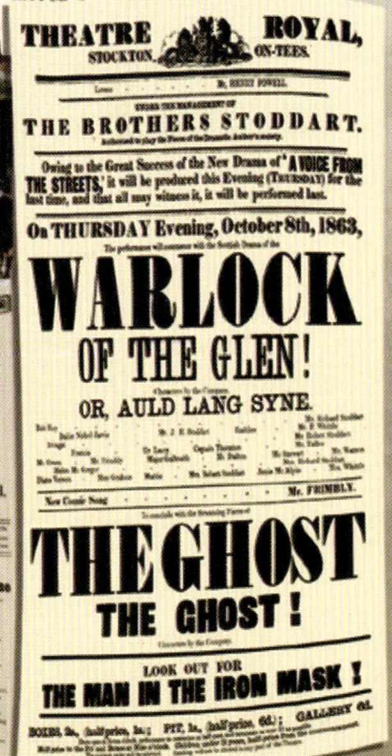

1891: the Grand Theatre and Opera House in Bishop Street before the fire

FIRE AT THE "GRAND" THEATRE, STOCKTON.

The original Theatre Royal in Green Dragon Yard opened in 1766 by Thomas Bates, enjoyed considerable success - artistes from several London theatres appearing there. The renowned William Cobbett M.P. came in 1832. On the evening of Monday 7 October 1833 the world famous Paganini performed to a full house, prices for a Box being doubled for the night to 38p. In 1866 it opened as The Oxford a music hall; by 1874 it was owned by the Salvation Army; eventually it became J.F. Smith & Co's Nebo Confectionery factory.

It will be learnt, from an advertisement in our succeeding columns, that the celebrated Paganini, after his performance here to-morrow night, will proceed to Stockton, where he purposes having a concert on Monday evening. The greatest anxiety prevails in both places to hear and see this unrivalled musician and extraordinary man.

1833, Oct. 7.—The celebrated Paganini exhibited his wonderful performance on the violin, in the Stockton theatre. The receipts were about £80, the admission to the boxes (which were crowded) being, on this occasion, 7s. 6d.; pit, 4s.; gallery, 2s. 6d.

THE
HOME
OF
MUSICAL COMEDY,
STIRRING DRAMA,
and VAUDEVILLE.
➡ Where EVERYBODY goes !
THE
Hippodrome
THEATRE OF VARIETIES,
Dovecot Street.
STOCKTON-ON-TEES.

NO TIME TO
BE LOST
———
RECONSTRUCTION
OF STOCKTON
CINEMA
———
GUTTED BY FIRE
———
THE Hippodrome Theatre at Stockton which, excepting the main foyer and the dressing-rooms, was gutted by fire about two months ago, is to be rebuilt on modern lines, and it is expected that the work will be commenced in a few days. The dressing-rooms and certain of the old walls will be retained, but the interior will be completely new. The site has been cleared of the piles of burnt and twisted debris from the fire, and a start will be made with the rebuilding as soon as the plans have been passed.

Fire struck other entertainment venues too. In October 1892 The Grand Theatre on Bishop Street suffered considerable fire damage. In 1932 the Hippodrome Theatre was gutted by fire and was reconstructed. It was a cinema as well as a variety theatre.

LAST NIGHT
OF
Miss FOOTE's
ENGAGEMENT.
And for her Benefit.
Theatre, Stockton.
On Thursday Evening, July 20th, 1826,
On which occasion will be presented Shakespeare's admired pastoral Comedy of
As you Like it.
...
Rosalind ... Miss FOOTE
In which Character she will sing
THE CUCKOO SONG,
And speak the Original Epilogue.
...
A Favourite Song, by Mr. Bywater.
A Comic Song, by Mr. Bland.
...
Weathercock.
...
Variella, ... Miss FOOTE
In which she will sing the favourite Air of
"Far, far from me my Lover flies" and the Celebrated Masquerade Song.
...
Tickets to be had and Places taken of T. JENNETT.
BOXES, 3s.—PIT, 2s.—GALL. 1s.
NO HALF PRICE during Miss Foote's Engagement.
Doors to be open at 6 before 7 o'Clock, and to begin at 8 till past 7.
No Admittance behind the Scenes. Mr. Parker, Manager.
Printed at T. Jennett's Office, Stockton.

THE EXCHANGE HALL,
STOCKTON-on-TEES.
Mr. Barnby's CONCERTS

Miss JESSIE BOND
and
Mr. RUTLAND BARRINGTON.

MONDAY, November 9th, 1891.	FRIDAY, JANUARY 22nd, 1892.
ARTISTS:	ARTISTS:
Mdlle. Rosina Isidor	Madame BLANCHE STONE-BARTON
Miss DEWS	Miss MEREDYTH ELLIOTT.
Mr. Braxton Smith,	Mr. EDWARD LLOYD
SIGNOR FOLI,	Mr. TURNER DOYLE.
Senor Albeniz,	Mr. WATKIN MILLS.
Herr David Popper,	MONS. JOHANNES WOLFF.
	Mr. W. C. HANN.
Musical Director & Conductor	ACCOMPANIST
Mr. F. T. WATKIS.	Mr. MARTINUS SIEVEKING.

MUSICAL
DUOLOGUES
AND
MONOLOGUES
IN COSTUME.

Friday, October 9th, 1891.

BOROUGH HALL, STOCKTON-ON-TEES.
Mr. FELIX CRUSE'S
MUSICAL EVENING,
Tuesday, January the 19th, 1892.

ARTISTS:
MADAME D'ALMERIA - - Soprano. | Miss ELLY LEMPFERT - - Piano.
The Manchester Quartette Party
1st VIOLIN - SIGNOR RISEGARI, | VIOLA - Mr. EDMUND NICHOLS.
2nd " - Mr. THEO. LAWSON. | VIOLONCELLO - Herr CARL FUCHS.

ADMISSION:
Dress Seats, 5/-; Gallery (Reserved), 3/-; Back Seats, 1/-
Doors open at 7-45. Commence at 8 o'clock. Carriages 10-15.
Plan of the Hall may be seen and Seats reserved, free of charge, by Subscribers on and after Wednesday, Jan 6th; by non-Subscribers on and after Monday, Jan. 11th, at Mr. APPLEBY'S, Bookseller, High Street, Stockton.

1832, Nov. 13.—Wm. Cobbett, M.P., lectured in the theatre, Stockton, on Parliamentary reform, sinecures, pensions, tithes, &c., to a very crowded house. He lectured the previous evening at Darlington.

MAISON - DE - DANSE. STOCKTON.
VICTORY DANCE. TO-NIGHT.
commencing 8 p.m. to 1 a.m. Admission
3/6. MODERN DANCING to JACK
MARWOOD & HIS ORCHESTRA.

STOCKTON ON TEES (INCLUDING THORNABY, YARM, NORTON & BILLINGHAM): A COLOURFUL PAST

IVY CLOSE...THE DANCE BANDS...MAISON DE DANSE...   THE CINEMAS...AND THE BEATLES

FILM, TALKIES, AND STAGE

Varied Career of Miss Ivy Close

THE HERALD.
SATURDAY, APRIL 4, 1908.

Ivy Close (Mrs Elwin Neame) with her family

Ivy Close, born in Stockton on 15 July 1890, became the town's own film star. After winning the Daily Mirror's 'Most Beautiful Woman' contest in 1908, Ivy married Elwin Neame in 1912 and went on to become a silent movie star during the era of Charlie Chaplin. She made her first film, 'The Lure of London' in 1914. In 1916, she sailed to New York and there made 44 films before retiring in 1922 to look after her children. Ivy's father, John, a watchmaker, was born in Stockton in 1868. Her mother was from Consett.

Elwin's sudden death in a road accident led to a failed attempt to ressurect her career in America. Ivy returned to the UK for the rest of her life. She died in a nursing home on 4 December 1968, reported as 'surrounded by her scrapbooks and press cuttings'. Her son Ronald, born in 1911, became famous for his work on films (including classic movies 'In Which We Serve', 'Brief Encounter' & 'Great Expectations'). Great-Grandson, Gareth Neame, a TV producer, has worked on Downton Abbey and Bridgerton.

Dance bands were popular in Stockton

PALAIS-DE-DANSE, SKINNER STREET
STOCKTON. V.E. CELEBRATIONS.
Special Attraction. Two Broadcasting
Bands. Leslie Jiver Hutchinson (coloured
B.B.C. Band), Jack O'Boyle's Broadcasting Band. Dancing 7—12. Old & New.
FRIDAY. MAY 11th. Tickets 5/- each
at the Palais de Danse, also Ingle's Ltd.,
Tobacconists. and 88, Norton-road.

The dance band era meant dancing the night away. A favourite venue was the Maison de Dance built in 1921 on the burnt out shell of the Theatre Royal. Jack Marwood was the resident bandleader for 44 years. Prime Minister (& Stockton M.P.), Harold McMillan celebrated his election as an M.P. there in 1924. During the war soldiers and airmen from RAF Thornaby packed out the dance floor; VE Night in 1945, was one of the busiest nights ever held there. Many famous orchestras played at the Maison - including Joe Loss, Ambrose & Lew Stone. It was a sad night in 1964 when it finally closed - the dance band era was no more.

With eleven cinema's in the Stockton area, choosing a film to see in at the cinema in the 1930's & 1940's was not always easy

STOCKTON HIPPODROME

GLOBE STOCKTON

EMPIRE. STOCKTON

REGAL Stockton

WUTHERING HEIGHTS
MERLE OBERON
LAURENCE OLIVIER

PLAZA — STOCKTON
DOUBLE INDEMNITY
with
Fred MacMurray   Barbara Stanwyck
Edward G. Robinson
Thursday—Margaret Lockwood in
BEDELIA

WIFE, HUSBAND AND FRIEND
LORETTA YOUNG, WARNER BAXTER
and BINNIE BARNES
also THE GORILLA with the
RITZ BROTHERS

THE MAYFAIR CINEMA

CENTRAL HALL   **QUEEN'S Cinema**

CINEMA   **MODERNE**
NORTON-ON-TEES

The Empire was previously Castlegate Theatre, converted into a cinema in 1912.

BARRY'S

GLOBE THEATRE STOCKTON
Advance Booking for
THE BEATLES
Opens Wednesday, 10 a.m.

In 1913 the Globe was the first cinema built in Stockton. It was rebuilt in 1925 and again in the 1930's as a theatre. When this failed, ABC Cinema's opened it in 1937 as a cinema though it later became a venue for popular variety during the 1950's, with acts ranging from Buddy Holly in 1958 to the Beatles in November 1962.

LUXURIOUS CINEMA
STOCKTON MAYOR OPENS THE REGAL

The Regal Cinema in the High Street, opened 22 April 1935. Adjacent to the Borough Hall, it became the Odeon Cinema, 12 March 1945.

STOCKTON RACES...SPORT OF KINGS...& OF STOCKTON FOLK

Race meetings held at The Carrs, have a documented history dating back to the summer of 1724. These popular gatherings in Stockton, started with a mayoral procession from the Town Hall. Alongside the races, attendees could go to cock-fighting exhibitions, assembly balls, and a bustling fair. The races themselves typically comprised Sweepstakes with heats, with prizes awarded each evening. However, when The Carrs changed ownership in 1816, racing activities were temporarily halted until December 1824, when they were resumed once again.

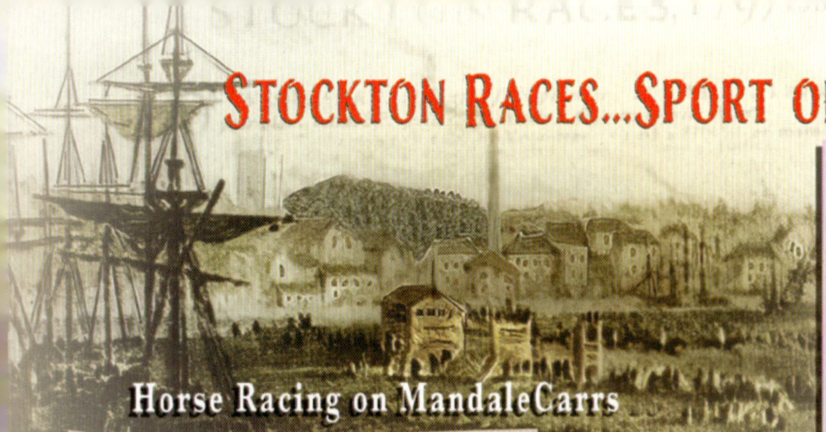

Horse Racing on MandaleCarrs

1732

THE
Newcastle Courant.
SATURDAY, MAY 27, 1732.

Stockton RACES.

TO be run for on the *Carr* opposite the Town of *Stockton* upon *Tees*, in the County of *Durham*, on Thursday the 6th Day of *July* next, a Plate of the full Value of 20 l. by any Horse, Mare, or Gelding that is no more than 4 Years old this Grass, to be certified under the Hand of the Breeder, carrying 9 Stone Weight, Saddle and Bridle excluded; to run 3 heats, 3 times about the said *Carr* to a heat, (being computed two Miles and an half or thereabouts) paying at Entrance 2 Guineas.

ON Friday the 7th Day of *July*, a give and take Plate of the full Value of 12 l. will be run for on the same Place, by any Horse, Mare, or Gelding that hath never won the Value of 10 l. in Plate or Money at one Time, those of 14 hands high to carry 10 Stone, Saddle and Bridle included; and all above or under that Size to carry, or be allowed Weight for Inches, as is usual in such Plates, and to run 3 heats, five Times about the said *Carr* to a heat, paying at Entrance one Guinea.

AND on Saturday the 8th of *July* will be run for on the same Place, a Plate of the Value of 30 l. by any Horse, Mare, or Gelding, being no more than 5 Years old this Grass, and to be certified under the Hand of the Breeder, carrying 10 Stone, Saddle and Bridle included, to run 3 Heats, four Times about the said *Carr* to a Heat, paying at Entrance 3 Guineas; four or more to run for each of the said Plates, or no Race. All Horses, *&c.* that run for the said 20 l. plate and 30 l. plate, to be shewn in the said *Carr*, and enter'd at the Serjeant's House in *Stockton*, aforesaid, on Tuesday, the 4th Day of *July*, between the Hours of 2 and 6 in the Afternoon of the same Day; and the Horses, *&c.* to run for the said give and take Plate, to be shewn and measur'd at such Place as shall be appointed by the Mayor on Thursday next before the said Day of running for the same, and to be book'd at the Serjeant's House, aforesaid, between the Hours of 9 and 12 in the Forenoon, of the same Day. All Horses, *&c.* running for any of the said Plates, to be govern'd by Articles for that Purpose to be produced; and if any Difference shall happen to arise, the same shall be adjusted by the Mayor, Aldermen and Steward of *Stockton*, aforesaid, or any 3 of them.

N. B. The ancient Fair at *Stockton*, aforesaid, will begin on Friday the 7th Day of *July*, aforesaid, when and where will be Sold all Sorts of Merchandizes: And on the Day following, Cattle, Sheep, and Horses, all Toll-free.

1734

Stockton RACES.

ON *Tuesday* the 10th of *September* next, will be run for, in the *Carr* opposite to the Town of *Stockton* upon *Tees*, in the County of *Durham*, a Purse of fifteen Guineas, by Horses, *&c.* no more than four Years old, 3 Heats, three Times round the said *Carr* to a Heat, carrying nine Stone, Bridle and Saddle included, paying at Entrance one Guinea and an half.

ON *Wednesday* the 11th, a Purse of ten Guineas, by any Horse, *&c.* that never won before the Value of ten Pounds in Plate or Money at one Time; to run three Heats, 5 Times round the said *Carr* to a Heat; Horses, *&c.* 14 Hands high to carry ten Stone, and those under or above that Size to be allowed or carry Weight for Inches, as is usual in Give and Take Plates, paying at Entrance one Guinea.

ON *Thursday* the 12th, a Purse of twenty Guineas, by Horses, *&c.* no more than five Years old, 3 Heats, four Times round the said *Carr* to a Heat, carrying ten Stone, Saddle and Bridle included, and paying at Entrance two Guineas.

The four Years old and five Years old Horses, *&c.* to be shewn in the said *Carr*, and enter'd at the House ...

1732

STOCKTON RACES.

TO be run for on the usual Course, in the Carr, opposite to the Town of Stockton, in the County of Durham, on Wednesday the Tenth Day of September next, a Plate of the full Value of Fifteen Guineas, by any Horse, &c. no more than four Years old the last Grass, carrying nine Stone, Bridle and Saddle included, three Heats, three Times about the said Carr to a Heat; paying at Entrance one Guinea and an half.

On Thursday the Eleventh Day of September, a Give and Take Plate, of the full Value of Ten Guineas, three Heats, five Times round the said Carr to a Heat, by any Horse, &c. that never won at one Time more than ten Guineas in Plate or Money (Matches excepted.) Horses, &c. fourteen Hands to carry nine Stone, Saddle and Bridle included; and those above or under that Size, to carry or be allowed Weight for Inches, as usual; paying at Entrance one Guinea.

On Friday the Twelveth Day of September, a Plate of the full Value of Twenty Guineas, by any Horse, &c. no more than five Years old the last Grass, carrying ten Stone, three Heats, Bridle and Saddle included, four Times round the said Carr to a Heat; paying at Entrance two Guineas.

And on Saturday the Thirteenth Day of September, will be given gratis, a Purse of Five Guineas, to be run for by any Horse, &c. that never run for or won at any one Time, Plate or Money to the Value of Five Pounds (Matches excepted.) Horses, &c. fourteen Hands to carry ten Stone, Saddle and Bridle included; and those under or above that Size to carry or be allowed Weight for Inches, as usual; to run three Heats, four Times round the said Carr to a Heat. The first Horse each Heat to win Twenty Shillings, the second Ten Shillings, and the third Five Shillings.

The Horses, &c. limited to Age, to be sufficiently certified for, under the Hands of the respective Breeders, and to enter at the House of Mr. Benjamin Scaife in Stockton aforesaid, on Thursday next before the Time of Running, between the Hours of Three and Six in the Afternoon. And the Horses, &c. for the Give and Take Plate, to be measured and entered at the said Mr. Scaife's on the Day following, between the Hours of Two and Six in the Afternoon. And the Horses, &c. to run for the Purse, to be measured and entered at the said Place, on the Wednesday before the Day of Running between the Hours of Eight and Twelve in the Forenoon; four or more to run for each Plate, or no Race, and be subject to Articles.

☞ There will be also a Mane of Cocks fought in the Forenoon of each Day, during the Races, at the said Mr. Scaife's Pit, between the Gentlemen of Richmondshire and the Gentlemen of Gisborough, for Four Guineas a Battle, and Fifty Guineas the Main or odd Battle; shewing Forty One Cocks on each Side.

NB. There will be an Assembly kept every Night during the Races.

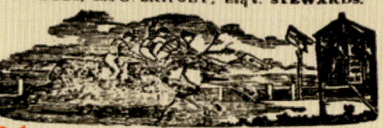

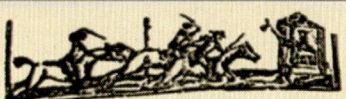

STOCKTON RACES, 1797.

ON WEDNESDAY, *the 13th of September* A SWEEPSTAKES *of 10 g. each*, ...

Same Day, ...

ON THURSDAY *the 14th*, A SWEEPSTAKES *of 10 g. each, p.p. by 4 year olds*, ...

Same Day A MAIDEN PLATE *of 50l. for Horses, &c. that never won the Value of 50l in* ...

Mr. Robinson's ch. filly, Hippona, 3 years old — Orange
Sir R Williamson's bay colt, Sloven, 3 years old — Harlequin
Mr Gregson's brown colt, 4 years old — Pink
Mr. Briscoe's bay colt, 3 years old — Green
Mr. Vevers's bay filly, 4 years old
Mr. Wilson's ch. colt, Little Hine, 3 years old
Mr Richardson's bay Colt, brother to Paleflower, 4 years old
Mr Coates's bay filly by Young Mark, 3 years old
Mr. Hutton's ch. colt Rockwood 4 years old

1797

ON FRIDAY *the 15th*, A HUNTERS SWEEPSTAKES *of Five Guineas each* ...

Same Day, 50l. *for all Ages*. ...

Sir R Williamson's bay horse, Bangtail 5 years old
Sir H. V. Tempest's ch. horse, Charger 5 years old
Sir Thomas Gascoigne's grey colt, Opposition, 4 years old

ON SATURDAY the 16th, A MATCH between Mr. Jefferson's ch. filly, ... and Mr. Hutton's ... Lydia, by Ruler, ...

N. B. No Person will be allowed to go upon the Race-ground on Horseback—Carriages as usual. Nor will any Person be allowed to go to the Founder's Stand, except the Stewards and Clerk of the Race — The Plates will be paid each Evening at the House where the winning Horse stands.

Major RUSSELL, } Stewards.
T. MEYNELL, Esq. }

☞ *Ordinaries, Assemblies, Plays, Cockings, &c. as usual.*

ATKINSON, Printer and Bookseller, near the DOVE-COTE

STOCKTON RACES, 1825.

THURSDAY, AUG. 18.—A Sweepstakes of 10 guineas each, p. p. with 20 guineas added for all ages. Three years old, 7st.; four, 8st. 3lb.; five, 9st.; six and aged, 9st. 4lb. Four pounds allowed to maiden horses at the time of naming. Three and four years old fillies allowed 3lb. Two miles.

Mr Russell's b c Caccia Piatti, 4 years old
Mr Riddale's c g Carouser, 4 years old
Mr Darnell's b g Chronicle, by Ebor, 4 years old
Mr Heseltine's g c Vengeance, by Revenue, 3 years old
Mr Jaques's c c by Whisker, out of Merryfield's dam, 3 years old
Mr Parkinson's b f by Whisker, dam by Woodpecker, 4 years old
Mr J. Robinson's b f by Catton, dam by Hambletonian, 3 yrs old

Fifty Pounds for maiden horses. Three years old, 6st. 10lb.; four, 8st.; five, 8st. 9lb.; six and aged, 8st. 12lb. Mares and geldings allowed 3lb. Heats, two miles.

Lord Tyrconnell's Cravat
Mr Clarke's br g Mexico, 5 years old
Mr Kirby's c m by Antrossan, 4 years old
Mr Parkinson's b f by Whisker, 4 years old
Mr ...'s br f Isabella, 3 years old

1825

STOCKTON RACES, 1831.

J. BELL, and G. SKIPSEY, Esqs. STEWARDS.

To start each day precisely at 2 o'Clock.

1831

Thursday, August 11th.

A SWEEPSTAKES of 10 sov. each, p. p. with 20 sov. added, for all ages; ... Mares and Geldings allowed 3lb. — Two Miles.

A MAIDEN PLATE of FIFTY POUNDS; ... Mares and Geldings allowed 3lb. — Two Mile Heats.

Friday, August 12th.

A GOLD CUP, value One Hundred Sovereigns, by a Subscription of 10 sov. each, with 20 sov. added, the surplus (if any) in specie; three year olds, 6st. 7lb. four, 8st. five, 8st. 9lb. six and aged, 9st. A winner of any of the great Subscriptions or Sweepstakes at York August Meeting, 1831, to carry 3lb. extra, (Handicaps excepted.) Mares and Geldings allowed 3lb. — TWO MILES AND A DISTANCE.

Mr Dickson's c. m. Lucy, by Tramp, 5 y. o.
Sir H. Williamson's br. f. Margaret, by Swiss, 3 y. o.
Mr Sutton's c. c. The Barber, by Figaro, 4 y. o.
Mr Wormald's b. c. Bullet, by Cannon Ball, 4 y. o.
Mr Bell's b. h. Chancellor, by Catton, 5 y. o.
Mr Russell's br. c. Brown Stout, by Jack Spigot, 5 y. o.
Duke of Leeds's c. m. Jenny Mills, 6 y. o.
Mr Hustler's b. c. Orangeman, 5 y. o.

The WYNYARD STAKES of 7 sov. each, p. p. with 30 sov. added by the Marquis of Londonderry, for horses that never won a Gold Cup, or £100, at any one time, in Plate or Stakes, before the day of naming; three year olds, 7st. four, 8st. 3lb. five and upwards, 8st. 10lb. Mares and Geldings allowed 3lb. The second Horse to receive back his Stake. — TWO MILE HEATS.

Mr Sutton's b. c. Welbeck, dam by Walton, 4 y. o.
Mr Reeves's b. c. Will o' the Wall, 3 y. o.
Mr Jaques's br. m. by Swiss, 3 y. o.
Mr Bower's br c. Chancellor, by Minos 3 y. o.

Saturday, August 13th.

A SWEEPSTAKES of 10 sov. each, p. p. for horses, &c. not thorough bred; ... — Two Miles.

FIFTY POUNDS for all ages; ... — TWO MILE HEATS.

A HUNTERS STAKE, of 5 sov. each, with 20 added, for Horses, not thorough bred, bona fide the property of those residing within 12 miles of Stockton. To close on Friday Night, and be handicaped before 12 on Saturday. Heats—A mile and a Distance.

It is desired that all Stakes, and Entrances be paid to the Clerk of the Course, before ... o'Clock on the day of running; and that all persons will clear the Course on the ringing of the Bell for Saddling, and observe the same during the Race. All Dogs seen on the Course will be destroyed. Admittance, to Persons riding on the Course, —Horses, 1s. — Gigs, 2s. — Carriages, 2s. 6d. each. Admittance to the Stand, 1s. 6d. each, or for the three days, 4s. Tickets to be had at the Town Hall.

An ASSEMBLY at the Town Hall, on Friday, Dancing to commence at ½ past nine.
An ORDINARY at the Black Lion, each day, at 1 o'Clock, and another immediately after the Races.

BOAT RACES, and STEAM PACKET PLEASURING, each day.
A PAIR OF COCKS upon the Sod, at Charlton's Pit, at 10 o'Clock.
CRICKET MATCHES, &c.
A Celebrated PLAY and FARCE, (see Bills of the day) at the Theatre, each ... day

J. Appleton, Printer and Bookseller, Stockton.

STEWARDS OF THE RACES.

On SATURDAY Evening, OCTOBER, 19th, 1811.

Will be presented Mrs. Inchbald's Comedy of

Wives as they Were,

AND

Maids as they are.

Sir David Dudley,	Mr LANCASTER.
Mr Norberry	Mr FAULKNER
Mr Bronzely	Mr HOLMES
Sir William Dorrillon	Mr RAMBLE
Mr Oliver,	Mr BARTLEY
Mr Rennic	Mr DARLEY.
Lady Mary Raffle	Mrs CAMDEN
Miss Dorrillon	Mrs DAWSON
Mrs Placid	Mrs CAMDEN

A COMIC SONG

By Mr LANCASTER.

To conclude with the Farce of

Ways & Means

OR A TRIP TO DOVER.

Sir David Dudley,	Mr LANCASTER,
Old Random	Mr RAMBLE
Young Random	Mr HOLMES
Sir Tivy Gaunt	Mr FAULKNER
Scruple	Mr DARLEY.
Tiptoe	Mr BARTLEY
Random	Mr APPLEBY
Kitty	Mrs WARN
Peggy	Mrs CAMDEN

S. Appleyard, Printer Stockton.

The three-day autumn race meeting commenced on Wednesday, October 16, 1811. As well as Town Hall assemblies the Theatre in the Green Dragon Yard was open, offering a special performance on Saturday, October 19. Two plays acclaimed in London were selected by race stewards, E.D. Shafto and W.C. Pierse.

STOCKTON RACES.—In consequence of the falling off in these races, a public meeting was held in the Long Room, Black Lion Hotel, Stockton, on Friday last, for the purpose of devising the best means for the improvement of the races. The meeting was respectably and numerously attended, and a committee of the leading gentlemen of the town and neighbourhood was appointed to carry the object of the meeting into effect. Among other means, it is intended to make an application to W. Russell, Esq., of Brancepeth Castle, for the use of some ground of his at Mandale, about a mile from Stockton, as a race-course; and should this application be acceded to—and from Mr Russell's well-known liberality of disposition there can be little doubt of it—Stockton will then be able to boast of a race-ground second to none in the kingdom. Other mea-

In August 1836 a public meeting was convened in the Long Room at the Black Lion Hotel to consider the future of racing at Stockton including renting land at Mandale, to establish a new racecourse. Deciding to improve the current course for 1837 a new stand, 'supported by sturdy brick pillars' was built as well as other enhancements to the course. Crowds returned but other developments were to cloud the horizon and eventually end racing here.

1839 STOCKTON RACES MOVE TO A FARM IN BILLINGHAM

1838, Aug. 31.—One of the stands on the Stockton race ground fell with above 100 persons, one of whom had his arm broken. A young woman was also much injured this day, being knocked down by one of the horses whilst she was crossing over the course.

Summer 1838 was a difficult time for racing on The Carrs. A stand collapsed on 31 August and a woman crossing the course, was badly injured after colliding with a horse. A month later on 29 September plans were announced for South Stockton, a new development on The Carrs ending race meetings there.

STOCKTON RACES.

TO THE SUPPORTERS OF THE TURF.

MY LORDS AND GENTLEMEN,—It may perhaps not be generally known that the town of Stockton-upon-Tees, is no longer in possession of a race course, that ground having been recently purchased by a wealthy company of speculators for building a new town, to be called "South Stockton." Consequently, if Stockton Races are to be continued, the time has now arrived that a new race course should immediately be prepared, otherwise it will be impossible to get it into a proper state against the usual time the races take place. A committee was appointed at the last race ordinary, to endeavour to procure ground for a new course, which I much regret they have not been able to accomplish. I am well aware of the difficulty there is in obtaining suitable ground for that purpose permanently, immediately in the neighbourhood, at a reasonable annual rent. However, rather than the races should go down, if the supporters of the turf will come forward with a subscription adequate to the expense of preparing a new course, which will cost from £200 to £300, I will furnish one myself on my own property, and have no objection to let it for a lease of twenty years, on reasonable terms. The land is situated at Tibbersly, near Portrack, within two miles of Stockton, and contiguous to the Tees. Steamboats may land passengers on the race ground, from either Stockton or Middlesbrough in the short space of ten minutes, and there is a good road for carriages to it; also by the Clarence and Stockton and Darlington Railways are each within half a mile of it. I have described the situation of the ground, and now take the liberty of laying a plan of the course before the public.

Subscription lists for making the new course are at all the principal inns in Stockton, and I feel honoured in stating, headed with the very handsome subscription of £50, by his Grace the Duke of Cleveland. Before I conclude, I beg to observe that should the committee be able to procure any other ground permanently, between this time and the first day of January next, which they may consider better adapted for a race course, I shall be exceedingly glad, as I have no wish that my land be old be used for that purpose, but, as I before observed, rather than the races should go down, I will willingly give it up.

I have the honour to remain,
My Lords and Gentlemen,
Your most obedient, and very humble servant
JOHN JACKSON,
Clerk of the Course.

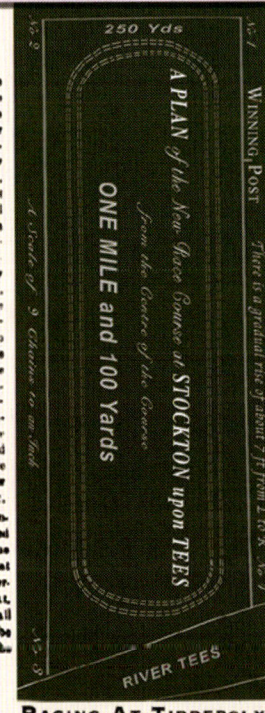

250 Yds

A PLAN of the New Race Course at STOCKTON upon TEES

From the Centre of the Course

WINNING POST

ONE MILE and 100 Yards

A Scale of 9 Chains to an Inch

There is a gradual rise of about 7 ft. from L to R

RIVER TEES

RACING AT TIBBERSLY: JACKSON'S PLAN

In November 1838, John Jackson, clerk of Stockton Races, outlined a plan to use his own land at Tibbersly Farm, Billingham. The course was accessible by steamboat from Stockton and Middlesbrough and close to the Clarence and Stockton & Darlington Railways with several footpaths leading to the course. Donations to cover the £300 costs started with £50 from the Duke of Cleveland as subscriber lists were posted in all local taverns and inns.

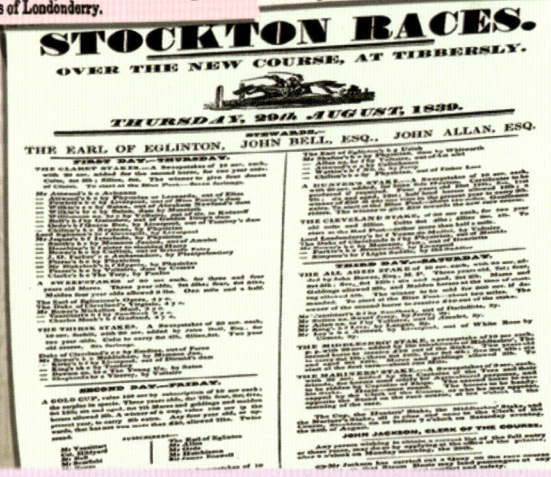

STOCKTON RACES, 1839.
OVER THE NEW COURSE AT TIBBERSLY.

To Week after York August Meeting.

STEWARDS,
THE EARL OF EGLINTON—JOHN BELL, ESQ.
JOHN ALLAN, ESQ.

FIRST DAY.—THE CLARET STA...
closed with 20 subs.

STOCKTON RACES.—A report is in circulation in Stockton and its neighbourhood that the Duke of Wellington and Sir Robert Peel, with others of the nobility and gentry, who are shortly expected at Wynyard, the seat of the Marquis of Londonderry, will honour the races with their presence.

The Marquis and Marchioness of Londonderry, accompanied by the Duke of Buccleugh, attended Stockton races on Friday. The ball in the Assembly Rooms was led off by the Duke of Buccleugh and the Marchioness of Londonderry.

STOCKTON.

These races commenced on Thursday last, over the new course at Tibbersly, which was universally admired for its excellent order and picturesque scenery; and the greatest credit is due to Mr. Jackson, not only for making a race course in so short a time, inferior to none in the kingdom of the same size, but also for the excellent stabling and other conveniences he has made for the accommodation of the race horses and trainers.—On Thursday morning, the booths on the course, about twenty-four or twenty-five in number, each sporting a flag at the top, waving with the wind, could be seen a great distance and it had a very good effect, and several of them were fitted up in the most comfortable manner, and provided such dinners as would not disgrace a gentleman's table; we were most happy to see the dining rooms with comfortable chairs and tables.

Workmen are at present employed in building an elegant Grand Stand, at Wynyard, for the accommodation of the Duke and Duchess of Cambridge, and the other illustrious visitors, who are expected to honour Stockton Races with their company during the latter part of this month. The stand, after being fitted up in a style suitable for the reception of the distinguished party, will then be removed to the New Course at Tibbersly, and there placed in an advantageous situation for viewing the races.

STOCKTON RACES.

OVER THE NEW COURSE, AT TIBBERSLY.

THURSDAY, 29th AUGUST, 1839.

THE EARL OF EGLINTON, STEWARDS, JOHN BELL, ESQ., JOHN ALLAN, ESQ.

Racing began at Tibbersly in August 1839. Spectators from the Stockton steamboat faced a long walk across a field. The new course with its beautiful views southwards of the Cleveland Hills and rural setting, was much admired. Jackson worked hard to improve facilities. In 1842 an ornamental archway decorated with flowers, greeted the Marquis of Londonderry's guests with an 'elegant Grand Stand' for Ladies, being built at Wynyard and transported to the course. The Marquis of Londonderry's patronage brought the Duke & Duchess of Cambridge, Duke of Buccleuch, Duke of Wellington and Sir Robert Peel to see the racing at Tibbersly. The most famous race at Tibbersly was the mare Beeswing's Stockton Gold Cup victory by a head from arch rival, Ararat, in August 1839.

RACING AT TIBBERSLY FARM BILLINGHAM 1839-1846

STOCKTON RACE WEEK

The rise in popularity of racing at Stockton, coupled with the expansion of holidays for workers and enhanced transport connections throughout the region, helped to establish Stockton Raceweek become an unofficial local holiday. Numerous industries planned their summer schedule to align with the August meeting at Stockton, and it was common for shops in Middlesbrough and Stockton to close for a half day during the races. However, the eruption of war in 1914, brought uncertainty for the plans of local industries to close during Stockton Raceweek.

LOCAL WORKS AND RACE WEEK.

This morning a representative of the "North-Eastern Daily Gazette" addressed the following query to the principal Middlesbrough firms:—

Will your works be closed down next week for the usual Race Week holiday, or will work proceed?

The answers received were as follows:—

Sir B. Samuelson and Co. — as possible work will proceed as usual.
R. Hull and Co. — Cannot tell at present.
Dorman, Long and Co. — Closed for repairs.
Opera, Mills and Co. — Works as usual.
North-Eastern Steelworks —

WORKS AND RACE WEEK.

IMPORTANT STATEMENT BY MR ARTHUR COOPER

Mr Arthur Cooper, Managing Director of the North-Eastern Steelworks, Middlesbrough, made the following statement to-day to the North Eastern Daily Gazette:—

"We recognise how important it is to our workpeople and their families that our works should be in operation...

TEES-SIDE RACE WEEK PLANS.

On inquiry at Messrs Bolckow, Vaughan and Co.'s works it was stated that work would proceed as usual next week. Messrs Richardson, Westgarth & have decided to close down for the Stockton Race holiday.

1914: It's war and queries about Race Week are in the local news headlines

January 1846

TO BE LET,
And entered upon at May-day next, TIBBERSLEY HOUSE, with the FARM and RACE COURSE, containing 152 Acres, more or less, in the Parish of Billingham, Stockton-on-Tees. The Hind at Tibbersley will show the Farm, and for further Particulars apply to Mr Crofton, Holywell, near Durham.

The death of John Jackson on December 22, 1845, at the age of 51, cast doubt on the future of racing at Tibbersly. By January 24, 1846, the farm was already being advertised as 'To Let.' However, in May 1846, it was announced that the August race meeting would proceed as planned, with Mr. John Gray from Newcastle serving as Clerk to the Course. Although the first two days of the event saw good attendances, the initiation of a subscription to relocate the racing to another venue signified the inevitable conclusion of racing activities at Tibbersly.

STOCKTON RACES.—A subscription is in operation for raising a sufficient sum for the formation of a race-course at Mandall, so that the races this year may be revived at that place, which is situated most conveniently for the purpose. A number of gentlemen have already subscribed towards accomplishing the undertaking, which is estimated to cost £500. The formation of the course, which is now staked out, and the making of the approaches to it, will, it is expected, be completed in less than a month.

1855

It took 10 years for racing to return - at Mandale Bottoms, a venue first considered in 1836. Revived by new and energetic management led by Thomas Craggs, a forceful Clerk of the Course, the new venue was funded through subscriptions. The first race on the Mandale course, the Mandale Trial Stakes on Thursday 6 September 1855, was won by Caledonian. The Stockton Grand Stand Company formed in 1859, ensured financial stability - including owning the Grandstand within 20 years. The future of racing at Stockton seemed to be assured.

Stockton-on-Tees, January 28th, 1869.

STOCKTON GRAND STAND COMPANY (LIMITED).

Notice is Hereby Given, that the Tenth General Meeting of the above Company will be held on Wednesday, the Third day of February next, at the .... Hotel, in Stockton, at Eight o'clock in the Evening.

By order of the Directors,

Thomas Craggs,
Secretary.

1887

SKETCHES AT STOCKTON RACES.

A humourous reflection on Stockton Races in 1887

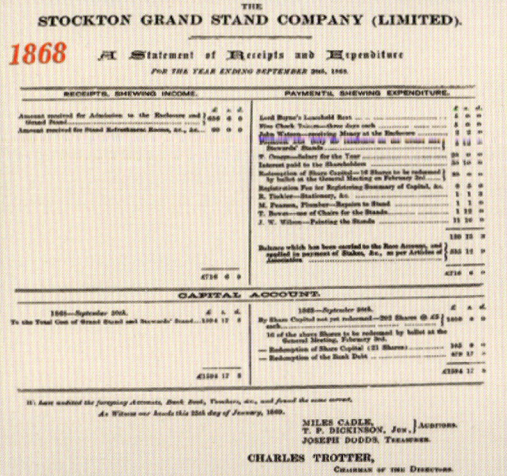

THE
STOCKTON GRAND STAND COMPANY (LIMITED).

1868

A Statement of Receipts and Expenditure
FOR THE YEAR ENDING SEPTEMBER 30th, 1868.

MILES CADLE,
T. P. DICKINSON, Jun.} AUDITORS.
JOSEPH DODDS, TREASURER.

CHARLES TROTTER,
CHAIRMAN OF THE DIRECTORS.

The Stockton Grand Stand Company Ltd. oversaw the accounts for racing at Stockton

RACING AT MANDALE BOTTOMS: 1855 TO 1981

1905

THE SPORTS GAZETTE. SATURDAY. AUGUST 19. 1905.

STOCKTON RACECOURSE.
THE NEW GRANDSTAND.

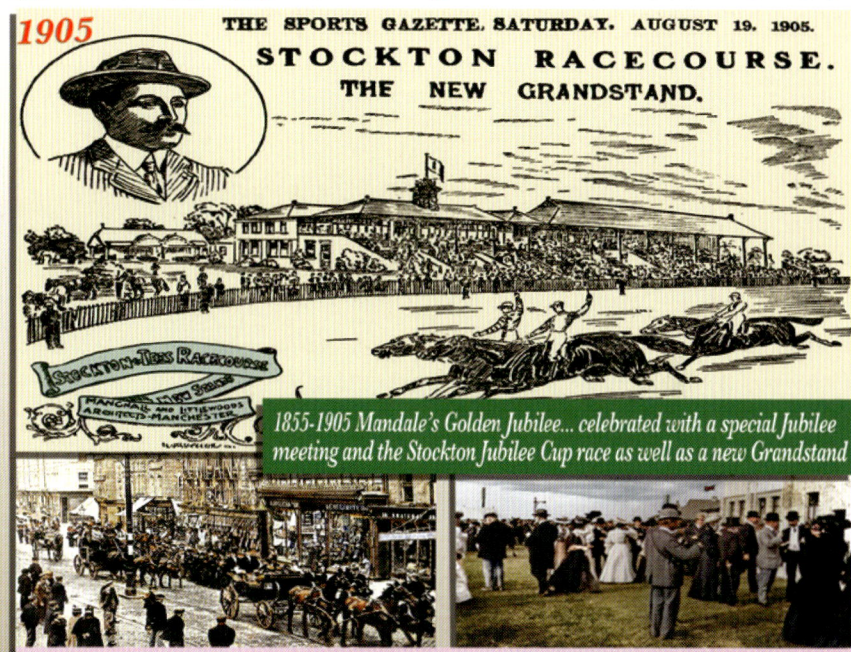

1855-1905 Mandale's Golden Jubilee... celebrated with a special Jubilee meeting and the Stockton Jubilee Cup race as well as a new Grandstand

LEFT: Lord Londonderry's party are driven down Stockton High Street to attend Stockton Race meeting....RIGHT: crowds gather outside the new grandstand at Mandale

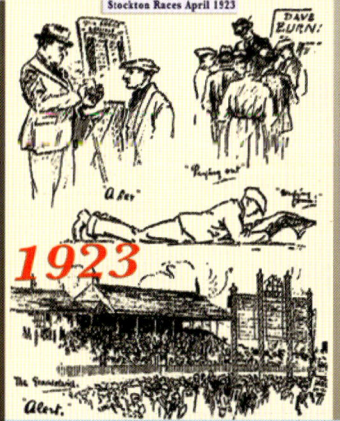

Stockton Races April 1923

1923

In 1955 the centenary of racing at Mandale was celebrated with a special meeting.

STOCKTON 2nd SPRING MEETING
SATURDAY MAY 16th 1942
OFFICIAL RACE CARD 1d

1942

STOCKTON
CORONATION
MEETING

SATURDAY 4th JULY
1953

OFFICIAL PROGRAMME
PRICE ONE SHILLING

The Centenary Programme
SATURDAY, JULY 2nd, 1955

2.30.—STOKESLEY APPRENTICE STAKES for four-year-olds and upwards. — One mile one furlong.	£200
3. 0.—YARUM PLATE Handicap for three-year-olds and upwards.—Six furlongs.	£500
3.30.—CARRS STAKES for two-year-olds only.—Six furlongs.	£1,000
4. 0.—DURHAM COUNTY PLATE for three-year-olds and upwards. — One mile.	£1,000
4.30.—MANDALE CENTENARY STAKES Handicap for three-year-olds only.—Two and a half miles.	£1,600
5. 0.—TIBBERSLEY STAKES for two-year-olds only.—Five furlongs.	£250

ADMISSION CHARGES:

First Ring .... 22s 6d (including 7s 2d tax)
Second Ring .... 9s 0d (including 2s 8d tax)
Course .... 3s 6d (including 10d tax)
Car Park 3s 6d : Buses 10s

Stockton became one of the leading courses in the north - one of the few northern venues to remain open during World War Two. Time caught up however with racing ending on 16 June 1981 due to falling attendances.

7 July 1904...Buffalo Bill's Wild West Comes To Stockton

ONE DAY ONLY.
STOCKTON,
THURSDAY, JULY 7th,
Near Tram Terminus, NORTON.

BUFFALO BILL'S WILD WEST AND

Congress of Rough Riders of the World.

HEADED AND PERSONALLY INTRODUCED BY

COL. W. F. CODY (BUFFALO BILL)

NOW MAKING POSITIVELY ITS FINAL TOUR OF GREAT BRITAIN, WILL NEVER RETURN. SEE IT NOW OR NEVER! THREE SPECIAL TRAINS, 800 PEOPLE, 500 HORSES.

The one Exhibition in all the World that has no Counterpart.

EXCLUSIVELY ITS OWN CREATION.

Not the Imitation of Fancy, but the Stupendous Realism of Facts.

ALL LONDON PRONOUNCED IT SUPREMELY ORIGINAL AND GREAT.

Brimful of Life, Action, and Thrilling Interest, crowded with Historical Fact and Correct Information, presenting with Historical Accuracy the Exciting, Sanguinary, and Romantic Scenes of Pioneer Life on the Plains, in the Forest, and at the Foot Hills during the early days of

THE STORY OF AMERICAN PROGRESS,

In which will participate Redskin Braves, Western Frontiersmen, Scouts Hunters and Cowboys in True Pictures of Border Life on the Western American Plains. Attack upon the Emigrant Train. Pony Express Riding. Famous Deadwood Stage "Hold-up." Burning of a Settler's Cabin.

INDIAN WAR DANCES AND PASTIMES.

Cowboy Fun. Lassoing Wild Horses. Riding Bucking Broncos.

The Chase, Capture, and Punishment of a Horse Thief.

BUFFALO BILL, THE MASTER EXPONENT

of Horseback Marksmanship in his wonderful exhibition of Shooting while riding a galloping Horse.

AT STOCKTON.

Buffalo Bill's Wild West and Congress of Rough Riders, which gave a performance on Thursday, was voted a huge success. A large concourse of people gathered to witness the imposing spectacle of animated pictures of the picturesque life on the Western American Plains, which showed primitive horsemen who had attained great fame, together with their counterparts of modern military horsemanship. Amongst the cleverest feats of the afternoon was that of Johnny Baker, the celebrated young American marksman, who enjoys the reputation of being the best "crack" in the world. Perhaps the most wonderful and sensational item was the performance given by Carter, the Cowboy cyclist, who jumped on his bicycle across a chasm of 56 feet, covering a distance in the plunge of 17 feet. The performance was repeated in the evening.

BATTLE OF THE LITTLE BIG HORN.

The Awful Reality of Furious Conflict and Massacre in Savage Warfare presented with Perfect Historical Accuracy of Detail, introducing 800 Indian Chiefs, Braves, and Warriors, Soldiers, Scouts, and Horses, with every accessory of Arms, Accoutrements, and Savage Decoration, whose Inconceivably Overpowering Apotheosis of Mortal Combat is the Illustrious Tableaux of

CUSTER'S LAST STAND AND HEROIC FALL.

THE WORLD WILL NEVER SEE ITS LIKE AGAIN!

EVERYTHING PRESENTED IS REALISM ITSELF.

THE VAST ARENA ILLUMINATED AT NIGHT BY SPECIAL ELECTRIC LIGHT PLANTS.

THE ENTIRE GRAND PROGRAMME

Will positively be presented undivided and uncurtailed.

TWICE DAILY,

RAIN OR SHINE!

AFTERNOONS AT 2.   EVENINGS AT 8.

Doors open at 1 and 7 p.m.

ONE TICKET ADMITS TO ALL ADVERTISED ATTRACTIONS.

PRICES OF ADMISSION:—

1s, 2s, 3s, 4s; Box Seats, 5s and 7s 6d. Children under 10 years half-price to all except 1s Seats.

All Seats are Numbered, except those at 1s and 2s. No Tickets under 4s sold in advance. Tickets at all prices on sale on the grounds at hours of opening, and Tickets at 4s, 5s, and 7s 6d on Sale 9 a.m. the day of exhibition at S. S. Eades, 71, High-street, Stockton-on-Tees.

Will Exhibit at

DARLINGTON, July 6th.
STOCKTON, July 7th.
MIDDLESBROUGH, July 8th.
WEST HARTLEPOOL, July 9th.
NEWCASTLE, One Week, July 11th to July 16th.

Buffalo Bill embarked on a tour of England during the summer of 1904, which spanned the entire country, including the North East. This journey included performances at various venues throughout the region. On Thursday, July 7th, the show arrived in Stockton where they set up in The Long Field, Durham Road, Norton End. The logistical feat of transporting the show required three special trains to accommodate 800 men and 500 horses as they travelled from town to town. Ticket prices ranged from one shilling (5p) to seven shillings and sixpence (37p), covering access to all the shows offered including the Battle of the Little Big Horn. There were two performances in Stockton and they drew large crowds before the entourage moved on to their next destination - Graham's Field off Parliament Road in Middlesbrough.

'Ye Olde Cherry Faire Races'

The origins of the Cherry Fair are shrouded in the mists of time, but its date, the 18th of July, coincides with the ripening of cherries. By the 19th century, the fair had evolved into an annual celebration, featuring many fun-filled activities in the High Street. Among these were the popular Donkey Derby, various rides, a diverse array of races, and, naturally, an abundance of food offerings for sale. As depicted in this image from 1904, the Donkey Derby took place at Stockton FC's Victoria Football Ground.

Messin' about on the river...

The first regatta on the River Tees was in 1825 in honour of the Duke of Cleveland who was a steward at Cup Day at Stockton Races on The Carrs adjoining the river. The boat races took place between the heats on the race course. Rowing was a very popular sport at Stockton with several rowing clubs formed.

TEES AMATEUR BOATING CLUB REGATTA. 1894

STOCKTON.

TEES CHALLENGE CUP.

THE MEDAL.

ALONG THE BANKS.

THE STOCKTON CREW.

ON THE SLAG BANKS.

MR FRANK COOKE. (STOCKTON STROKE.)

WATCHING THE CLUB RACE.

ISOLATED.

The Tees Regatta 1894 was notable for the Stockton Boat Crew following up their recent Ironmasters' Cup victory by winning the Tees Challenge Cup against Middlesbrough A.B.C. for the first time since 1883. Large crowds gathered to watch the race from Thornaby High Wood to the Railway Bridge.

Enjoying a pleasure trip on SS Gondolier on the Tees at Stockton 1905.

Stockton and Thornaby Rowing Club. 1905

OPENING OF THE NEW BOATHOUSE BY MR R. ROPNER, JUN., J.P.

STOCKTON & THORNABY ROWING CLUB

Robert Ropner Jun PRESIDENT of the Club.

E.F. Popple Hon Secretary.

James Nicholson Captain.

Going for a spin.

The new boathouse at the Stockton and Thornaby Rowing Club was opened 30 May 1905, by Robert Ropner Jnr J.P., before a large gathering of members. The opening ceremony with several speeches continued at the Ship Launch Inn on the Quayside with food and musical entertainment.

or enjoying the splash of the swimming pool

1892

OPENING OF THE NEW BATHS AT STOCKTON.

Since the latter end of September, 1890, Stockton has been deprived of the Corporation Baths and Washhouses, which have been entirely reconstructed during the interval. A handsome building now replaces the old structure, and they were publicly opened on Friday last week. The large swimming bath, which, of course, takes up the main portion of the interior of the building, is 75 feet in length and 27 feet broad, and has a capacity of 60,000 gallons of water. The bath is lined with Farnley Iron Company's white-glazed bricks, and in depth ranges from 4 feet to 6 feet 6 inches. There are 40 dressing compartments surrounding the bath, and above these boxes is a gallery running round three sides of the lofty hall and supported on twelve iron columns. A dozen second-class slipper baths are placed on one side, whilst a vapour and shower bath are provided at each end, together with additional accommodation. On the remaining side other twelve slipper baths may be inserted in case of necessity. The swimming hall is heated with steam pipes in such a manner that a comfortable temperature may be registered during all seasons. On each side of the main entrance there are smaller departments. On the one side eight first-class gentlemen's "slippers" are fitted up, whilst the same apartment contains

NEW BATHS FOR STOCKTON.

OPENING CEREMONY AND GALA.

The old baths of the Stockton Corporation were closed on the 27th September, 1890, and yesterday the splendid new baths and washhouses which have been erected on the same site at a cost of over £7,000 were formally opened. Mr Campbell, the Corporation surveyor, seems to have utilised to good advantage the area of 1,120 square yards which were at his disposal. The entrances are as before, in Portrack-lane, and respectively for men and women, the corridors being divided by the pay office of Mr Power, the baths manager, in which there is an electric indicator communicating with every bath and room in the building. To the right of the men's entrance is the boiler and engine-house, the former horizontal and 24 feet long and the latter vertical and of eight horse-power. Passing the engine-house, a winding staircase leads to comfortably matted corridor in which are eight first-class

SLIPPER BATHS

for gentlemen, and also a Russian vapour bath and a shower bath. There is a waiting-room in this corridor, and the bath floors have been laid with cork matting, a warm and comforting provision. Messrs Carter & Co., of Stockton, it may be remarked, supplying the upholstery throughout. Returning to and proceeding along the entrance corridor, the magnificent hall containing the

SWIMMING BATH

is reached, which is said to be one of the finest

OPENING NEW BATHS AND WASH-HOUSES AT STOCKTON.

The new Stockton Baths & Wash-houses on Portrack Lane were opened to great public acclaim on Friday 19 February 1892 by Mayor John Burn. The old baths, closed in September 1890, 'had been much missed'. The Corporation justified the £6,346 cost with the 'hope that the baths would prove.. a great public utility'. The swimming bath was almost 25 metre long and it was considered to be 'one of the finest in the kingdom'. There was also a Russian vapour bath and eight slipper baths. To complete the celebrations there was a swimming gala and a water polo match between Darlington and Stockton on the evening with Stockton victorious by 3-0. New wash-houses were also available for use.

Swimming Gala at Stockton.

1904

Swimming galas and water sports were always very popular with the Stockton public.

Fancy a bike ride?

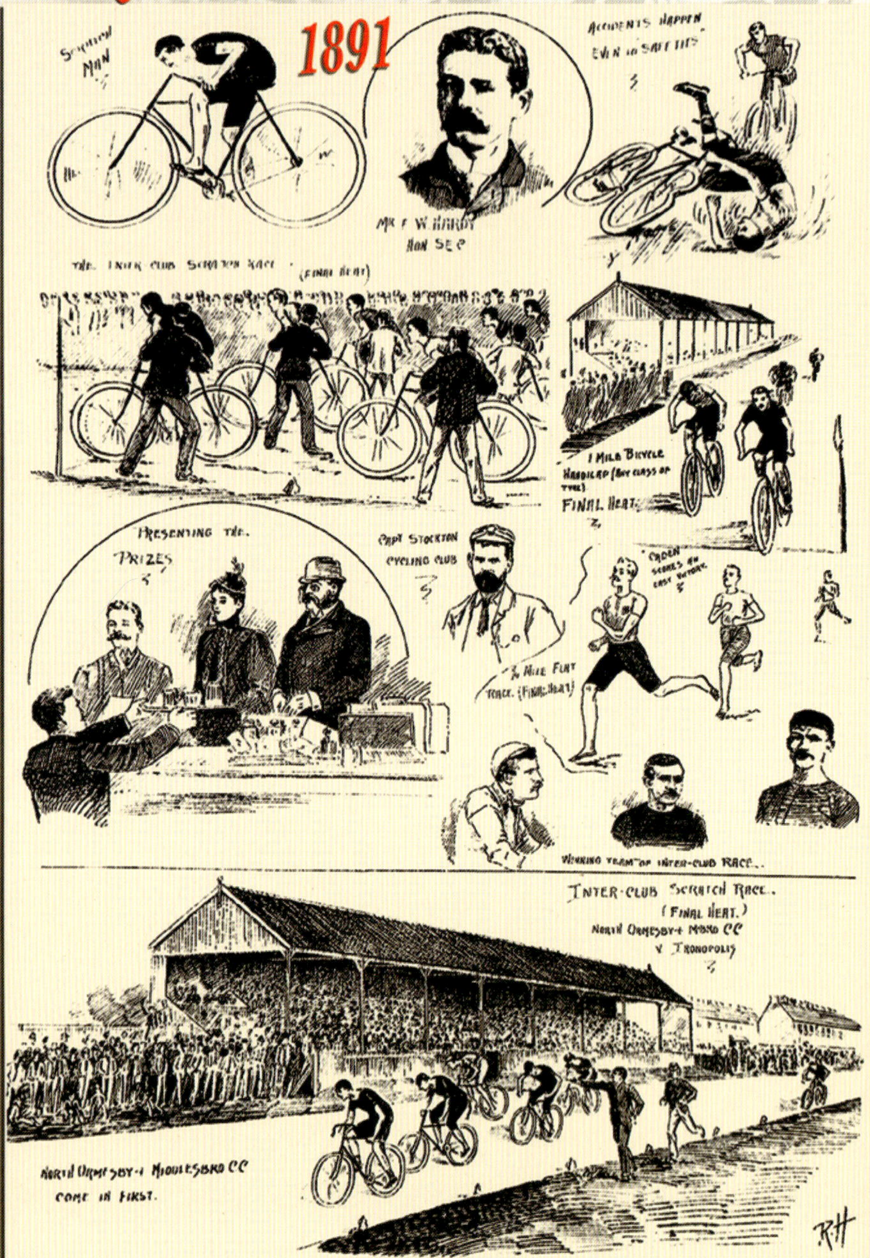

1891

SKETCHES AT THE
STOCKTON CYCLING CLUB AMATEUR RACE MEETING.

Cycling became popular in Stockton after the 'safety model' was introduced in 1885. There were several cycling clubs in the town with competitive races held across the region - including Victoria Park Stockton. For many however, the social aspect of cycling was the attraction, with organised rides to country villages & tea rooms and annual 'Sports Events' for all members.

The popularity of cycling saw several cycle shops opening in Stockton. Over one million cycles were sold nationally during the 1890's.

Just having a good time...

STOCKTON SPORTS.

1904

1892

SKETCHES AT THE
COSTUME & BLOSSOM BICYCLE PARADE AT STOCKTON.

ATHLETIC SPORTS.

STOCKTON CYCLING CLUB.

To-day the thirteenth annual Athletic Sports in connection with the Stockton Cycling Sports, were held on Victoria Football Ground in the presence of a large company. The chief officials of the meet were:—Judge, Dr W. J. Beatty, J.P. (president), assistant-judges, Messrs H D Parsons, F. W. Hardy, W. Hutchinson, F. J. Forster, and Major Smith; umpires, Messrs T. Borrow, J. Nattrass, N. Todd, J. Moss, S. Wood, T. E. Thompson; handicappers and timekeepers, Messrs W. H. Harrison and G. M. Todd; honorand starter Mr W. Robinson; hon. secretary Mr Tom Shaw. There were six different events including 120 yards flat race, for which there were 75 entries; half-mile bicycle handicap 30 entries; 440 yards flat race, 45 entries; one mile bicycle handicap, 79 entries; one mile flat race 45 entries; one mile bicycle scratch race for the Ropner Challenge Cup, four entries, making a total entry of 247, which, on the aggregate, is higher than last year, the increase being in connection with the foot races.

DETAILS OF THE RACING:—
120 YARDS.
HEAT WINNERS

STOCKTON CYCLING CLUB SPORTS

1903

ALL OUT!

THE MAYOR

THE PROCESSION IN THE MILE RACE

1.8 TURN OUT OUT OF 1.8 ENTRIES

DURING THE INTERVAL THE OFFICIALS LOOK PLEASANT

THEY WAS ALL OUT

LOOK OUT FOR THE LUCKY BIRD KEY

WAITING THEIR TURN

THOMAS LOOKS TO SEE WHERE HIS OPPONENTS ARE IN THE 440 YARDS

J.T. RUSSELL WINS THE ROPNER CHALLENGE CUP THE 2ND TIME

J.T. RUSSELL WINNER OF THREE EVENTS IN ONE DAY

THE ROPNER CHALLENGE CUP WON BY J.T. RUSSELL NOW HIS OWN PROPERTY HAVING WON IT THREE TIMES IN SUCCESSION

FINISH OF THE MILE SCRATCH RACE

A COMPETITOR FALLS INTO THE POT.

A LITTLE ENCOURAGEMENT TO THE WINNER OF THE MILE RACE.

FINISH OF THE 440 YARDS.

STOCKTON SPORTS.

This afternoon, in brilliant weather, the fourteenth annual amateur athletic sports in connection with the Stockton Cycling Club were commenced on the Victoria Ground. The chief officials of the meet were:—Judge, Dr. W. J. Beatty, J.P., assistant-judges, Messrs H. D. Parsons, F. W. Hardy, W. Hutchinson, Major Smith, and F. J. Forster, umpires, Messrs T. Borrow, J. Nattrass, N. Todd, S. Wood, E. Thompson, and J. L. Bainbridge; handicappers and timekeepers, Messrs W. H. Harrison and G. M. Todd; starter, Mr W. Robinson; number board Messrs E. Bartlett, R. L. Welford, J. Borrow, and G. Everson; telephone, Mr E Morton; clerk of the course, Mr J. Batsworth; hon. secretary, Mr Tom Shaw. There were six events, which found the following entries:—120 Yards Flat Race (handicap), 90 runners; 440 Yards Flat Race (handicap), 43; One Mile Flat Race (handicap), 44; Half-mile Bicycle Handicap, 52; One Mile Bicycle Handicap, 29; and One Mile Bicycle Scratch Race, 9; making a total entry of 247. There was a good company round the ropes.

RESULTS OF THE RACING.
HALF-MILE BICYCLE.
1. J. T. RUSSELL, N.O. & M.C.C. (30).
2. G T. POUNDER, Sedgefield C.C. (88).
3. J. SETTLE, Billingham (90).
Won by inches, after a good race; third man two lengths behind. Time, 1 min 10.4 sec.

These images show just some of *the events from the era when cy-cling was a popular pursuit for many people. Special events were organised most summer weekends, including fancy dress parades and themed cycling days. Most cycling clubs pro-moted a strong social life for club members with dances, con-certs and dinners held across the year.*

Whitsuntide & the 'Richmond Cyclists Meet'

North York and **South Durham Cyclists Meet, 1893**

Richmond

1930

WHITSUNTIDE 1930 LONG NEWTON: STOCKTON CYCLISTS EN ROUTE TO THE 'RICHMOND MEET'

The most important event for many club members was the annual 'Richmond Cyclists Meet' held at Whitsuntide, attracting riders from across the region who enjoyed a variety of events held in the picturesque town of Richmond during the holiday weekend. The event, which began in 1893, was celebrated with some ceremonial exchanges between the Mayor of Richmond and Mayor of Stockton. The cyclists raised a lot of money for local charities - a perfect weekend!

1933

STOCKTON CYCLISTS RIDING TO THE 'RICHMOND MEET'

CYCLISTS' MEET AT RICHMOND

LIST OF CLUB RUNS DURING MONTH OF JUNE.

The run programme of the above club for June is as follows:—
2nd (Saturday), Carlton-in-Durham; 3rd (Sunday), Swainby; 6th (Wednesday), Wolviston; 9th (Saturday), Stokesley; 10th (Sunday), Hutton Rudby; 13th (Wednesday), Newton-under-Roseberry; 16th (Saturday), Seaton Carew; 17th (Sunday), Chop Gate; 20th (Wednesday), Seamer; 23rd (Saturday), Worsall; 24th (Sunday), Stainton (N.C.U. Jubilee Rally); 27th (Wednesday), Redcar; 30th (Saturday), Appleton-Wiske.

The run to Chop Gate on the 17th will start at 10 a.m., all Wednesday runs at 6.30 p.m., and all other runs at 2.30 p.m., all from Park-road South.

CYCLING

WEEK'S CLUB RUNS.

The following are the cycle club runs arranged for next week:—

SUNDAY, JUNE 12th.
Bohemian Club to Redcar
Sedgefield Club to Redcar at 9 a.m.

MONDAY, JUNE 13th.
Darlington Club (both a et-one) to Mansfield (from Piercebridge), at 6.30 and 6.15 p.m.
Darlington Wednesday Club to Crasswick and Barton at 6.30 and 6.15 p.m. Assemble Horse Market. Ladies' section to Maldleton-one-Row.

WEDNESDAY, JUNE 15th.
Darlington Wednesday Club (ladies' and gents' sections), impromptu, at 2.15 and 6.15 p.m.
St. Augustine's Club to Aldbro' at 6.30 p.m.
Darlington Club (combined run) to Richmond, at 6.15 and 6.30 p.m. Assemble top of Houndgate.
Sedgefield Club to Bishopton, 6.30 p.m.

THURSDAY, JUNE 16th.
Stockton Club, impromptu, 6.30

SATURDAY, JUNE 18th.
Darlington Wednesday Club to Hutton Rudby (combined run) at 2 p.m. Assemble Bondgate.
Stockton Club to Redcar, 2 p.m.
St. Augustine's Club (both sections) to Northallerton, 2.30 p.m.
Cleveland Road Club (both sections) to Bedale 2.15 p.m.
Darlington Club, impromptu, 2.30 p.m. Assemble Middlesbrough High School.
Sedgefield Club to Middlesbrough, 1.30.

Although the major meetings were a main attraction it was the weekly runs that kept many cycling clubs running. Often ending at local attractions such as Marton Bungalow they proved a highly popular part of being a member of a club.

THE SPORTS GAZETTE. SATURDAY. JUNE 2. 1928.

THE RICHMOND MEET

N.Y. & S.D. CYCLISTS HOLD ANNUAL CARNIVAL.

MR "BILLY" THOMPSON'S SUCCESS AS PRESIDENT.

NEW FURNESS CUP HOLDERS.

(By "T.A.K.")

Richmond was again en fête at Whitsuntide, when the N.Y. & S.D. Cyclists held their great festival.

Mr "Billy" Thompson, of Middlesbrough, who was President this year, proved himself a fine sportsman, and led the merry-making with great zest.

As usual, the wheelers devoted their efforts to charitable objects, and raised substantial sums for needy institutions at Richmond.

During the proceedings the Mayor of Richmond invested the president with his jewel of office, and he also presented a special jewel to Mr S. P. Thorpe, the president of Stockton Cycling Club, as a token of gratitude from the cyclists for his services to the meet as hon. secretary and treasurer for two years.

Shortly before midnight a number of the members of the meet may have been noticed unobtrusively making their way in the direction of the Mayor's Parlour. They were answering a summons to attend the annual meeting of the extremely ancient and very venerable Order of Merrie Meads, which was held at the midnight hour.

P. G. M. Newton presided, and although the strictest secrecy was maintained with regard to the business transacted, it is permitted to report that the Meads absolutely refused to entertain an application from the Persians, the purpose of which was an amalgamation of the two bodies. They also officially declined to recognise any wars that may be held on the future and intimated that anyone who indulges in future did so at their own risk.

Sunday.

The weather was fair, but inclined to be dull when the wheelers awoke on Sunday morning and prepared for the business of the day. The first function was the special service in the Parish Church at which there was an excellent attendance.

Help for Charities.

The hon. secretary and treasurer, Mr A. J. Hargreaves, who also responded, declared that the Meet that year had been an undoubted success. The collection in the Parish Church in aid of the Victoria District Hospital, had realised more than £22, which was much better than last year.

In spite of the bad weather about £10 was raised by the Sunday afternoon concert in aid of the Mayor's Fund for the district nurse, and the Ovington concert for Edwin Turner's Memorial Fund had also realised £10.

The money collected for the Victoria Hospital amounted to more than £5. The collection realised by the Ceremony.

'Scrum down'...Stockton Rugby Club

1886: EARLY WEEKS

The Stockton Rugby Club, which was only recently formed, have already issued their card of fixtures, containing, in the small space of time allotted H. Benington, the hon. secretary, a good number of representative matches. The club has still several dates open, and will be glad to hear from secretaries of other clubs with whom engagements have not yet been made with a view to making one.

1887: FIRST AGM

STOCKTON RUGBY FOOTBALL CLUB.—Last Friday the first annual meeting of this Club was held in the Victoria Coffee Palace, High-street, the Rev. J. C. Fellowes presiding.—Mr H. Benington, the hon. sec., read a report, which stated that the Club had had a fairly successful season. Two games had been won, two drawn, and four lost. Considering all the circumstances, the prospects of the Club were very bright. The Club has joined the Durham County Rugby Union, and has also entered for the county cup competition. It is hoped the Club will next season have a much better ground than at present. The receipts amounted to £25 6s 4d, and there was a balance in hand of £2 13s 3d, with no outstanding accounts to discharge. There are 86 financial members of the Club. The following officers were appointed:—President, the Rev. H. Martin, Vicar of Stockton; vice-presidents, Messrs T. Wrightson, C. Arthur Head, G. M. Watson, W. E. Fawcett, Wm. Whitwell, Major Ropner, J. W. P. Page, Geo. Newby, A. E. Crosby, E. J. Vie, Wm. Dodshon, C. J. Archer, A. Hutchinson, F. L. Dodds, W. C. Langley; captain, the Rev. J. C. Fellowes; vice-captain, Mr H. S. Cadle; committee, Messrs G. M. Hogg, Taylor, Nattrass, Braithwaite, Bennett, and Smiles; secretaries, Messrs H. Benington and R. D. Hogg. Mr H. S. Cadle was elected the club's representative on the county committee.

1888: TOUGH AWAY TRIP

FOOTBALL NOTES.

THE Rugby team had anything but a pleasant experience of it at Sunderland last week. The Wearsiders not only defeated our "pets," but (perhaps carelessly) added insult to injury, for when the Stocktonians arrived at their destination there was no one to meet them at the Station, and not knowing where to put up they were obliged to charter about half a dozen cabs at their own expense to convey the team and a few enthusiastic supporters, direct to the Ashbrooke Ground. Arrived there, not a soul of the opposition party was to be found. The captain began to think that there must have been some mistake in the arrangement of the match, and "wanted" the "blood" of the poor secretary, but his conjecture was wrong, for after patiently waiting for one solid hour the Stocktonians had the satisfaction (!) of seeing the Sunderland full-back come strolling in at the gate, followed at intervals by the remainder of the fifteen, who arrived by twos and threes. This is shocking bad form on the part of a club like Sunderland. They must have known perfectly well the time when the Stockton team would arrive, and ought to have made proper arrangements for their reception.

Rugby Football.

1889

STOCKTON

v.

Mossley

Saturday, January 12th

Bowesfield Lane Ground.

Admission 6d. Ladies and Members Free.

Grand Stand 3d. extra.

STOCKTON RUGBY CLUB.

The annual general meeting of this Club was held in the Palatine Hotel on Thursday, Dr. J. H. Clegg presiding. The report submitted by Mr A. Braithwaite (hon. sec.) stated that the past season had not been successful either with respect to matches or finances. The Club numbered 134 members, as compared with 106 in the previous season, or an increase of 28. The first fifteen had thirty matches arranged (exclusive of Cup ties), but of these only 17 were played, and 13 cancelled for various reasons. Of the 17 matches played 2 were won, 5 drawn, and 10 lost. The second fifteen played 15 matches, winning 3, losing 5, and drawing 1. The expenses were very heavy last season. The receipts amounted to £106 19s 10½d, and the expenditure to £104 10s 8½d, leaving a credit balance of £2 4s 2d. There were outstanding debts amounting to £37 3s 8d. Allowing for unpaid subscriptions, donations promised, and the assets of the Club, the net deficit was £7.—on the motion of the Chairman the report was adopted. The following officers were elected:—Major Ropner, J.P., president; Mr J. J. Fowler, captain first 15; Mr E. J. Merryweather, deputy; Mr W. H. Nattrass, captain second 15; Mr A. Holmes, deputy; Messrs A. Braithwaite and E. S. Cadle, hon. secs.

1889: AGM

THE prospects of the Stockton Rugby Club are somewhat improved since last season. The increase of employment in the district has attracted hither many young men from South Yorkshire, where the handling game is most in favour; and several of these have represented a desire to join the club. Its ranks being thus recruited by well-known players, it will have a better opportunity of selecting a good representative team every Saturday in the coming winter to uphold the honour of our ancient borough against the Rugby forces of the North country. Last Saturday the club had its opening match, when the old players of last season were pitted against the new importations, and proved themselves well able to hold their own. The recruits are a stalwart lot, but they had the disadvantage of being new to each other, and showed great need of diligent practice to bring them up to the standard of Stockton's old contagent. The latter were in very fair form, and carried off the honours of the day by 2 goals 3 tries 3 minors to 1 minor. Learmore, " Lane " Brown, and W. H. Nattrass were among the pick of the lot. Amos Lowe, a well-known goal-kicker from Cleckheaton, is the strength of the new arrivals.

1890: NEW SEASON HOPES

STOCKTON RUGBY DEFEATED AT GATESHEAD.

STOCKTON RUGBY sent its first team to Gateshead last Saturday, and they travelled so late that it was five o'clock before they made their appearance within the ropes at the North Durham ground. Conning kicked off against the wind and hill, and the home team pressed all the first half, but the Stockton backs prevented them getting over, and only two minors resulted from the play. Stockton had slightly the best of the game for a few minutes after changing ends, but the home backs by a little good, passing changed the venue of the play. Bailey made a brilliant run, and being collared on the goal line passed to John Hall, who secured a try, which was converted by Hutchinson. Conning also secured a try, and at the close the score stood in favour of North Durham by one goal, one try, and six minors to nil. For the visitors W. H. Nattrass, Lane Brown, and Jacobs acquitted themselves very creditably.

1890: TURNING UP LATE!

The Stockton Rugby Football Club seem to be in a flourishing condition judging from the report which was submitted at the annual meeting. Out of 16 matches played last season, nine were won, six lost, and one drawn. The club has also a good financial position, and after paying off the debt on the pavilion they have still a good balance. This club, which has been established over 10 years, was never in a better condition than at present. Messrs Nattrass and Brown were appointed hon. secretaries.

1895: IN A GOOD PLACE

STOCKTON DEFEATED AGAIN.

The officials and players of the Stockton Rugby Club do not go the way to get much public patronage. Their unpunctuality is notorious, and hence people are shy of attending the matches. Last Saturday Stockton had an engagement with the Hartlepool Rovers' second team, and it might have been supposed that they would have been anxious to make the best of the daylight. Three o'clock, the time for the kick off, arrived, and the spectators began to muster, but only one or two players were to be seen kicking at ball about.

Ten minutes later the visitors arrived in a body, ready stripped for the fray. Then folks began to enquire where were the Stockton men. The answer was forthcoming at last— they were sitting comfortably in the parlour of their favourite "pub." This led to a message being sent to know if they had forgotten the time, and presently their lordships came bustling up in a desperate hurry. The match was twenty-five minutes late in starting, and hence short time had to be played, as it became too dark before the end of the game.

1895: LATE AGAIN!

Bowesfield Lane was the home of Stockton Rugby Club, when it was formed in 1886. Fortunes were mixed in the early years with a regular fixture list soon established. One of the highlights of that era was the visit of a Maori team watched by a then record crowd. The Club was also developing it's social side with Drama Nights and holding monthly dances in the Exchange Hall. In 1895, the Club had paid off the debt on their pavilion and balanced their accounts though there were still problems remaining - including punctuality at games!

A Friend in Need · Tackling a Tackler · Wide Throw up · Full Back · A Tres Easter · Piet Tennis · Refreshments · Cup Tie Tackling · Bravo Sadler · Well Collared

RUGBY FOOTBALL SKETCHES. 1889
STOCKTON v. HUMBLEDON.

FOOTBALLIST HISTRIONS AT STOCKTON.—Last night, the Temperance Hall, Stockton, was well filled on the occasion of the second annual dramatic entertainment given by the members of the Stockton Rugby Football Club. The performance was under the patronage of His Excellency the Marquis of Londonderry, K.G., Sir H. M. Havelock-Allen, M.P., Mr Jos. Dodds, M.P., and the High Sheriff of Durham (Mr David Dale, J.P.). Byron's charming little comedy, "Weak Woman," had been selected for representation. Mr Lloyd Claraunge, of the Theatre Royal, kindly supplied the requisite stage accessories and dresses, and the musical portion of the programme was supplied by Mr Woolman's String Band.

SKETCHES AT THE STOCKTON RUGBY FOOTBALL CLUB DRAMATIC ENTERTAINMENT.

Hon Secretary · Frederick Volspane · Captain Ginger · Mr A. Devonshire Hon Treasurer · Mrs Gwyn & Capt Ginger · End of Act I

1889

5 November 1888: a famous game at Stockton

I HEAR the Stockton Rugby club is negotiating for a match with the now celebrated Maori team, which will be in this district in a week or two. I hope they will be successful, as I feel sure the venture would prove a success from a financial point of view, as well as providing a great treat for the football-loving community of this neighbourhood.

THE MAORI FOOTBALL TEAM.

The team of Maori Rugby Union football players, which has arrived in England from Melbourne, consists of six full-blooded Maoris and 15 half-castes, the other four being of pure European descent, but they were all born in New Zealand. All the players are amateurs in the strictest sense of the word. Since the organisation of the team they played nine matches in New Zealand against the leading teams, winning seven and losing two. At Melbourne they played two games, one being won easily and the other drawn. At the latter place they entered the field wearing their native mats, some of which are very valuable. The mats were afterwards handed to an attendant. The men drew marked admiration at Melbourne for their fine physique, strength, and remarkable activity. One of their leading players played without his boots. The names of the members of the team are J. Warbrick (captain), W. Warbrick...

SKETCHES AT THE RUGBY FOOTBALL MATCH.
MAORIS v. STOCKTON.

GRAND
Rugby Football
MATCH!
MAORIS
(New Zealand Football Team)
v.
STOCKTON
Monday, 5th November.

Bowesfield Lane Grounds.

KICK-OFF 2-30 P.M.

Admission 6d. Grand Stand 6d. extra

THE MAORI TEAM AT STOCKTON.

The Stockton Rugby Club, who have made for themselves name and fame in local fields during the past two seasons, have been fortunate enough to secure a fixture with the Maori football team now making a tour of this country, and who reached Stockton from Newcastle yesterday. One of the finest expositions of the tackling game ever seen on Teesside was consequently witnessed on the Bowesfield-lane Ground yesterday afternoon by a large concourse of spectators, estimated to number not less than 3,000. The game was an unusually fast one throughout, and the operation of the new rules rendered it a remarkably open one. Stockton won the toss, and wisely elected to play with the wind in the first half. Pease secured the ball from the kick-off and after a smart run passed to Ropner, who, however, was off-side, and the visitors were allowed a free kick.

Extracts from the match report

...sides throughout. The visitors, however, were evidently possessed of the better stamina. They were remarkably swift, quick and clever in passing, and stronger in the scrimmages, in which they showed themselves adepts at screwing. The two teams were subsequently entertained to dinner in the Borough Hall by the Stockton Club. Teams:—

Maories.—Back, M'Causland; three-quarter backs, C. Maddigan, W. Warbreck, and J. Gage; half-backs, J. Elliot, Tami, F. Warbreck; forwards, Tairon, Renne, Williams, Kamwals, R. Warbreck, Maynard, Lee, and Anderson. Umpire, Mr J. Warbreck.

Stockton.—Back, E. J. Merryweather; three-quarter backs, R. Williams (capt.), R. Appleton, J. H. Smeddle; half-backs, E. S. Richardson, C. J. Sadler; forwards, Rev. J. C. Fellowes, J. J. Fowler, F. R. Pease, W. Hodgson, D. Terry, R. Ropner, W. Ropner, W. Tiend, J. Jones. Umpire, Mr C. Mountford, Darlington. Referee, Mr F. B. Junor, Durham.

NEW ZEALAND NATIVE FOOTBALL REPRESENTATIVES.

STOCKTON THEATRE ROYAL.—Last evening this theatre was crowded, mainly by players and admirers of the handling game of football, the performances being under the patronage of the Stockton Rugby and Maori teams. The play was "The Private Secretary," produced by Hawtrey's "No. 1" Company. Everything was done to make the play a spectacular success, and the merits of the company were such as to ensure them a warm reception. The *Rev. Robert Spalding* of the play was very capably delineated by Mr Arthur Helmore, who received adequate support from the other *dramatis personæ*.

More than 3,000 people came to the Bowesfield Lane ground to see the game. They were not disappointed as the game was fast and open. Afterwards the victorious Maori team were entertained to dinner in the Borough Hall by Stockton Rugby Club with Club President, Dr J H Clegg in the Chair. There were toasts to both teams and speeches from both team captains. Joe Warbreck, the Maori captain, said he hoped the new rules for the game now in force would give it greater appeal! Both teams then attended the Theatre Royal where they received a boisterous welcome before watching a perfomance of 'The Private Secretary'.

Stockton Football Club..the early years

Formed in 1882, Stockton joined the Northern League in 1889, becoming one of the league's top clubs, finishing 1st in 1898. In 1899 they won the FA Amateur Cup - they won again in 1903 & 1912. Middlesbrough were arch rivals.

1888.03.17 CLEVELAND CUP FINAL LOST 3-0 TO M'BRO

STOCKTON ASSOCIATION FOOTBALL CLUB. —The committee of this Club has now definitely secured the Victoria Recreation Ground, and intend at once to drain and level it for the coming season. The site is large enough to get a full-sized playing ground—viz., 120 yards by 80 yards, and it is the intention of the committee to erect a commodious grand stand, make a cinder path round the field of play, place turnstiles at entrance, provide exits at both ends of the ground (north and south), and make every other arrangement for the comfort of their patrons. When completed the ground will be equal to any in the North. The membership of the association is rapidly increasing. Several of the members come with good reputations, so that it is hoped that the Club will be able to put two strong teams in the field.

WALTER BORRIE, Stockton.

WALTER BORRIE has played the game since the formation of the Stockton Club, 5 years ago. For the first 2 seasons he attended to the Secretarial duties of the Club, but since then the Captaincy has been entrusted to him, and the duties of this office he now discharges in a manner satisfactory to all who feel interested in the Stockton Club's welfare. His position on the field is right wing half back. He is a strong energetic player and kicks with good power, but he has had to relinquish the game during the past few weeks owing to disablement. He is 24 years of age, 5 feet 9 inches high and weighs 11 st. 6 lbs., a weight which he is able to use to some good purpose.

1888: STOCKTON DECIDED TO MOVE TO THE VICTORIA RECREATION GROUND. DEVELOPMENT INCLUDED A GRANDSTAND & TURNSTILES. WALTER BORRIE WAS CLUB CAPTAIN

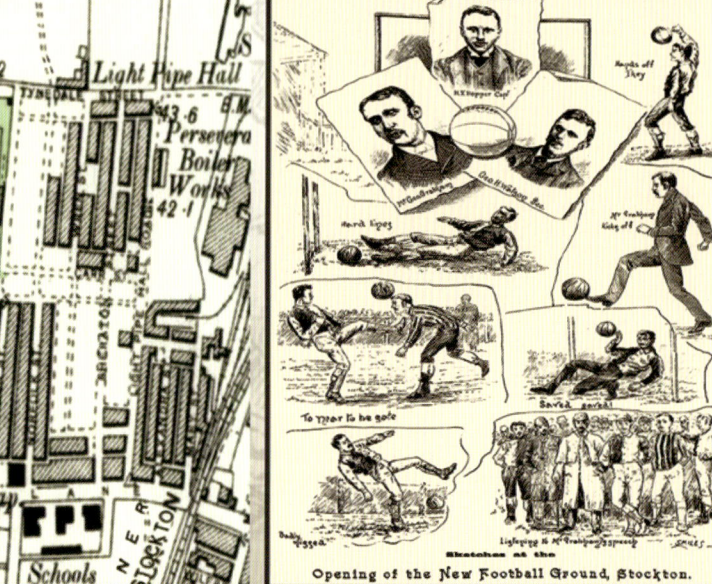

Opening of the New Football Ground, Stockton.

1888.09.15: THE GROUND OPENS WITH A GAME v NOTTINGHAM WANDERERS WHO WON 2-0

FOOTBALL SKETCHES. STOCKTON v. MIDDLESBROUGH

1889.09.07: OVER 6,000 STOCKTON FANS SEE M'BRO RECORD A 5-1 VICTORY

Football Sketches——Stockton and District v. West Bromwich Albion.

1889.04.23: MORE THAN 5,000 FANS CAME TO SEE THE FAMOUS WEST BROMWICH ALBION TEAM, TO RAISE FUNDS FOR THE CRICKET CLUB. STOCKTON PLAYED WELL BUT LOST 3-2

CLEVELAND FOOTBALL CUP FINAL SIX. MIDDLESBROUGH v. STOCKTON.

1890.03.29: M'BRO WIN THE CLEVELAND CUP FINAL 1-0 v STOCKTON

*Map extract reproduced from 1895 Twenty-Five inch series, with the kind permission of the Ordnance Survey

1890.09.13: Stockton Record A 3-0 Win Against M'bro At Linthorpe Road Ground

1890.11.29: Another Fiesty Game At Stockton v M'bro In Wintry Conditions Saw M'bro Win 5-2 & Stockton's Robert Shaw Carried Off With A Leg Injury

1891.02.14: Cleveland Cup Semi Final & A Record Stockton Crowd See A 2-0 Win

1891.03.21: Cleveland Cup Final & 12,000 Fans See Stockton Win 2-0 At Linthorpe Road, M'bro

Team captain Robert Shaw (right full-back) was born at Paisley 24.2.1870. He had played for Abercorn before joining Stockton in 1889. He soon became a highly rated player with county honours and he was also very popular with the Stockton fans.

This Is The Medal That Stockton Player Robert Shaw Was Presented With

1891.11.21: Victoria Ground: 8,000 Fans See Stockton Draw 1-1 With M'bro Ironopolis

1892.03.05: Cleveland Cup Semi-Final & A Big Crowd Of 10,000 See Stockton Lose 4-0 To M'bro

One of the north's strongest clubs..

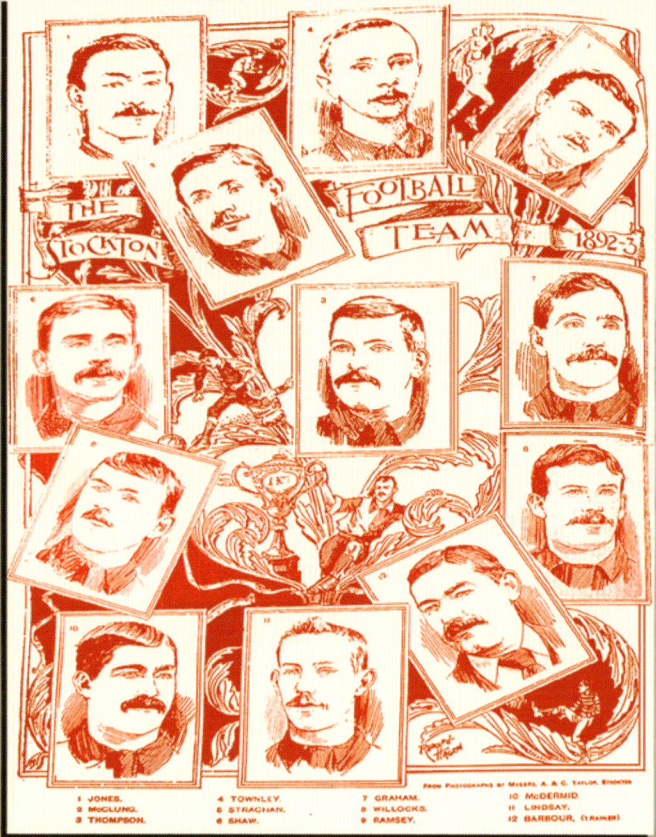

Stockton had finally won the F.A. Amateur Cup in 1899 and in 1903 they won it again when they defeated Oxford City 1-0 in another replay at Darlington after a 0-0 draw in the first game held at Elm Park Reading.

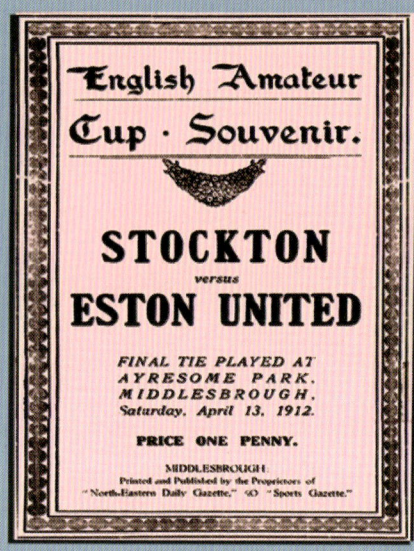

English Amateur Cup · Souvenir.

STOCKTON versus ESTON UNITED

FINAL TIE PLAYED AT AYRESOME PARK, MIDDLESBROUGH. Saturday, April 13. 1912.

PRICE ONE PENNY.

MIDDLESBROUGH: Printed and Published by the Proprietors of "North-Eastern Daily Gazette," & "Sports Gazette."

FA Amateur Cup Winners 1912

In 1897 Stockton reached the FA Amateur Cup Final for the first time. A large crowd of fans saw a 1-1 draw with favourites, Old Carthusians at Tufnell Park in London. Stockton led, had a goal disallowed before conceding an equaliser. Stockton lost the replay at Darlington, 4-1. This is a runners-up medal from that year.

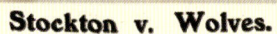

Stockton v. Wolves.

Stockton's success in the FA Cup brought Wolves to the Victoria Ground. A big crowd saw Wolves win 4-1.

WHY NOT?

In 1900 there was even talk of a united team from Stockton applying to join the Football League Second Division as it was felt the town could support this venture but it never came to fruition.

In 1912, Stockton became the first club to win the FA Amateur Cup three times when they defeated Eston United 1-0 after a 1-1 draw. Both games were held at Ayresome Park and almost 20,000 watched the final. By now Stockton were one of the strongest clubs in the north of England.

Stockton F.C. 1894-1895
Winners of the Durham Challenge Cup

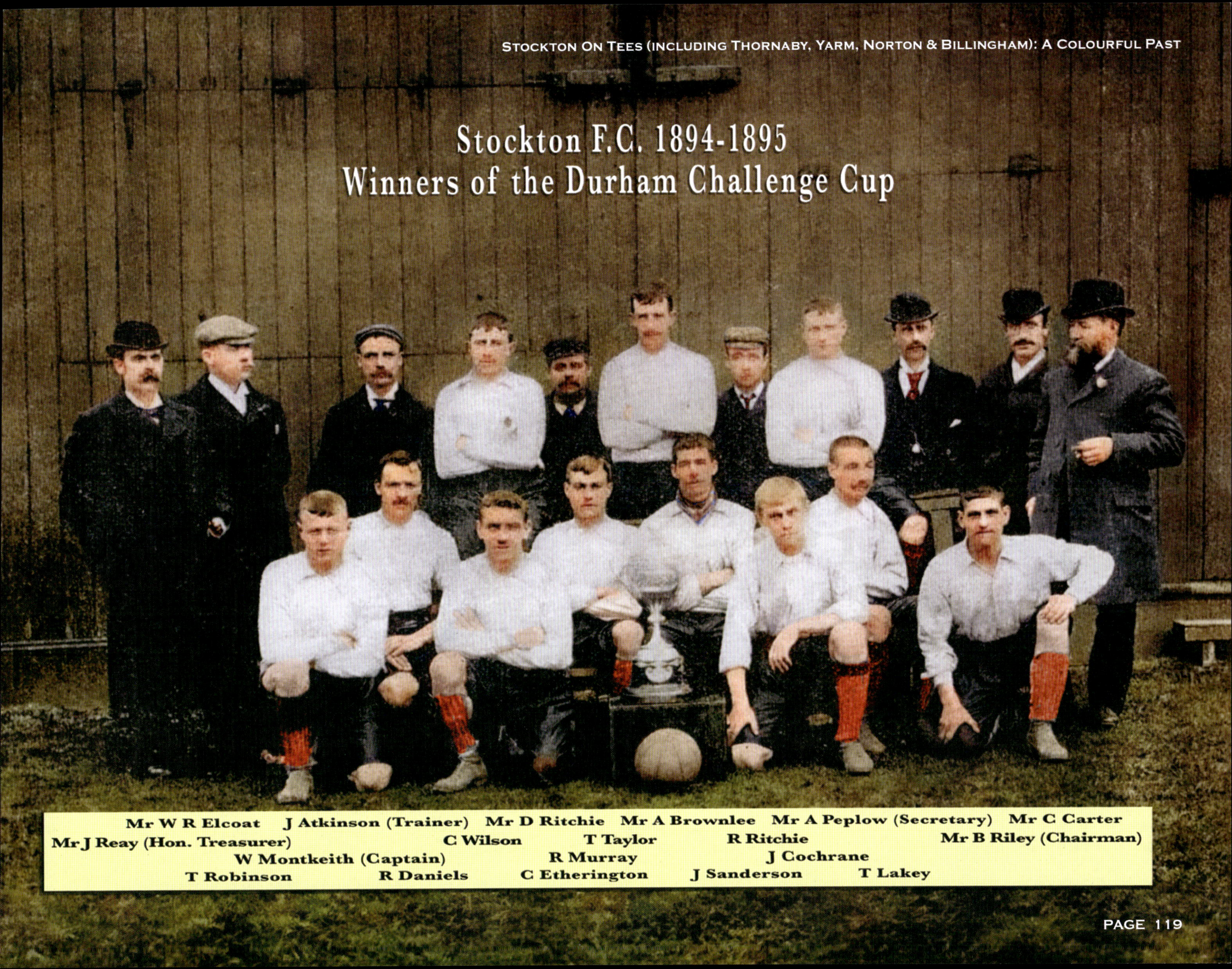

Mr W R Elcoat	J Atkinson (Trainer)	Mr D Ritchie	Mr A Brownlee	Mr A Peplow (Secretary)	Mr C Carter
Mr J Reay (Hon. Treasurer)		C Wilson	T Taylor	R Ritchie	Mr B Riley (Chairman)
	W Montkeith (Captain)		R Murray	J Cochrane	
T Robinson	R Daniels	C Etherington	J Sanderson	T Lakey	

Stockton Cricket Club 1890
Winners of Durham Cup

J Potts   T Swanson   JD Welford   A Scott   T Hill   M Heavisides   WR Hornby   A Atkinson

J Wright (Scorer)   AW Welch (Captain)   W Scott   FH Welch   RC Ellerton   H Windle (Umpire)

15 MAY 1851..A FINE SUMMER DAY AT STOCKTON CRICKET CLUB

A close look at the score book shows John Wisden batting no.6 for the All England XI

1814

1814, Sept. 13.—A cricket match for £100 was played in a field near Preston, by 11 gentlemen of Stockton and the same number of Yarm. Yarm, 1st innings, 45; 2nd ditto, 18—total, 63: Stockton, 1st innings, 24; 2nd ditto, 36—total, 60. Yarm had only one man out in the 2nd innings. Each side had 2 umpires.

Cricket in Stockton has a long history - it's known that a game versus Yarm took place on 13 September 1814 and a club was established in 1816. Under the Presidency of Dr. William Richardson from the mid-1840s the club became one of the strongest in the area hosting games against an All-England XI on six occasions between 1847 and 1859 – though it was only in 1858 that Stockton finally defeated the opposition - an event celebrated with a display of fireworks on the south side of The Square. In 1851, John Wisden, later associated with the cricket almanacks, played for the All-England team, as recorded in the Stockton score book.

1847: First visit of an All England XI

The corporation of Stockton have given £25 towards defraying the expences of the cricket match to be played this month, at Stockton, between eleven of all England and twenty-two of the Stockton Cricket Club.

1847, Sept. 23.—A cricket match, which lasted 3 days, was played at Stockton by 22 gentlemen of that town and of the North Riding of York with 11 of All England, which terminated as follows:—All England, 1st innings 55; 2nd innings 118; total, 173.—Stockton, &c., 1st innings 56; 2nd innings 73; total, 129; All England winning by a majority of 44. The All Englanders paid several visits to Stockton after this time.

1851

CRICKET AT STOCKTON.—Eleven of England v. 22 of Stockton and the district.—This match terminated on Saturday evening. An unusual feature in the score of this match was, that whilst in the first innings of the eleven there were five double figures, there were in their second as many as eight bats which produced the like result. They gained quite a triumph, their score being 121 and 176; total 297: while the twenty-two scored 96 and 97, total 193; the eleven thus winning by 104 runs.

CRICKET.
Just published, price 16s.,
ROBY'S ALL ENGLAND ELEVEN CRICKET MATCH SCORING BOOK, as used at their matches for 1851, showing at one view the result of every ball, and the certainty of arriving at true averages.

"There is little doubt, when Cricketers, engaged in great and important matches, look into it, that they will adopt Mr. Roby's system, and thank us for bringing it under their notice."—ED. ERA.

Also, just published, 3d edition, foolscap folio, price 1s. 6d. THE ALL ENGLAND CRICKET MATCH SCORING BOOK, on same plan as above, adapted for two elevens.
London: Simpkin, address on receipt of Meller, bookseller, Sto

UNDER THE PATRONAGE OF THE NOBLEMEN AND GENTLEMEN OF THE MARYLEBONE AND SURREY COUNTY CLUBS.
E. BALL, AND W. PAGE, CRICKET BAT KENNINGTON-ROW, facing KENNINGTON-COMMON, and STUMP MANUFACTURERS, No. respectfully to inform Noblemen, Gentlemen, and Cricketers generally, that they have now a large stock of well-seasoned Bats of first rate quality; also Improved Tubular and plain India-rubber gloves, leg guards, spiked soles for Cricket shoes and every article required in the game of Cricket. The bats have the especial patronage of the Universities of Oxford and Cambridge, and the Surrey County Clubs. Catapultas of improved construction. Superior whalebone-handled bats, well known for strength and durability, cannot be surpassed. Page's is the only place in London where balls are made on the premises. Orders promptly forwarded to all parts of the Kingdom on receipt of remittance.
Visitors to the Exhibition are requested to examine E. and

Just Published, by Baily Brothers, Cornhill, the Fifth Edition of
THE CRICKETERS' MANUAL.
By "BAT," showing the Character, History, Elements, and Laws of Cricket.—A Chapter of Curiosities—List of the principal Players—List of provincial Metropolitan and Suburban Clubs—Sketches of Mr. A. Mynn and Fuller Pilch—Rules for the formation of Clubs—Cricketing Songs, with choruses—Cricket Recitations; and a fund of useful and interesting information.
172 pages, bound in Cloth, Lettered and Gilt, Price ONE SHILLING.
"The Cricketer's Manual teems with merit."—Bell's Life
"The Cricketers' Manual is a comprehensive little volume, and stored with good materials for the lovers of bat, ball, and wicket."—Sporting Magazine.
Eighteen postage stamps, addressed to "Bat," 4, Beaufort Buildings, Strand, will ensure a copy per return.

The increase in newspaper ads reflects the growing interest in cricket

Seasons in the sun

Reminiscences of the Old ... Stockton Cricket Club.

By M. HEAVISIDES.

"He is the whole Encyclopedia of Facts"
— *Emerson.*

In the year 1814, a great cricket match, for £100 aside, between Stockton and Yarm, was played in a field opposite Potato Hall—a name given to a toll-bar and a group of cottages in Yarm Road contiguous to the stile giving entrance to the fields leading to Hartburn. Yarm won easily. Each side had two umpires. I may add that Tommy Marshall (the old Stockton umpire) and my father were the last survivors of the Stockton eleven referred to.

The first mention I find of the Stockton Club appears in the Annals of Stockton-on-Tees written by my father, in which is stated that the Stockton Cricket Club was established in 1816, though there is no doubt that for many years before that date the game was played in and about the ancient borough.

In 1847 the All-England Eleven visited Stockton for the first time. The match was played in a field on Murray's Farm, still standing westward of the Bowesfield Ironworks, and the scores were as follows:—

All England ... ... 1st innings 55, 2nd innings 118
Stockton & North Yorkshire „ „ 56, „ „ 73

The chronicler of the time, speaking of the second day's play, says:—
"The ground on this day presented a most animated and joyous scene—the sun shone in cloudless splendour—the playing was excellent on both sides—and upwards of three thousand admiring spectators were present,

Michael Heavisides & the early days of Stockton Cricket Club.

STOCKTON CRICKET CLUB CONCERT.

THE MAGNIFICENT BAND OF THE

COLDSTREAM GUARDS IN THE STOCKTON EXCHANGE HALL,

On Wednesday Evening, NOVEMBER 16th. **1891**

The Programme will include:—"La Tarantelle de Belphegor;" the Overtures—"Der Freischütz" and "William Tell;" Selections from "Lohengrin," "Cavallerio Rusticana," "Gondoliers," "Forge in the Forest," Grand March, "La Reine de Saba." Solos for Cornet, "Dear Heart;" Euphonium, "In Cellar Cool" (old German drinking song); Bassoon, "Lucy Long;" Two Piccolos, "Nightingale and Thrush;" also, **LONDON COSTERMONGER SONGS, &c.**

Doors open at 7.   Admission—1s., 2s. and 3s.   Reserved Seats. 3s. 6d

Seat Plan at Frank Appleby's.   Tickets from Frank Appleby, High Street (Telephone No. 4504);   Heavisides & Son, Finkle Street; and the Stockton Cricket Club Committee.

STOCKTON CRICKET CLUB: A FEW MEMORIES

1898: ARTHUR WELCH TOOK 10-48 V NORTH ORMESBY

20 JUNE 1896: PRESENTATION MADE TO CLUB CAPTAIN ARTHUR WELCH TO MARK HIS RECENT MARRIAGE.

1908

1925

RAIN STOPS PLAY v DARLINGTON GRANGEFIELD 23 MAY 1927

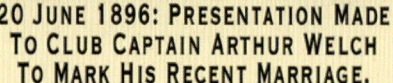

STOCKTON V NORTON

1903

STOCKTON v REDCAR

1904

---

4 June 1892: First game at Grangefield

OPENING OF THE NEW GROUND. STOCKTON V. CONSTABLE BURTON.

The opening match on the new ground of the Stockton Club, which has been laid out at a cost of £1,200, was played on Saturday between the above teams, in fine weather, and before a thin attendance of spectators. The ground is situated at the western extremity of the borough, about a quarter of a mile further from the town than the Victoria Ground. The Constable Burton team, who are recognised as one of the best organisations in the North of England, arrived at Stockton during the forenoon, and were entertained to luncheon at the Queen's Hotel by the Stockton Club. Wickets were pitched at half-past one, and the visitors winning the toss elected to bat.

Stockton played their early games at several venues including Bowesfield Lane, Hartburn Fields and Portrack Lane, before they moved to Grangefield in 1891 - the first game was against Constable Burton on 4 June 1892. Stockton were now members of the Durham League but after poor attendances they joined the North Yorkshire South Durham League in 1896. In their second season, they won the Championship after defeating rivals Middlesbrough in a play off as both teams had finished

---

May 1896: Stockton members of the NYSD

STOCKTON V DARLINGTON.
(North York and South Durham League.)

There was a fair attendance on the Stockton Ground on Saturday, in fine weather, to witness this match. The visitors won the toss, and elected to bat, and they sent in A. P. Whitwell and H. Ensor, to the bowling of A. W. Welch and Hawkyard. Both batsmen were disposed of for ducks, and three more wickets were down for a total of 58

Racing of a diferent kind...Freddie Dixon

THRILLING RACE

F. W. DIXON COMES UP SMILING

VICTORY AT BROOKLANDS

ALTHOUGH still looking quite ill, Freddie Dixon, Middlesbrough's famous motor racing star, made a dramatic reappearance on the Brooklands track on Monday, and signalised his presence by a brilliant victory.

The most exciting race of the whole day was the British Mountain Handicap of laps round the mountain course.

This Mr. Dixon won hands down, from such other mountain course experts Flight-Lieut. Staniland Eccles—with very latest type of Grand Prix Bugatti Shuttleworth, with an Alfa Romeo; Co and Fairfield, with the British E.R. Pat Driscoll, with the Monoposto Aus and other fine drivers.

Freddie was in the middle of the on handicap, receiving 32 seconds fr the scratch man, Shuttleworth, but gy 43 seconds to the limit man, Richard with a Riley.

Freddie's own little Riley was as as any on the corners, and down straight a hurtling projectile which of the other cars could match for sp

74 MILES AN HOUR

He gradually overtook the in front of him and held off ca an hour by 40 7 'blew up'' errific stra Riley, cat Hill on Brool scene w the f s t ....

FREDDIE DIXON, the popular Middlesbrough racing motorist, in the Riley which he was driving in the Junior Car Club's International Trophy Race at Brooklands. He was competing against many famous drivers.

FRED DIXON WAS NEARLY A CHAUFFEUR!

SPEED ACE'S PLANS FOR MOTOR-CYCLE FACTORY

HIS OWN IDEA

FETED BY MIDDLESBRO' COLLEAGUES

"HAD it not been for the gloom of trade depression Freddie Dixon would have been manufacturing motor-cycles in Middlesbrough to-day," said Mr W. Ryan, in proposing the toast of Fred Dixon at a complimentary dinner to the famous Middlesbrough racing motorist in the Middlesbrough and District Motor Club headquarters, was attended by the Mayor of Middlesbrough (Councillor A. Cooper); Mr G A. Reed (president of the Yorks Centre A.C.U.), Mr Cyril Paul, the well-known racing driver, and Dr Burnett (Saltburn Urban District Council), Mr John Gjers, the president, was in the chair.

Mr Ryan added that the machine that would have been manufactured was Fred's own invention, and it would have caused a re-olution in motor-cycle design and performance.

If it had not been for Freddie's individual geni and objection to uniform Mr It revealed, he might have been lost racing world, which h born r as a chauffeur.

...CLINED

... d such a success as McAdam's loyer tried to a uniform, but a star of Brook game

FRED DIXON THIRD

Thrills in the Le Mans Grand Prix

Fred Dixon, the Middlesbrough racing motorist, was one of the drivers in the car which gained third place in the 24-hour Le Mans Grand Prix, which started at p.m. Saturday and finished 4 p.m. yesterday. The winning car was an Alfa Romeo (Chinetti and Etincelin). Sebilleau and Delaroche, in a Riley, were second, whilst Dixon and Paul, also in a Riley, were third, being 16 laps behind the winner.

Raymond Summer (Alfa Romeo) was leading when his car caught fire and he had to withdraw. Mrs Gwenda Stewart also had to retire owing to oil feed trouble.

APRIL 1934: FREDDIE DIXON AND HIS BROOKLANDS PARTNER, CYRIL PAUL, AT WORK IN HIS GARAGE IN MIDDLESBROUGH TUNING UP TWO SIX-CYLINDERED RILEYS FOR RACING AT BROOKLANDS AND LE MANS

Freddie Dixon, born in Alliance St Stockton in 1892, became famous for racing motorcycles and racing cars. He rode in the Isle of Man TT races from 1912 until 1928 becoming the only rider to have won both the solo and sidecar race. In 1932 Freddie had his first major car race, The Ulster T.T. at Ards driving a Riley 9. In 1933 he won the March Sprint Handicap at Brooklands & at Donnington. He then finished 3rd at Le Mans. A fine mechanic he invented a revolutionary banking sidecar & four wheel steering for cars. A memorable but often controversial figure Freddie Dixon had his issues with the authorities. He died suddenly on 5 November 1956.

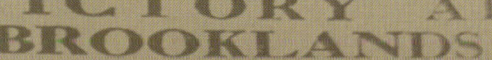

4 OCTOBER 1893: THE OPENING OF ROPNER PARK

DECLARING THE PARK OPEN.

THE DEPARTURE.

THE 1ST NRYV ARTILLERY FIRING THE ROYAL SALUTE.

ALD HIND CHAIRMAN OF PARK COMMITTEE.

THE PROCESSION PASSING HIGH STREET.

FIREWORKS IN PARK.

MR K F CAMPBELL AMICE BOROUGH ENGINEER.

ROYAL VISIT TO STOCKTON.

ROYAL VISIT!

For a Refreshing Cup of

TEA OR COFFEE

VISIT

BARROWCLIFF'S

ORIENTAL CAFE,

4, DOVECOT ST., STOCKTON.

OPEN from 9 a.m. to 7 p.m., or

The CAFE, 65, High Street

(Opposite Stirling's Cleveland House).

ROYAL VISIT.

Next Week's Issue of the

THE PROPRIETORS OF THE

NORTHERN REVIEW

Will commence the commemoration of the Royal Year of publication by the issue of

A SPECIAL

ROYAL VISIT

DOUBLE NUMBER

WHICH WILL BE

READY OCTOBER 4.

IT WILL CONTAIN SPLENDID

DOUBLE-PAGED COLOURED PLATE,

LITHOGRAPHED IN

4 COLOURS ON GLAZED PLATE PAPER.

PORTRAITS of the DUKE & DUCHESS of YORK and the MAYOR of STOCKTON; Coloured Drawings of Park Entrance, Triumphal Arches, etc.

24 Pages Matter & Coloured Supplement will be enclosed in a Special Cover. Printed in Gold. DESCRIPTION & PLAN of ROUTE. PROGRAMME of PROCEEDINGS, etc.

PRICE **TWOPENCE.**

¶ This Edition will be published at great expense, and as only a limited supply will be printed, orders should be given to Newsagents at once to prevent disappointment.

ORDERS WILL HAVE PREFERENCE, ACCORDING TO DATE RECEIVED.

PLAN OF ROUTE
OF PROCESSION.

THE PARK

HARTBURN LANE

YARM ROAD

YARM LANE

DURHAM ROAD

STATION

HIGH STREET NORTON ROAD

RIVER

In 1890 Stockton Corporation discussed buying thirty-six acres of land on the outskirts of Stockton to be used as parkland. When it was decided not to go ahead with this because of the finance involved, Major Robert Ropner of Preston Hall offered to donate 36 acres of land (valued at £10,000) at Hartburn Fields. Stockton Corporation added a further 4 acres to increase the size of the Park to 40 acres. It cost £24,000 to lay out the Park which was on the edge of the town, commanding fine views of the Cleveland Hills to the south, with Hartburn village to the west and a new development of large houses to the north, close to Oxbridge Lane. Having stayed overnight at Wynyard Park, the Duke and Duchess of York travelled to Stockton where huge crowds cheered as they went down the High Street. At the Park the Mayor, Robert Ropner, greeted them. Watched by a large crowd, including 350 schoolchildren, the opening ceremony took place. As a memento, His Royal Highness was handed a gold key. There was an offical luncheon at the Exchange Hall after which the Duke and Duchess left from Stockton Station at 4.45pm for York.

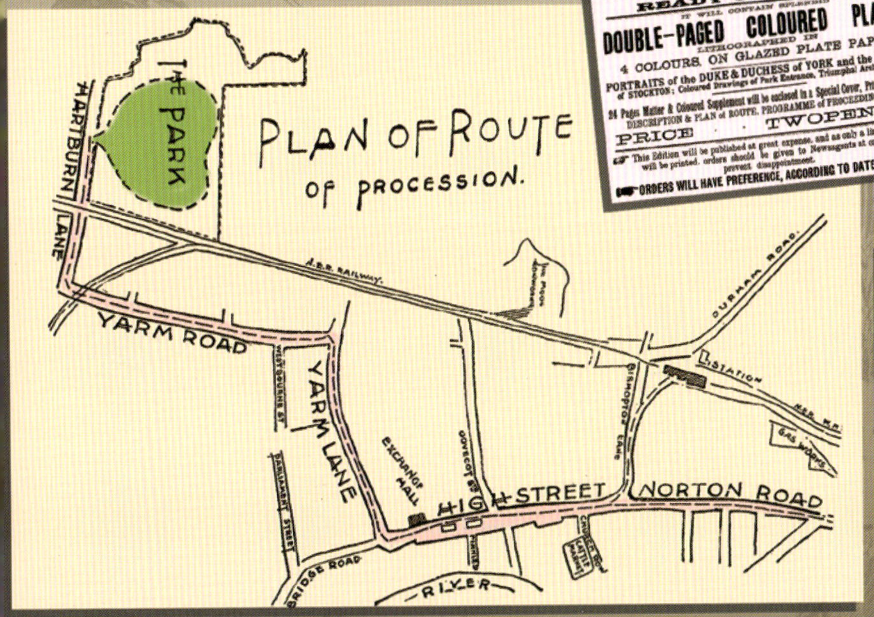

Royal Visits: The entire route from the entrance of Norton to South Stockton Station was decorated most lavishly and resplendently. Indeed the villages of Billingham and Wolviston were also gay, and at the latter village the dainty triplets of the late Capt. Young, of Wolviston Hall, presented H.R.H. with bouquets. Stockton and South Stockton throughout the route were lined with miles of Venetian masts, and acres of bunting floated in the air. There were some most massive triumphal arches, one at the north end of High Street, representing the Marble Arch, and one at the south end of the street, an ancient castle gateway, with flanking towers, arch and portcullis. Immense grand stands were erected, several of them by private individuals, notably the late Mr. Dodds, M.P., who, with his characteristic consideration, provided one in Norton Road, especially for the Workhouse children. A gigantic stand was placed near the Alms Houses ....

A Royal Day

DUKE OF YORK AND PRINCESS MAY

THE DUKE AND DUCHESS OF YORK IN STOCKTON.

OPENING OF THE ROPNER PARK.

A MAGNIFICENT RECEPTION.

IMPOSING PROCESSIONS AND CEREMONIES.

His Royal Highness was requested by the Mayor to declare the Park open, and at the same time his Worship presented H.R.H. with a magnificent gold key as a memento of the occasion. Miss Elsa Ropner, youngest daughter of the Mayor and Mayoress, then stepped forward and presented the Duchess with a lovely bouquet of flowers, which H.R.H. graciously accepted. The Duke then briefly replied to the address from the civic body, and declared the Park open. He thanked the citizens

THE ILLUMINATIONS AT STOCKTON.

As an appropriate conclusion to the proceedings of yesterday at Stockton the Ropner Park was brilliantly illuminated at the cost of the Mayor, who also provided a fine display of fireworks. The work was carried out in a most efficient manner by Messrs Pain and Co., of London. When night came on little fairy lights sprang up all over the Park, outlining the buildings, flower beds, and footpaths, presenting a very effective scene from a distance. The two fountains were almost covered with van-coloured lights, but the principal effect was obtained at the bandstand, which was completely covered with lamps of various colours giving it a striking effect.

A large fireworks display in the park ended a memorable day.

Enjoying a day in the Park 1896

The lake in Ropner Park in 1896. The rural location is clearly visible here with Oxbridge Farm on the left and Grangefield Farm in the distance on the horizon. The area close to the Park is being developed and West Villas on Oxbridge Lane, with their long gardens to the Park boundary are immediately behind the lake. The vegetation in the Park is yet to mature as it is only 3 years after it opened.

The Fountain in Ropner Park

ROPNER PARK, STOCKTON.

THE WEST HARTLEPOOL OLD OPERATIC PRIZE
BAND

Will give Two Concerts on SUNDAY FIRST,
Commencing Afternoon 3 o'clock, Evening 7.30.27

The cast-iron fountain in Ropner Park quickly became a popular gathering place for people enjoying time to relax. Located on one of the main pathways, the fountain stood close to the Bandstand which can be seen here in the distance.

The Pavilion

Standing on the north side of the Park, close to the tennis courts, the Pavilion with its cafe, was another popular location for visitors. Behind is one of the terrraced houses in Hampton Road.

Sir Robert Ropner Bt., M.P., V.D., J.P.

Preston Hall.

Residence of Major Ropner.

Presented by Major Ropner.

Major Ropner J.P.C.C.

Hartbury field from Spring Street bridge.

Major Ropner and the New Park for Stockton.

THE PROCEEDINGS IN THE COUNCIL CHAMBER.

MAJOR ROPNER J.P.

ENTERING THE BANQUETING HALL.

FIDES ET FORTI

BANQUET IN THE BOROUGH HALL

Presentation to MAJOR ROPNER of the Freedom of the Borough of Stockton.

The Reception.

The Mayor of Stockton's (Major Ropner) Ball.

Sir Robert Ropner born in Magdeburg, Prussia in 1838, emigrated to England when he was 19. He settled in West Hartlepool where he founded the Ropner Shipping Company in 1874. In 1888 he acquired the shipping company, Pearse Lockwood at Stockton which he developed to become one of the largest shipping firms in the country, employing over 1,000 people. He bought Preston Hall in 1881 for £27,500; he progressed in civic life too becoming Mayor of Stockton in 1893 and being awarded the Freedom of the Borough. He was High Sheriff of Durham in 1896 and the M.P. for Stockton from 1900 to 1910. Knighted in 1902 he was created Baronet of Preston Hall & Skutterskelfe Hall in 1904. During the Great War he served in the DLI. Sir Robert Ropner died on 26 February 1924 - surely one of the town's greatest benefactors.

1917...A SPECIAL ROYAL VISIT

The Tees Conservancy Commission.

VISIT OF THEIR MAJESTIES, THE KING AND QUEEN,
Thursday, 14th June, 1917.

Enclosed is Official Programme of the Royal Visit.

The Tees Commissioners will be pleased if you will favor them with your Company at **11-40** a.m. prompt, to-morrow (Thursday), on board their S.T. "William Fallows," or other Steamer, which will be moored in the Middlesbrough Dock Entrance, Middlesbrough.

Lunch will be provided at the close of the Inspection.

Kindly produce this Invitation.

JOHN H. AMOS,
General Manager.

Middlesbrough,
June 13, 1917.

11-50 a.m. Embark on Tees Conservancy Commissioners Steam Tug and proceed up the river to Stockton-on-Tees.

During the journey the Works on the banks of the Tees will be pointed out by the Chairman of the Commission and the General Manager, Mr. John H. Amos.

12·30 p.m.
Disembark at Stockton Corporation Quay, when the Royal Party will be received by the Lord Lieutenant of the County of Durham (the Right Honourable the Earl of Durham, K.G., P.C., &c.), and the Mayor and Mayoress of Stockton (Ald. and Mrs. John Harrison).

'Welcome to Stockton ma'am!'

Finkle Street

'Good afternoon Your Majesty'

Programme of the Visit

OF

THEIR MAJESTIES THE KING AND QUEEN

To the Merchant Shipbuilding Yards and Steel Rolling Mills on the River Tees at South Bank, Middlesbrough, and Stockton; also the Hartlepools.

Thursday, 14th June, 1917.

PROGRAMME of Their Majesties' Visit to the Merchant Shipbuilding Yards and Steel Rolling Mills on the River Tees at South Bank, Middlesbrough, and Stockton; also the Hartlepools.

Thursday, 14th June, 1917.

10·0 a.m. Royal Train arrives at South Bank Railway Station.

Received by the Lord Lieutenant for the North Riding of Yorkshire—Sir Hugh Bell, Bart.

The Right Honourable Lord Knaresborough, Chairman of the North Eastern Railway Co.

The Chairman of the Eston Urban District Council—Robert Brown, Esq.

Rear Admiral Grant; and

Brigadier-General A. J. Mullins, Commander of the Tees Garrison.

10·5 a.m. Motor to Smith's Dock Company, Ld., South Bank.

10·10 a.m. Arrive. Received by Launcelot Smith, Esq. (Chairman of the Company).

Inspect the Building of Mine Sweepers, Dry Docks and Engine Works.

12·35 p.m. Walk to the Shipbuilding Yard of Messrs. R. Ropner & Sons, Ld.

Received by Mr. Leonard Ropner.

10·35 a.m. Leave by motor for the Shipbuilding Yard of W. Harkess & Son, Ld., Middlesbrough.

10·45 a.m. Arrive. Received by Joseph Calvert, Esq., Mayor, and the Mayoress, on behalf of the County Borough of Middlesbrough, and William Harkess, Esq., Chairman of the Company, who will conduct the Royal Party round the Yard.

Inspect the Building of Patrol Boats.

11·5 a.m. Walk to the Shipbuilding Yard of Sir Raylton Dixon & Co., Ld.

Received by Harald Dixon, Esq., Chairman of the Company.

Inspect Frozen Meat Ship (building), 2 Standard Ship (building) and the Joiners Shop.

Refreshments for the Royal Party will be served from 11·30 a.m. to 11·45 a.m.

11·50 a.m. Walk to Middlesbrough Dock Entrance.

The Royal Party will be received by Sir Hugh Bell, Bart., Chairman of the Tees Commission, who will present the Mayor and Mayoress of Thornaby-on-Tees.

Embark on Tees Conservancy Commissioners Steam Tug and proceed up the river to Stockton-on-Tees.

During the journey the Works on the banks of the Tees will be pointed out by the Chairman of the Commission and the General Manager, Mr. John H. Amos.

12·30 p.m. Disembark at Stockton Corporation Quay, when the Royal Party will be received by the Lord Lieutenant of the County of Durham (the Right Honourable the Earl of Durham, K.G., P.C., &c.), and the Mayor and Mayoress of Stockton (Ald. and Mrs. John Harnson).

12·35 p.m. Walk to the Shipbuilding Yard of Messrs. R. Ropner & Sons, Ld.

Received by Mr. Leonard Ropner.

Inspect Shipbuilding Yard, Power House and Pneumatic Plant.

12·55 p.m. Proceed by motor to Works of South Durham Steel & Iron Co., Ld.—Steel Rolling Mills.

Received by the Right Honourable Lord Furness, Chairman of the Company, who will conduct the Royal Party round the Works.

Inspect the Steel Furnaces and the New Ship Plate Mill. This Mill is the largest Ship Plate Rolling Mill in the United Kingdom.

1·20 p.m. Proceed by motor to Stockton-on-Tees Railway Station.

1·30 p.m. Entrain for the Hartlepools.

After the royal couple had left, luncheon with the Mayor of Stockton at the Queen's Hotel.

The King and Queen walked through the old part of Stockton to Ropner's shipyard, via Calvert Lane, Thistle Green & Hunter's Lane watched by a cheering if slightly bemused crowd.

Queen Mary chatted quite freely with a line of munition girls enquiring about the nature of the work, expressing the opinion that the 9½ hours worked by the girls, was a long day for them.

Tour Of Shipyards And Rolling Mills.
WORKERS' ENTHUSIASTIC GREETING.

In spite of the necessarily brief stay at the various establishments, the King and Queen found time to speak encouraging and homely words to individual workers

'Your Majesty..'

Queen Mary shakes the hand of veteran shipyard worker, Thomas Spark, who had worked 48 years in the yard.

Stockton Station

In 1852 the Leeds Northern Railway, extended from Melmerby to Billingham, via Northallerton, Yarm, Eaglescliffe and Stockton where the station opened on 2 June 1852 - though it was renamed North Stockton by 1853. In 1890 it was decided to re-develop the station with two through-platforms, waiting and refreshment rooms as well as an arched glass-panelled roof - an elegant building worthy of a town of importance in the history of railways. The new development was complete by 1893 with the station reverting back to its original name – Stockton.

NORTH EASTERN RAILWAY.
Kildale

NORTH EASTERN RAILWAY
From STOCKTON.
CASTLE HOWARD

NORTH EASTERN RAILWAY.
From STOCKTON.
TRENHOLME BAR

NORTH EASTERN RAILWAY.
From STOCKTON.
West Rounton Gates

NORTH EASTERN RAILWAY.
From STOCKTON.
SEATON CAREW

NORTH EASTERN RAILWAY
TADCASTER

South Stockton or is it Thornaby?

Many people today are unaware of the name of South Stockton yet for almost fifty years it was the name given to the urban community which proudly became the Borough of Thornaby on Tees in 1892. Other names of communities such as Mandale or Erimus are largely forgotten too - we will remember them here. This section also recalls the days when RAF Thornaby was an important part of the military defence of our country. Presented in colour are some memories of those iconic times.

OLD THORNABY 1908

The old village of Thornaby was a small settlement centred on the village green, with its 11thc Church of St Peter ad Vincula. Originally dedicated to St Mary Magdalene it fell into disuse in 1858 when St Paul's opened, but was restored in 1908. Until 1869 the cemetery on the Green was in use but overcrowding led to a cemetery being opened on Acklam Road in 1870.

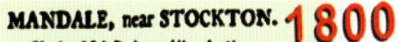

Mandale

With the French Revolution causing national concern over grain supplies, the late 18th century saw several windmills constructed in the area around the Tees estuary. On 4 October 1800 the Newcastle Courant announced the public auction in Stockton of a newly constructed 'Wind Corn-Mill' at Mandale with 'three dwelling houses, Granaries, a Kiln' and 4½ acres of land'. An improving road system and a quay on the Mandale loop of the River Tees, offered transport links to local markets and those further afield.

This was the only road between South Stockton and Middlesbrough until the road to Newport opened in 1858. These are the cottages at Mandale and Mandale Bridge. This site stood on a bluff high above the River Tees before the Mandale Cut opened 18 September 1810. This effectively left Lord Harewood's Mandale Mill isolated and cut off from access to the sea. Compensation of £2,000 was paid to Lord Harewood. In 1814 the mill was rebuilt due to leaning forward. The granary building remained until the early 1900's.

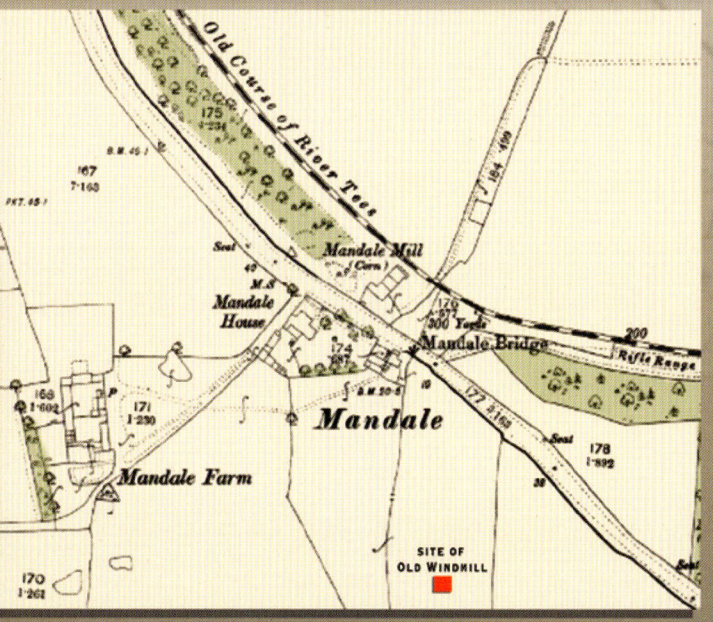

The old Mandale Mill that had stood south of the bridge, was destroyed by fire in May 1891. It was never rebuilt. There were several cottages here including an inn, Mandale Farm and Mandale House. The only reference to 'Mandale' now is the name of a road.

South Stockton

Thornaby's development as a separate borough began in the late nineteenth century. The original settlement, South Stockton, was established in 1838 when William Smith, who had owned a pottery works just north of Thornaby village since 1825, purchased 110 acres of land south of the river and sold the plots to speculators. As construction took place near the level crossing and Stockton Bridge, the rapidly growing community became known as South Stockton.

With its prime location, available land, and improving transport infrastructure, South Stockton became an attractive area for development. This commercial growth spurred community development, and by 1845, there was a request for the town to have its own post office. The advertisements below highlight South Stockton's increasing appeal—a place that, with the establishment of the Borough of Thornaby in 1892, would ultimately disappear.

YORKSHIRE AGRICULTURAL SOCIETY.
GREAT SHOW
AT
SOUTH STOCKTON-ON-TEES.
PROGRAMME.

1863

TUESDAY, Aug. 4th.	Trials of Implements, Steam Ploughs, Grass Mowers, &c. Admission 1s.
WEDNESDAY, Aug. 5th.	Show Yard open at Ten a.m. Admission 2s. 6d., Ladies 1s.
THURSDAY, Aug. 6th.	Show Yard open at Eight a.m. Admission 1s.
FRIDAY, Aug. 7th.	Show Yard open at Eight a.m. Admission 1s.

For Cheap Trains see Railway Bills.

JOHN HANNAM, Secretary.

Kirk Deighton, Wetherby.

YORKSHIRE
AGRICULTURAL SOCIETY.

Meeting at South Stockton-on-...

STOCKTON, ...

Sir,

I send herewith Posting...
which I will thank you to cause to be p...
most prominent place in your neigh...
as possible, and inform me the cost, w...
remit in Postage Stamps by Post Office...

Yours obediently,

JOSEPH DOD...

YORKSHIRE AGRICULTURAL SOCIETY.—The preparations for the forthcoming show of this society, at South Stockton-on-Tees, are fast approaching completion. The contractors, Messrs. Wood, of York, have completed the long lines of substantial sheds for the stock and implements; and the external fencing is finished. The Stockton and Darlington Railway Company have completed a branch line into the show yard, and the pontoon bridge over the Tees will be ready for use in a few days. This will place the show yard in immediate proximity to the town of Stockton-on-Tees, which is on the opposite side of the river, and is in the county of Durham.

Cheap trains will run on Thursday and Friday from all parts of the county of York and the north of England. The trials of grass mowers, &c., and the trials of steam ploughs, reapers, and other implements, commence, it will be seen, on Tuesday. The public dinner of the society will be held in the show yard, on Wednesday, the 5th, at 5 o'clock. The price of tickets has been fixed at 6d., in order that all classes of farmers may meet together. A handsome pavilion has been erected for the occasion.

Holding the Yorkshire Show at South Stockton in August 1863 was a huge event. Easy access from Stockton was put in place with a special rail line and pontoon bridge across the river. The location with its view of the nearby hills was a huge success with big crowds on all three days.

South Stockton-upon-Tees.

PART of the arrangement for the New Town to be called South Stockton being now complete, any Person wishing to purchase or take Sites upon long Lease or Ground Rent, may be accommodated. Suitable situations are apportioned for Commercial and Manufacturing purposes, which possess all the advantages which can be desired, being in connection with the Tees both above and below the Bridge, and having almost hourly communication by Railway with Darlington, Middlesbro', Yarm, the large and increasingly populous district of the Auclands, and will shortly be connected with Northallerton, Thirsk, Easingwold, York, and nearly all the Manufacturing Districts in the Kingdom, by the Great North of England Railway. Many of the Sites suitable for Commercial and Manufacturing purposes, can have the advantage of a Branch Railway running direct into them for their own private use.

For Persons connected with Shipping, such as Brokers, Coal Fitters, and Masters of Ships, it is most convenient, as within 12 minutes they can go from their own House to Middlesbro' or Port Clarence, to Darlington in half an hour or 40 minutes, and to the Coal Districts in an hour and a half.

The Town is divided into convenient and spacious Streets for Dwelling-houses, of all sizes. That part selected for Genteel Dwellings is most pleasantly situated on an eminence commanding an extensive view of the Cleveland Hills and the river Tees from the Sea to Stockton, and is allowed by Professional Gentlemen to be one of the most healthy situations in the Neighbourhood.

The Property is Freehold, and the parochial Assessment a mere Trifle.

There are several Acres of Land to be Let on long Lease for Gardens.

The Plan may be seen, and further Particulars known on application to Mr. WM. SMITH, Stafford, near Stockton-on Tees.

September, 1838.

1838

SOUTH STOCKTON-UPON-TEES.
VALUABLE CORN MILL AND OTHER PROPERTY FOR SALE.
MESSRS BARKER AND HENDERSON

Are instructed to offer
FOR SALE BY AUCTION,

At the House of Mr Holberry, the Rokeby Hotel, in South Stockton, on Tuesday the 23rd Day of May, 1843, at two o'Clock in the Afternoon, in the following Lots,

(Subject to such Conditions as shall be then and there produced)

Lot 1. **A**LL that valuable STEAM CORN MILL, situate in South Stockton, now in the Occupation of Mr James Paylor, together with two good Dwelling Houses, Stable, Yard, with every other Convenience attached thereto.

Lot 2. A good COTTAGE, adjoining Lot 1, situate in Montague Street, in the Occupation of James Graham.

Lot 3. An excellent HOUSE, containing 5 Rooms, large Shop, Cellar, Yard, and every other suitable Convenience attached thereto, fronting Trafalgar Street and Montague Street.

Lot 4. All that HOUSE and SHOP, situate in Trafalgar Street, containing 5 Rooms, Cellar, Yard, and other Conveniences attached thereto, now in the Occupation of Mr John Heron, Draper, &c.

Lot 5. All that large and elegant HOUSE and SHOP, situate in Trafalgar Street, containing seven Rooms, Shop, large Yard, Cellar, and every necessary Convenience attached thereto, now in the Occupation of Mr James Paylor.

The Whole of the above Property is Freehold, and having been recently built of the best Materials, presents a favourable Opportunity for any Person wishing to purchase.

The Corn Mill is capable of doing an extensive Business, and in excellent Condition.

The Premises may be viewed, and all further Particulars may be ascertained, on Application to Mr James Paylor, at South Stockton.

Possession may be had immediately. **1843**

A memorial, signed by nearly all the inhabitants of South Stockton, has been forwarded to the Postmaster-General, with a view to secure the establishment of a post-office in that town. It is also in contemplation to build a new church, near the cotton factory, which is being considerably enlarged, and also to provide a weekly market.

1845

SOUTH STOCKTON.
TO BE SOLD OR LET,

ALL that newly-erected GLASS BOTTLE HOUSE, with the Warehouses, Offices, Wharf, Yard, and Buildings thereto belonging, situate at South Stockton, in the county of York, and called or known by the name of the Tees Glass Bottle House.

The above Premises are in excellent Order and Repair, and are admirably situated for a Glass Bottle Manufactory, the same having the River Tees adjoining on one side thereof, and the Stockton and Darlington Railway on the other; thus, from the Situation affording every Facility for the obtaining of Coals, Lime, and other necessary Materials, for the purposes of Manufacture, at as low a Rate as can be procured by Bottle Houses on the Tyne and Wear, and presenting a ready and easy Shipment for Bottles.

Also, all those 30 Cottages, with upwards of Half an Acre of Ground adjoining the above-mentioned Premises; the Cottages have neat Gardens fronting the same, and necessary Conveniences and Buildings thereto belonging.

The above-mentioned Cottages and Land may be Sold either together with, or separately, from the first above-mentioned Premises; or the same may be Let to any Purchaser or Lessee of the Bottle Manufactory. The Parochial Rates are very low.

Further Particulars may be obtained on Application to Mr T. Skinner, Solicitor, Stockton, who will send a Person to show the Premises.

Stockton, Nov. 27, 1843. **1843**

SOUTH STOCKTON-ON-TEES.

TO BE SOLD BY AUCTION, at the Black Lion Hotel, in Stockton-on-Tees, in the county of Durham, on Wednesday, the 16th day of March, 1853, at 3 o'clock in the afternoon, for 3 precisely, in One Lot, and (subject to such conditions as will be read at the time of sale,)

Messrs. FISHER & SON, AUCTIONEERS,

All that valuable FREEHOLD ESTATE, known as the "SOUTH STOCKTON ESTATE," situate at South Stockton-on-Tees, in the county of York, containing 20a. 3a. 9r. of valuable BUILDING GROUND.

And all that Extensive Building, lately used as a COTTON MILL, together with two Fifty-Horse-Power Condensing Steam-Engines, and Four Boilers in the centre of the Mill; also 950 feet of polished wrought iron Shafting, with pullies and gearing complete; and 1,300 feet of Steam Pipes. And, also, the GAS WORKS, with piping and taps to supply the building. The Mill is 81 yards long, 24 yards wide, and 5 stories in height.

This valuable and important property is intersected by the Stockton and Darlington Railway, and the road leading from Stockton to Guisbrough, and is close by the Stockton Station of the said Railway, and has a large Frontage to the River Tees, thus affording direct water and railway communication with all parts of the kingdom, which renders the situation most eligible for Mills, Manufactories, Shipyards, and any other mercantile purposes.

Notice has already been given to the Owner of this Estate, that part thereof will be required for the purpose of forming a Dock (by virtue of the powers contained in the Tees Conservancy Act), which undertaking will give an impetus to the Manufacturing, Shipbuilding, and other trades carried on at South Stockton, and will considerably enhance the value of this property, and make it a profitable investment for the capitalist. Part of the Land has been set out for building purposes.

Mr. JAMES KINGSTON, at the Mill, South Stockton, will, on application, show the Property, together with a plan thereof; and all further particulars may be obtained of Messrs. FISHER & SON, of 12, Kennedy, Manchester, or of Mr. SOWERBY, Solicitor, Stokesley, Yorkshire.

Stokesley, Feb. 19th, 1853. **1853**

SHOPPING IN VICTORIAN THORNABY

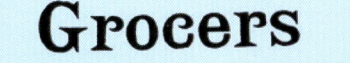
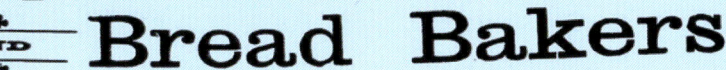

Victoria Bridge & the 1887 Jubilee

OPENING OF THE VICTORIA BRIDGE

The new bridge, which by special permission of Her Majesty has been named "The Victoria Bridge," was thrown open to the public on Monday, the 4th of April, without ceremony, it being then in an incomplete state. It has only recently been finished, and we believe it is not yet altogether out of the hands of the contractors. At the time when it first came into use we gave a detailed account of the new structure, which it is unnecessary now to repeat.

It is proposed to place upon the abutments of the bridge on either side the following inscriptions :—" This bridge was formally opened on the 20th of June, 1887, and has been named 'The Victoria Bridge' in commemoration of the fiftieth year of the reign of Her Most Gracious Majesty Queen Victoria. The bridge was gaily decorated for the occasion by a number of Venetian masts, ornamented by trophies, and connected by streamers of every imaginable colour. In the centre of the bridge on the south side a spacious stand was erected for the accommodation of guests invited to witness the ceremony, and in front of the stand a huge streamer bore the inscription. "Victoria Bridge.

JUNE 25, 1887.

THE JUBILEE.

On Monday Her Majesty Victoria, Queen of Great Britain and Ireland and Empress of India, completed the fiftieth year of her reign over the

CELEBRATIONS AT STOCKTON.

The ancient borough of Stockton-on-Tees was en fête on Monday in celebration of Her Majesty's Jubilee. A general holiday was proclaimed, and all the places of business were closed, while the operatives at the various works were also set at liberty for the day. The three banking houses closed their doors at noon, and did not resume business till Wednesday evening. The town presented a much more gay and festive appearance than it does on ordinary holidays by reason of the number of flags which were flying, especially in the High-street. The heat of the previous week having moderated, the weather was pleasant, though the sky was overcast in the earlier part of the day. The day was ushered in by merry peals from the Parish Church bells, which rang out at intervals during the day. Shortly after nine o'clock the children attending the public elementary schools in the borough assembled in the various schools to receive the Jubilee medals which the Mayor (Alderman Joseph Richardson, J.P.), has generously provided for them. These medals have on one side a portrait of Her Majesty, with the words "Jubilee of Her Majesty's reign, 1887," and on the outer rim—" Queen Victoria, born May 24th, 1819, ascended the Throne 20th June, 1837." On the other side as a representation of the Victoria Bridge, with the motto, "Victoria Bridge, Stockton-upon-Tees, officially opened June 20, 1887. Joseph Richardson, Mayor."

THE JUBILEE AT STOCKTON.

On Monday a meeting of the Jubilee Committee was held in the Town Hall, the Mayor (Alderman Richardson, J.P.) presiding. It was reported that to South Stockton £137 had been subscribed, and that including this amount the total subscriptions were £365 12s 6d.—The Mayor expressed the opinion that the amount was not sufficient. It was estimated that £200 would be required for children's teas, while a distribution of meats would cost £60 more. He thought if each member of the committee would undertake to obtain £5 more it would be...

Amidst the celebrations in Stockton of Queen Victoria's Golden Jubilee on Monday 20 June 1887, there was a very important local event - the opening of the new Victoria Bridge, named in commemoration of the fiftieth year of her reign. It replaced the old stone structure built in 1769. The bridge was 'gaily decorated...in the centre was a spacious stand....for guests invited to witness the ceremony...(and) in front of the stand a huge streamer..(with) the inscription "Victoria Bridge".'

It was quite a day - a public holiday marked by a civic procession along the decorated High Street to the parish church, followed by a luncheon. In the afternoon, a second procession made its way down Bridge Road to the opening ceremony. Children were treated to a free tea at local schools before joining the crowds at the Victoria Football Ground to sing the National Anthem. This was followed by various sports events. In the evening, the High Street buzzed with crowds enjoying performances by numerous bands. The day concluded with a spectacular fireworks display and a civic banquet in the Borough Hall.

JUBILEE SKETCHES

VICTORIA BRIDGE, STOCKTON

AN UNEXPECTED SHOWER

OPENING OF THE VICTORIA BRIDGE STOCKTON ON TEES

PRE 1887: OLD STOCKTON BRIDGE

Whitwell's Iron Works

Whitwell & Co's Iron Works, established in 1859, was one of the key employers in Thornaby. Located on a large site on the Carrs, there were six rolling mills and several coke ovens at the works, employing up to 700 men. The hazardous working conditions led to several fatalities over the years, including founder Thomas Whitwell.

SKETCHES of the INCORPORATION of THORNABY on TEES

Mr J. W. WATSON, Acting Town Clerk.

COUNCIL CHAMBER.

PROSPERITY TO TEES SIDE

TRIUMPHAL ARCH on the Bridge.

The FIVE LAMPS

MUNICIPAL BUILDINGS.

Mr W. ANDERSON, Mayor Elect.

STOCKTON BRIDGE.

Mr C. W. ANDERSON, Member of Incorporation Committee.

FREE LIBRARY.

Donor of Library.

T. WRIGHTSON ESQ. M.P.

PRINCIPAL DECORATED BUSINESS PLACES.

THORNABY PARISH CHURCH.

INCORPORATION OF THORNABY-ON-TEES.

On October 6, 1892, the incorporation of the Borough of Thornaby on Tees was celebrated with a day of decoration and ceremony, drawing huge crowds. The day had an added edge due to the rejection of Stockton Corporation's attempt to incorporate South Stockton into its borough. An afternoon holiday for all, including those in Stockton, saw events commence at the new Town Hall, where a procession of formal guests and many community representatives began at 2 p.m., led by the Thornaby Brass Band. Spectators lined the route from every vantage point. Back at the Town Hall, formal speeches were made, and the National Anthem was sung before children were treated to tea at schools around the town. As night fell, spectacular illuminations lit up the town. The day concluded with crowds heading to the racecourse to witness a spectacular fireworks display, which included a pyrotechnic show.

THE INCORPORATION OF THORNABY.
THE CHARTER DAY CELEBRATIONS
THE DECORATIONS.

Thornaby has never presented so gay an appearance as it does on this occasion. The Celebration Committee had arranged with Messrs Pain and Son, of London, to provide decorations for the main thoroughfare, and the result of their attention has been that Mandale road especially presents a very gay appearance. Appropriately enough, the entrance to the town from Stockton has received special attention. At the centre of the Victoria Bridge are placed a couple of tall and graceful Venetian masts, and from that point along Mandale road to the end of Harewood terrace there is a continuous line of the same, at intervals of 60 feet apart. These masts are alternately 25 and 22 feet high, covered with crimson cloth, and surmounted by golden spear heads, and banners float from the top. Each mast bears a handsome trophy of flags, with shield. At the end of the bridge a special display is made by a floral triumphal arch. From each side of the roadway springs a group of five Venetian masts, four blue and one crimson, bearing a platform filled with foliage and flowering plants, while on a higher level were five separate platforms, each bearing a graceful palm. The two buttresses were connected across the roadway by festoons of ever green and flowers, further decorated by lovely banners.

The celebration includes a children's tea, an old men's dinner, an illumination of the principal streets, and a display of fireworks.

THE BOROUGH OF THORNABY ON TEES

MANDALE ROAD

THE FIVE LAMPS

This view from the Town Hall, looks down Mandale Road towards the Five Lamps. It's a busy area - the National Provincial Bank, Thornaby Co-Op, grocers, drapers, coffee shops and places to eat. The Post Office is close to Archer Street & Pumphrey Sugar Mills.

The Five Lamps, a unique five-lantern gas lamp, at the junction of Mandale Road and George Street. A recognised Thornaby landmark this was a meeting place with speeches and rallies of religious and political groups common here. The original Five Lamps were presented to the town in 1874 by three local JP's to commemorate the extension of the boundaries of South Stockton. In the distance is the Public Library & Police Station.

Mandale Road from the Five Lamps (a gathering place across the years) at the entrance to George Street. Before the distant Town Hall there is Ebenezer Chapel, Prospect Place and a Home & Colonial store. On the left the Market Hall is behind the line of shop buildings.

Looking down Mandale Road towards Middlesbrough Road and Brewery Bank with Bon Lea Terrace (left) & Swathamore Terrace (right just past Sadler's Hotel in the foreground). This was a busy tram route with trams on their way from Middlesbrough to Norton.

Around Thornaby

Westbury Street in Thornaby was one of the roads which converged at the Five Lamps. Westbury Street School and the junction with Gilmour Street are on the left whilst the Roman Catholic Church is in the right foreground next to a Baptist Chapel. In the distance the Windmill Inn looks on to the Five Lamps square.

The Public Library in George Street opened on 8 June 1892 after being suggested by Alderman Thomas Wrightson J.P. Very popular with residents, a Children's Library was added in 1904 after a grant of £1,500 was received from the Andrew Carnegie Foundation. It was conveniently close to the National School.

HAREWOOD GARDENS & VICTORIA RECREATION GROUND

THORNABY'S "LUNGS."

Owing to landslips and other drawbacks there has been several weeks' unavoidable delay in the work of laying out and fencing the new Victoria Recreation Ground and the Harewood Pleasure Gardens at Thornaby, but it is expected that in the course of about a month both places will be completed and opened to the public. All that remains to be done is the asphalting of the footpaths, the construction of which is more advanced at the Pleasure Gardens than at the Recreation Ground. These open spaces will serve a very useful purpose for the public of Thornaby, and will add

vacant for a keeper's lodge. The present undertaking does not include a fountain or a bandstand; these we may state are matters which are being deferred in the hope that some generous donor may come forward with a gift of the kind which would hand his name down to posterity, and help to keep green his memory in the minds of the people. The contractors for the laying out of the ground is Messrs Robinson, of Stockton, and for the fencing Messrs Raybould, of Workington.

THE PLEASURE GARDENS.

The Pleasure Gardens occupy a charming site. They extend along Acklam-road from opposite St. Luke's Church to the old Mandale Mill, and command a full view of

considerably to the attractiveness of the town. The site of the Recreation Ground, which is 4½ acres in extent, was given to the borough as far back as October 13th, 1886, for that purpose, but it was not until two years ago, when Lord Harewood offered the site of the Pleasure Gardens of 32 acres, that the Corporation showed sufficient enterprise to enter upon a scheme for properly laying it out.

RECREATION GROUND.

The Recreation Ground, which is rectangular in shape, is bordered on the east by Cromwell-terrace, on the west by Park-terrace, on the north by Peel-street, and

Stockton Racecourse and the Cleveland Hills, the southern breeze from which will be felt with refreshing effect. These banks, which in years gone by formed the banks of the River Tees before its course was diverted, are naturally pretty, and there has not been quite so much time and money necessary to make them a pleasure resort for the public. The length of the gardens is about 1,000ft. The width varies at different points, but averages about 130 feet. Additional trees and shrubs have been planted, the grass plots have been improved, and a number of winding paths arranged with safe gradients. Here again a site has been preserved for a bandstand

PARKS FOR THORNABY.

Opening of Harewood Gardens and Victoria Grounds.

THE CEREMONY.

The public of Thornaby have patiently waited the opening of the new Victoria Recreation Grounds and Harewood Pleasure Gardens, which in the ordinary course of events should have taken place last summer, but at last their patience has met with its just reward, and the opening ceremonies were performed on Thursday.

The delay is accounted for by landslips and other drawbacks, but these have been successfully overcome. Up to the present there has been no place in the town where one could enjoy a few quiet hours in the open air, and, consequently, these open spaces will serve a very useful purpose for the public of Thornaby, and will add considerably to the attractiveness of the town.

The site of the Recreation Ground, which is 4½ acres in extent, was given to the borough as far back as October 13th, 1886, for that purpose, but it was not until three years ago, when Lord Harewood offered the site of the Pleasure Gardens, of 32 acres, that the Corporation showed sufficient enterprise to enter upon a scheme for properly laying it out.

The Recreation Ground, which is rectangular in shape, is bordered on the east by Cromwell-terrace, on the west by Park-terrace, on the north by Peel-street, and on the south by Victoria-road, and measures 680 feet by 315 feet.

Harewood Pleasure Gardens stretching from St Luke's Church to the site of the old Mandale Mill, were opened on 29 July 1909 by the Mayor of Thornaby along with the Victoria Recreation Grounds. The land donated by Lord Harewood in 1906, had been due for completion in 1908 but issues with landslips caused delays. There was a lack of formal gardens for local people to visit so it was very popular. Situated high above Stockton Racecourse it offered such a good view that the park was closed during race meetings to stop people taking advantage of the viewpoint.

1898: ELECTRIC TRAMS

In 1897 a Parliamentary Bill sanctioned the building of an electrified tram system from North Ormesby to Norton Green. The new service which began 16 July 1898, was one of most up-to-date systems of the time and for the first time provided a regular transport link across the main towns south of the Tees. This tram (with flower garlands) on Brewery Bank Thornaby reflects the celebratory joy of the new service.

THE WILDERNESS ROAD

One of the teams of men who maintained the tramlines whatever the weather. They are working on the Wilderness Road linking Newport to South Stockton, first laid out under an Act of Parliament of 1856 as part of the Middlesbrough to Stockton Turnpike. A single tram line ran along this stretch of the road with passing loops in place.

'TRAM IN THE WILDERNESS'

This tram is 'en route' from Middlesbrough to Stockton. It provides an idea of how much passengers on the upper deck and lower deck end were exposed to the elements.

The image was taken on the route from Newport to Thornaby, known locally as the Wilderness Road. Much of the route was single track with loops for passing. The land south of the Wilderness Road was part of Stockton Raceourse and Marsh Farm.

1875...The Erimus Licence

To the Overseers of the Poor of the Parish of Stockton-on-Tees, in the county of Durham, and to the Superintendent of Police of the district of Stockton aforesaid.

I, LEONARD CLOUGH, Innkeeper, now residing at Stockton-on-Tees, but formerly at Sunderland, in the county of Durham, DO HEREBY GIVE NOTICE, that it is my intention to apply at the General Annual Licensing Meeting, to be held at the Police Court in Stockton aforesaid, on the Twenty-fifth day of August next, for a LICENSE TO HOLD ANY EXCISE LICENSE OR LICENSES TO SELL BY RETAIL, under the "Intoxicating Liquor Licensing Act, 1872," all Intoxicating Liquors, to be consumed either on or off the house premises thereunto belonging, which are situate in the parish of Stockton aforesaid, at or near the Turnpike road leading from Stockton to Middlesbrough, of which premises Thomas Robert Maddison Plews, of Darlington, in the said county of Durham, Wine and Spirit Merchant, is the owner, of whom I rent them, and which premises are known by the name or sign of "The Erimus Hotel."

Given under my hand this Twenty-first day of July, 1875.

LEONARD CLOUGH.

Erimus

Erimus

SPORTS AT ERIMUS.

At a special meeting held at the Erimus Hotel on Wednesday, Mr Richbey in the chair, it was resolved to hold a series of Coronation Sports on June 27th inst., on a field adjoining (for residents of Erimus only. The following events were decided upon, for each of which three useful prizes will be given :—100 yards' handicap for boys under 15 years of age ; 100 yards handicap for men under 40 years of age ; 100 yards egg and spoon race for boys and girls ; 100 yards' skipping race for girls under 16 years of age ; shuttlecock competition for girls under 16 years of age ; 100 yards' three-legged race for men and boys ; 80 yards' sack race for men and boys (competitors find their own sacks) ; 80 yards' obstacle race for men and boys ; 80 yards' cap, jacket, and boot race for boys ; 80 yards' cap, jacket, and boot race for yards' race for single young women ; 80 yards' obstacle race for men and boys ; 80 yards' cap, jacket, and boot race for boys under 14 years of age ; 100 yards' walking race for women over 40 years of age ; 100 yards' race (consolation) for married men only, over 40 ; comic costume competition for boys under 16 years of age.

Special prize.—Councillor Coleman will give a box of cigars to winner of handicap for men ; Councillor Higgin will give boar's head to winner of consolation race ; Mr Abell will give two stones of flour to winner of walking race.

Sports to commence at 4 o'clock p.m. prompt. Starters, Messrs Hatten and Danks ; judges, Messrs Thompson and Morley ; clerk of the course, Mr Richbey, to whom all entries must be made.

1902: Celebrating the Coronation

The small community of Erimus was located on the road from South Stockton to Newport close to Stockton racecourse. Built in the mid-1870's to provide housing for workers in the local iron works, it consisted of the Erimus Hotel, Pioneer St. and Stainton St. The Erimus Hotel which opened in 1875, was well known to local people and racegoers too. Despite its small size, Erimus enjoyed a vibrant community life.

A selection of Thornaby churches

St Paul's Church was built on Thornaby Road in 1858, part of the development of South Stockton to the south. The land was given by Lord Harewood and St Paul's became the parish church in 1860. This land close to the church is still to be developed.

St Paul's Church is seen from a different perspective here. The tower was added after the original construction. Thornaby was made a separate parish from Stainton in 1844.

Opening on 31 March 1834, for workers at the Stafford Pottery, Stafford Place Methodist Chapel was the first church in South Stockton.

Harvest Festival at the Cleveland Wesleyan Church on Swathamore Terrace, which could hold 800 people.

St Luke's Church on the corner of Cobden and Mandale Road was consecrated in 1904 by the Archbishop of York.

Those sporting afternoons...

Thornaby had two strong soccer teams in the 1890's.

1898 Amateur Cup Semi Final
Middlesbrough v Thornaby.

THE AMATEUR CUP.

On account of the epidemic of small-pox at Middlesbrough an objection has been raised to the playing of the semi-final tie between Middlesbrough and Thornaby at Darlington on Saturday next. At a special meeting of the Amateur Cup Committee, held at 61, Chancery Lane, on Tuesday evening, it was decided to postpone the tie, an... also the final, fixed for March 26th, until the advice of the Local Government Board has been taken on the matter. The Committee will meet again on March 18th.

Now that the football season is nearing its end considerable interest is being manifested in the result of the various cup-ties, and so far as Thornaby is concerned I am glad to note that both the principal teams have had a successful time. The Thornaby team, indeed, are having a remarkable career in the run for the English Amateur Cup.

	P.	W.	L.	D.	For.	Agst.	Pts.
Thornaby	15	12	0	3	31	11	27
Grangetown	14	13	0	1	35	17	26
Thornaby Utopians	14	8	6	0	32	54	15
Brotton	10	8	2	0	27	11	15
Stockton St. John's	9	4	5	0	14	25	8
Middlesbro Res.	13	4	7	0	19	24	8
Billingham	12	3	5	3	12	15	9
South Bank Res.	10	2	6	2	19	27	6
Darlington Reserve	10		2	10	12	52	4
V W'tlepool N.E.R.	10	2	7	1	14	16	5

THORNABY formed in 1892, were in the Teesside League until 1898 when they joined the Northern League. Their best season was 1897-98 when they reached the Amateur Cup Semi Final beating Bishop Auckland, Sheffield & Darlington before losing to eventual winners, Middlesbrough. Playing at the Thornaby Cycling Track, they turned professional in 1900, joining the Northern Alliance before disbanding in 1902 due to finance issues.

THORNABY UTOPIANS formed in 1894, were also in the Teesside League until 1898 when they joined the Northern League. Their ground was in Peel Street. Finishing 2nd in their first season they were promoted to Division One but they disbanded in 1901 after two poor seasons.

Thornaby Cricket Club: Historic Days

29 June 1860

SPORTING.

CRICKET.

A NEW CRICKET CLUB.—By the praiseworthy exertions of Messrs. Howard Head, W. Whitwell, and several other enthusiastic admirers and patrons of the manly game of cricket, a club has been inaugurated in the rising suburb of South Stockton. Friday last was the opening day, when a friendly game was played on the new ground, which is situated in close proximity to the Railway Station. A moderate display of cricketing skill was exhibited on the occasion, the batting of Whitwell, Waton, Wright, and a very promising youth named John Watson, being very fair. The bowling of Messrs. Wine and Head was also extremely creditable—considering. A portion of the Corporation Band attended, and played on the occasion, under the leadership of Mr. Henry Brown. Mrs. Wright, the worthy hostess of the "Rokeby," occupied the refreshment booth, and Tommy Marshall and N. Darnton, of the Stockton Eleven, officiated as umpires.

South Stockton - a new cricket club

16 September 1893

CRICKET.

NORTH YORKSHIRE LEAGUE.

The annual meeting of the above League was held at Northallerton on Saturday, the president, Mr J. J. McLaren (Constable Burton) in the chair.—Mr T. S. Wheater (Thirsk), hon. secretary, read the financial statement, which showed that the season had ended with a balance in hand of £4 1s 9d. The winner of the championship of the League had been the Constable Burton Cricket Club with seven points, Redcar and Coatham coming next with five points, while Middlesbrough, Northallerton, and Thirsk were minus three points, and the Ironopolis Club (South Bank) minus four points.—On the motion of Mr A. Burns, seconded by the Rev. James Butler, the report and statement of accounts were unanimously adopted.—It was resolved that the above clubs form the League for next season, with power to add to their number.—The Thornaby Cricket Club was then included in the League; and it was agreed to invite the Ripon C.C. to join.

Thornaby admitted into the North Yorkshire League

6 May 1905

THE SPORTS GAZETTE. SATURDAY, MAY 6. 1905.

THORNABY CRICKET CLUB.

OPENING OF THE NEW GROUND BY SIR ROBERT ROPNER, M.P., TO-DAY.

Thornaby move to their new ground at Mandale

Thornaby Village Ladies Football team 21 October 1933, celebrating winning a tournament.

It is interesting to note that despite the Football Association's ban in 1921 on women playing football, the women's game had survived across the country with teams playing a few games each season. This photo appeared in local newspapers - evidence of the popularity of the women's game at this time.

ABOVE: Thornaby Cricket Club began as South Stockton in 1860 helped by wealthy local patrons. They joined the NYSD in 1893. They moved to their current ground on Mandale Road in May 1905 with Sir Robert Ropner M.P. performing the opening ceremony.

LEFT: Stafford Place Workers Cricket Club in 1902 is evidence that cricket was a popular game in Thornaby.

LOT 26 AT OLD THORNABY

After World War One, Thornaby expanded southwards with the auction in May 1920, of land from the Thornaby Village Estate, acting as a catalyst for development. The sale of Lots 4 and 26 in Old Thornaby were plots around the village green which were developed. The new properties, & behind them, Thornaby Hall, are visible beyond the entrance to Bassleton Lane, April 1934.

1920'S DEVELOPMENT

THORNABY ESTATE SALE.
At the Borough Hall, Stockton, yesterday afternoon, Messrs Ralph Appleton and Hall, offered for sale Thornaby Village estate of the late Mr G. T. Gilpin-Brown.

Old Thornaby village green in the early 1900's.

The auction of land from Thornaby Village estate in May 1920 opened up the development of Thornaby. The land, sold off as lots, became the urban landscape familiar today with many houses being built.

Thornaby Road

Oddfellows Arms before changes in 1914

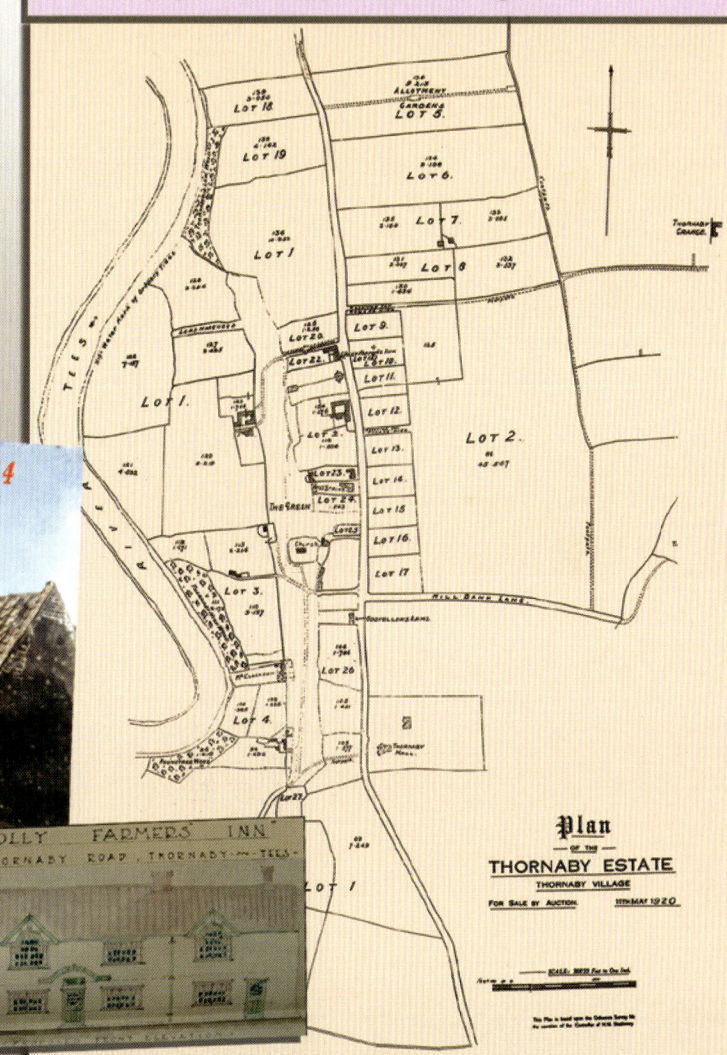

The auction was very successful - a cottage on the green & eight-acre small holding selling for £1,160, a house for £1,260 with other smaller cottages selling for between £500 to £650. The Jolly Farmers' Inn and two cottages went to Mrs Welch from Saltburn for £1500 - soon to be developed with a new front elevation - see extract from plans dated December 1923. The Thornaby Road view shows the entrance to RAF Thornaby opposite a distant lorry, whilst Thornaby Hall is behind trees to the right.

JOLLY FARMERS INN
THORNABY ROAD, THORNABY-ON-TEES

Plan
OF THE
THORNABY ESTATE
THORNABY VILLAGE
FOR SALE BY AUCTION 11th MAY 1920

Thornaby Hall.. at the centre of change

September 1929

In the late 1920's it was reported that negotiations were ongoing to purchase land close to Old Thornaby village - a sale that included Thornaby Hall, built in the 1870's by entrepreneur Webster Cuthbert. Industrialist and twice Mayor of Thornaby, John Robinson Crossthwaite had lived at the Hall since 1896. When he died in 1914, his wife remained at the Hall until 1929 when, along with adjacent land it was sold to the Air Ministry, as part of the plan to establish an air base in the lower Tees valley. The Hall became a well appointed Officers Mess.

From Gustav Hamel to the RAF

FIRST FLYING AT THORNABY

July 1912

AIR FLIGHTS ON TEES-SIDE.

On Saturday last Mr Gustav Hamel, the popular aviator, who so delighted thousands of people on Tees-side last Thursday with his exhibition of flying, again ascended ascended.

At Thornaby Mr Hamel gave an exhibition for an hour. Later in the afternoon Hamel set off from the field on a flight to Boldon, Sunderland. It was expected that he would cover the 25 miles between Thornaby and Sunderland in less than half an hour.

Upwards of 15,000 people gave Mr Gustav Hamel a rousing reception at Thornaby, on Saturday, as he appeared first like a black speck on the sky and gradually developing into what resembled a huge bird, until ultimately he revealed himself in his Bleriot monoplane and alighted in a field on a farm about a mile from the town.

There were many of the principal citizens waiting to greet him and shake hands. Having been photographed alongside of Supt. Cook, the aviator joined heartily in the laughter which followed a suggestion that he had been exceeding the speed limit.

Subsequently the spectators were treated to an exhibition of aviation of practically every description.

On Saturday 26 July 1912, Thornaby High Road was packed with crowds of people going to see Gustav Hamel give a spectacular display of flying. Up to 6,000 paid admission to a field at Vale Farm to see Hamel fly in from Redcar at 3.30; thousands more packed the nearby roads to catch a glimpse of Hamel's Bleriot Monoplane overhead. After an audience with the Mayor & other civic officials Hamel took off to fly to Sunderland - only to be forced to land by a bank of fog near Seaton Carew & returning for the evening to Middlesbrough.

A view in 1931 with 607 & 608 Squadron's Westland Wapiti aircraft and four Avro 504N's on the right. In the distance note the Water Tower - still under construction.

Thornaby airfield was officially opened on 29 September 1929 and No 608 Squadron Auxiliary Air Force was formed 17 March 1930 with the first aircraft, an Avro Lynx, arriving on 7 May 1930. It was kept at Catterick until the first hangars were completed

Squadron Leader W.Howard Davies, who had grown up at Elton Hall, was appointed Commanding Officer on 16 June 1930 whilst recruitment was ongoing. The first hangar was completed 24 July 1930 and the airmen's barrack block was completed in October 1930 with Thornaby Hall being the officer's mess.

By July 1931 the airfield was becoming established; the Squadron had eight officers and thirty-eight auxiliary airmen and training on flying service types of aircraft had started with the first summer camp also underway.

9FTS (Flying Training School) Thornaby Hawker Hart K5817 running up

Final check...

1931... early morning as the pilot of a Westfield Wapiti K1153 makes a final check of his maps

608 Squadron Wapiti and Avro 504n aircraft at Thornaby c1931

One fine morning...

Officers and pilots gather on the airfield as a parachute harness is checked prior to flying.

608 Squadron...one fine day

A Westland Wapiti with members of 608 Squadron at Thornaby Airfield.
Commanding Officer William Appleby Brown is second from the left.

THORNABY
608 (B) SQUADRON AUG 1933

L.A.C. MURDOCK. L.A.C. COOKE. L.A.C. BROWN. LAC PERCIVAL. L.A.C. ROWLANDS. L.A.C. SPARKS. SELF. LAC. SUTHERLAND. LAC MURRAY.

L.A.C. PAGAN. CPL. GIRLING. F/SGT. SADDINGTON. F/O. GROOM. CPL. JUKES. CPL. LEE. L.A.C. PAYE.

PHOTO CPL. G. BEWS (DEC)

608 Squadron..the early years

This image from 1934 provides an excellent view of the new airfield and the surrounding area. In the foreground is Old Thornaby village with houses around the green. Thornaby Road is mid-picture with the Oddfellows's Arms opposite a partly completed Mill Bank Lane. On the base itself hangars, maintenance & mess buildings around a runway with some Wapiti aircraft, are all visible. To the right, surrounded by trees, is Thornaby Hall whilst Stainsby Grange Farm is visible in the distance.

608 Squadron Hawker Demons at RAF Thornaby 1937

A special visitor at RAF Thornaby

King George VI inspecting pilots of the Hudson Conversion Flight, 1 November 1939

ASR Lancaster RF310 - 279 Squadron Airborne Lifeboat: RAF Thornaby 1945

We will remember...

SQUADRON COMMANDERS 1930 TO 1943

S/LDR W HOWARD DAVIES	JUNE 1930	- FEB 1933
S/LDR IWT THOMPSON	FEB 1933	- OCT 1934
S/LDR G H AMBLER	OCT 1934	- NOV 1938
W/CDR G SHAW DFC	NOV 1938	- MAY 1941
W/CDR R S DARBYSHIRE	MAY 1941	- NOV 1941
W/CDR P D R HUTCHINGS DSO AFC	NOV 1941	- FEB 1943

No. 608 COUNTY OF YORK (North Riding) SQUADRON AUXILIARY AIR FORCE.

R.A.F. STATION, THORNABY-ON-TEES.

OMNIBUS UNCULIS

THORNABY AIR CRASH

Pilot Killed

BLAZING 'PLANE IN WOOD

SERGEANTS' MESS R.A.F. STATION, THORNABY, YORKS.

Chocolate and Cigarette Ration Card

THORNABY AIR CRASH

Pilot Trapped In Burning Bomber

608, 2608, 3608 R.A.F. AUXILIARY SQUADR

Coronation Ball

JUNE 1ST, 1953

IN THE PALAIS DE DANSE STOCKTON-ON-TEES

Uniform or Evening Dress

DANCING 8-30—2 a.m.

Bob Potter's Orchestra

Running Buffet Bar 9—1 a.m.

608 (North Riding) Squadron Royal Auxiliary Air Force

21st Anniversary Dance

BATTLE OF BRITAIN ROYAL AIR FORCE "At Home"

SATURDAY, 16th SEPTEMBER, 1958

ROYAL AIR FORCE THORNABY

Airfield Opens 1 p.m.

Flying Display Commences 2 p.m.

BATTLE OF BRITAIN WEEK

ROYAL AIR FORCE at home

Saturday 19th September 1959

ROYAL AIR FORCE — THORNABY

ROYAL AIR FORCE THORNABY

AT HOME DAY

ALL PROCEEDS IN AID OF R.A.F. BENEVOLENT FUND

ROYAL AIR FORCE OFFICIAL PROGRAMME

EMPIRE AIR DAY

Memories from life at RAF Thornaby with 608 Squadron 1929-1958

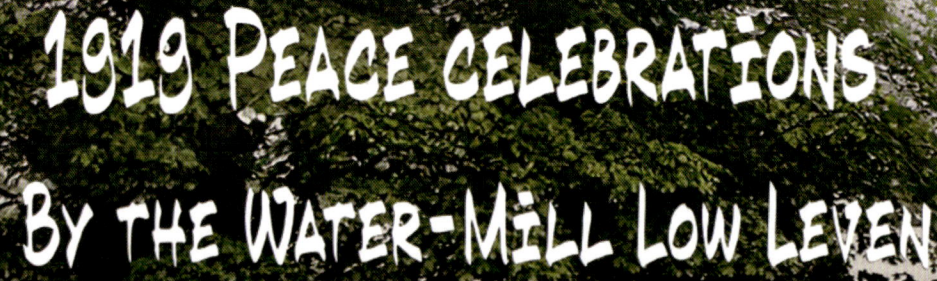

1919 Peace celebrations

By the Water-Mill Low Leven

Residents from High Leven and Ingleby Barwick
gather to celebrate peace after World War One

From Old Barwick to Yarm

It is hard to comprehend the changes that have transformed the area around Yarm and Ingleby Barwick - changes that have occurred in a relativley short period of time. Yarm of course, has a long history with its role as an important port in the region as well as a Benedictine monastery which survived three centuries until a visit from the officials of Henry VIII changed that forever. The modern day towns have grown away from the past but it is still there as this section sets out to show.

BARWICK LANE

Once known as High Leven Windmill, the old mill is seen here in quieter times

More snow to come?

Barwick Lane looking towards High Leven Windmill and High Leven

High Leven Windmill

Barwick

Sober Hall Windmill

Barwick Lane

High Leven Windmill & Walk To The Fox Covert

THE NEW INN.... MALTBY

Named the 'New Inn' when it opened to avoid any confusion with the nearby public house in the village, the establishment was managed by landlord John Tate, who was 72 years old and had been born in Maltby. Remarkably, the inn retained a water pump and gas lights until 1962. The decision of Scottish & Newcastle Breweries in March 1965 to build an executive-style hotel named the 'Yorkshire Dragoon' in the autumn of that year meant demolishing this quaint old building & cottages.

MALTBY... HALF MOON INN

INGLEBY BARWICK

In 1911, John Pain, born in Thornaby, was the licenced publican who lived here with his wife and two young sons.

Although customers were usually farmers and villagers, during the war men from RAF Thornaby were also regular visiters here - as well as going to visit the other inns featured in the local area. It was later named The Pathfinders

MALTBY... OAKLANDS

GREAT LOCAL STEEPLECHASE. MATCH FOR £200.

This (Monday) afternoon the match made between "Joe Bennett," 5 yrs old, owned by Mr R. Brunton, of Marton, and "Basso," an aged brown horse belonging to Mr R. Mewburn, farmer, of Berwick, near Yarm, was decided upon Mr Robinson's farm, at High Leven. The animals were to run over four miles of fair hunting country, at catchweight, with the sons of the owners up, and great interest was manifested in the result. A start was made exactly at 2·42 p.m., Joe Bennett taking a clear lead, which he held over the first fence. He was then pulled back, and Basso went away several lengths in advance, over the second and third fences, and thus order was maintained throughout, Basso clearing all his leaps without mishap, and winning by 50 or 60 yards. The time occupied from start to finish was 12½ minutes. The winner was taken home preceded by a brass band, which played "See the conquering hero comes." A great amount of money depended upon the result, Joe Bennett being made the favourite at 6 to 4, the bulk of the money going from Middlesbrough.

2 December 1872

The two mills at Sober Hall (top) and High Leven in Ingleby Barwick are depicted here on February 12, 1930, already in a state of disuse. High Leven had five floors, while a large granary was located next to the mill at Sober Hall. The exact dates of their construction are unknown, but Harrison suggests they were built to meet the needs of Stockton and possibly the new industrial town of South Stockton, eventually falling out of use due to competition from newer steam mills in South Stockton.

The 1911 Census records that John Thompson, a 59 year old farmer born in Ferryhill, lived here with his wife and two teenage sons.

HILTON

HIGH LEVEN

The Half Moon Inn 1907 (now The Fox Covert) was also a farm with barns and a blacksmith. The cottages at High Leven are still there today but the farm buildings next to the inn are no longer there.

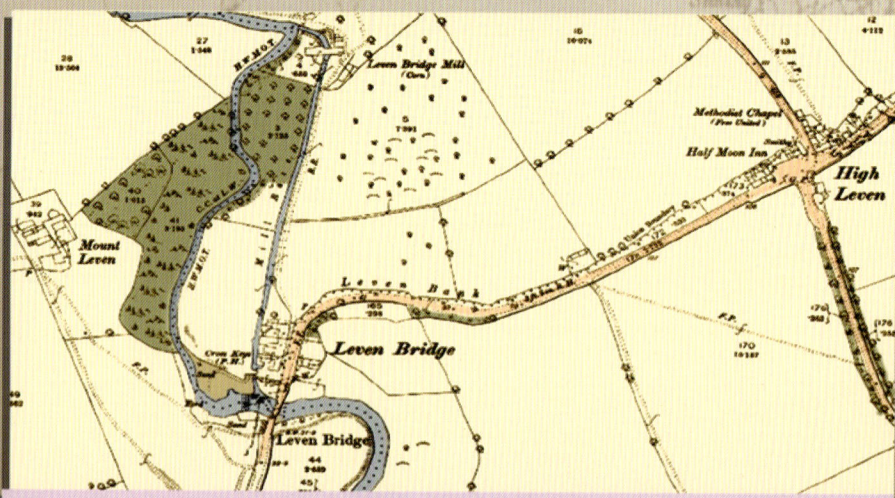

Hilton has remained largely unchanged over the years, a linear village development with cottages, a church, and a public house, The Falcon. Hilton Manor & Estate were the main local landowners but the sale of Hilton Manor (the house and 10 acres of land) in Darlington on September 17, 1953, brought change including the construction of new housing and eventual demolition of the Manor House.

This 1892 map shows Leven Bank road before it was modified in 1928 to make it safer by easing the sharp turn at the lower end. The Cross Keys Inn and the small shop, once part of the community there, are now just a memory.

Reproduced from 1895 Twenty-Five inch series, with the kind permission of the Ordnance Survey

LEVEN BRIDGE (OR LOW LEVEN)

The road from Yarm going over Leven Bridge, passed the cottages there and then took a very sharp bend before it ascends Leven Bank. There were a couple of serious road incidents on the bank before the road was modified in April 1928 when the old narrow lane was replaced by a wider modern road.

The Cross Keys Inn had several publicans over the years. William Farnuby, publican in 1891, lived in Stockton before coming to Leven Bridge where his occupation is given as a 'metal cleaner'. By 1901 he is registered as a 'general labourer'. This image, c1907, shows two women and a child stood at the door. Trade would be seasonal - Leven Bridge is featured in the North Eastern Daily Gazette as one of the area's beauty spots' - a summer attraction for local visitors.

BEAUTY SPOTS IN OUR DISTRICT.
June 1900

Afternoon Tea at Mrs Easby's Cottage Leven Bridge

Afternoon Tea at Leven Bridge 1903

Leven Bridge 1927

THE FALLS AT LEVEN BRIDGE

'WISH YOU WERE HERE!'
On holiday at Leven Bank in the 20's & 30's

THE CAMPING FIELD AND CHALETS

Leven Bridge was a popular destination in the 1920s and 1930s, attracting visitors throughout the year. The River Leven offered various water-based activities, and the area was served by the Cross Keys Inn and the Half Moon Inn at High Leven, making it a convenient break to stay. During an era when holidays were often taken locally, Leven Bridge provided an enjoyable retreat.

Watermills Along The Leven...

Leven Mill

Stone Mill (Weary Bank)

Crathorne Mill

Watermills (& windmills)* were a very common part of local life for communities in the pre-modern age. The three watermills shown here have long since ceased to be operational but they were once thriving centres at the heart of the economic cycle.

LEVEN BRIDGE MILL: *Harrison refers to the water corn mill at Leven Bridge, being left in a will in 1718. Being on the route to Yarm ensured the mill had a steady customer base. Heavisides notes the old mill has 'gone to decay' in 1901 but a mill was worked here until the 1920's (Harrison).*

STONE MILL (NEAR WEARY BANK): *this mill on the Leven was upstream from Foxton Bridge on the Weary Bank road located at the northern end of Middleton Wood. An adjacent weir drove the water wheel and the mill is mentioned in the thirteenth century (Harrison).*

CRATHORNE MILL: *there was a corn mill and a fulling mill here. As well as corn being milled (Crathorne Mill flour was promoted as the best flour in Middlesbrough) the bleaching of linen cloth was an ongoing trade. The mill was demolished in 1970.*

*The information here is researched on John K Harrison's excellent book 'Eight Centuries of Milling in North Yorkshire', second edition, 2008.

Crathorne 1907

In 1804 the turnpike road from Thirsk to Yarm was completed, passing through Crathorne. In 1907, children from the village school stand on the road with the Crathorne Arms just visible in the distance.

CLEVELAND WOMEN UNIONISTS DEMONSTRATION
CRATHORNE HALL

Cleveland Women Unionists met at Crathorne Hall on 22 July 1910, to listen to a speech from the Marchioness of Zetland, followed by tea and music entertainment in a marquee. The Crathorne Branch was an active group with strong political feelings on many events of the time.

YORKSHIRE,
In the North Riding.

Particulars
OF THE
VERY VALUABLE AND IMPORTANT
FREEHOLD MANORIAL FAMILY DOMAIN
KNOWN AS THE
CRATHORNE ESTATE,
WITH ITS
COURTS LEET, COURTS BARON, & OTHER MANORIAL RIGHTS,
COMPRISING NEARLY THE WHOLE OF
THE TOWNSHIP OF CRATHORNE,
FOUR MILES FROM THE STOCKTON AND DARLINGTON RAILWAY AT YARM, WITHIN TEN MILES OF
THE GREAT NORTH OF ENGLAND RAILWAY AT NORTHALLERTON, SIXTEEN MILES FROM
THE MARKET TOWN OF THIRSK, THIRTY-FIVE MILES FROM THE CITY OF YORK,
AND ONLY TWELVE HOURS JOURNEY FROM THE METROPOLIS.
The Estate consists of nearly
TWO THOUSAND TWO HUNDRED ACRES
OF RICH
ARABLE, MEADOW, PASTURE, AND WOOD LANDS,
IN A RING FENCE, DIVIDED INTO
MOST CONVENIENT FARMS WITH EXCELLENT HOMESTEADS,
A Water Corn Mill, with extensive Granaries attached,
AND THIRTY-FIVE WELL-BUILT COTTAGE HOUSES;
ABOUNDS WITH EVERY DESCRIPTION OF GAME, AND HAS AN EXCELLENT TROUT STREAM INTERSECTING
THE ENTIRE ESTATE
THE RENTAL
IS ALMOST TWO THOUSAND FIVE HUNDRED POUNDS A YEAR.
EXCLUSIVE OF
ONE HUNDRED AND THIRTY-THREE ACRES OF WOOD.
ALSO,
THE ADVOWSON OF THE RECTORY OF CRATHORNE
OF THE VALUE OF UPWARDS OF £500 A YEAR.
Which will be Sold by Auction,
BY MESSRS. RUSHWORTH AND JARVIS,
AT THE GEORGE HOTEL, IN YORK,
ON WEDNESDAY, OCTOBER 22nd, 1844, *AT TWO O'CLOCK IN THE AFTERNOON,*
IN TWO LOTS.

The Conditions of Sale will be Printed, and may be had fourteen days before the Sale.
Plans and descriptive Particulars may be had at the principal Hotels. The Estate may be viewed on
application to Mr. PAYER, Land Agent, Peckfield, Ferrybridge; to Mr. WILLIAM FLOUNDERS, of Crathorne;
to the AUCTIONEERS, at their Offices, Saville Row, Regent Street, and 10, Clarges Alley, Cardiff, London; or to
Messrs. BAXTER, Solicitors, Doncaster.

DONCASTER:
PRINTED BY R. HARTLEY, BOOKSELLER AND STATIONER, OPPOSITE THE MANSION-HOUSE, HIGH-STREET.

LEFT:
Notice of an auction held on 23 October 1844 in York when the Crathorne Estate, including 2,200 acres of land, a water-mill, and thirty five cottages in the village, was up for sale. The Dugdale family bought the estate and remain there today.

ABOVE:
Crathorne Hall seen from across the Leven valley, was the vision of Lionel Dugdale. An elegant house, Crathorne Hall, completed in June 1906, was the largest house built in the Edwardian era, containing 115 rooms - 41 of which were bedrooms.

Rounton Grange

Rounton Grange, an elegant country house in East Rounton, was designed in 1871 by renowned architect Philip Webb for Victorian ironmaster Sir Isaac Lowthian Bell. It symbolized entrepreneurial wealth. After the deaths of Sir Isaac and his son Sir Hugh Bell, the house faced heavy death duties and economic challenges, making it too costly to maintain. During World War II, it served as a refuge for evacuees and housed prisoners of war. Attempts to sell the property failed, leading to its demolition in 1954.

Sir Hugh Bell was the father of Gertrude Bell, famous writer, traveller, political adviser, and archaeologist.

OPENING OF THE LEEDS NORTHERN EXTENSION TO STOCKTON AND HARTLEPOOL.

The opening trip of the directors and shareholders of the Leeds Northern Railway Company, from Leeds to Hartlepool, takes place this day, the train starting from the Midland station 9.70 a.m. The Yarm contract commences at Picton, and extends to Stockton, when it forms a junction with the Clarence and Stockton railways, a length of 8½ miles. The greatest height, from the rim to the line of the railway, is about 65 feet. From the viaduct, the view of the town of Yarm, and of the valley up and down the river Tees, is very beautiful. The tide ascends three miles above this place. About a mile north of Yarm, is the Egglescliffe Junction.

Yarm-on Tees

One of the largest in England, the viaduct at Yarm, with 43 arches and spanning half a mile, was designed by Thomas Grainger. Built at a cost of £44,500 it was opened on 15 May 1852 when great crowds gathered to see a special train, carrying directors and shareholders of the Leeds Northern Railway Company, cross the viaduct on their journey to Stockton. Yarm Mill is visible south of the town.

A contemporary image of Yarm before the viaduct was built

The Spital Yarm

Once known as Spital Lane, the former A19, south from Yarm to Crathorne, is seen here in the late 1930's. The houses were built on land once belonging to the 'Yarm Estate', whilst the trees beyond were part of the grounds of the Friarage which formerly extended up Spital Lane to the Rose Hill and Hedley's Garden Nursery on the corner of Leven Road.

Yarm - Up for Sale!

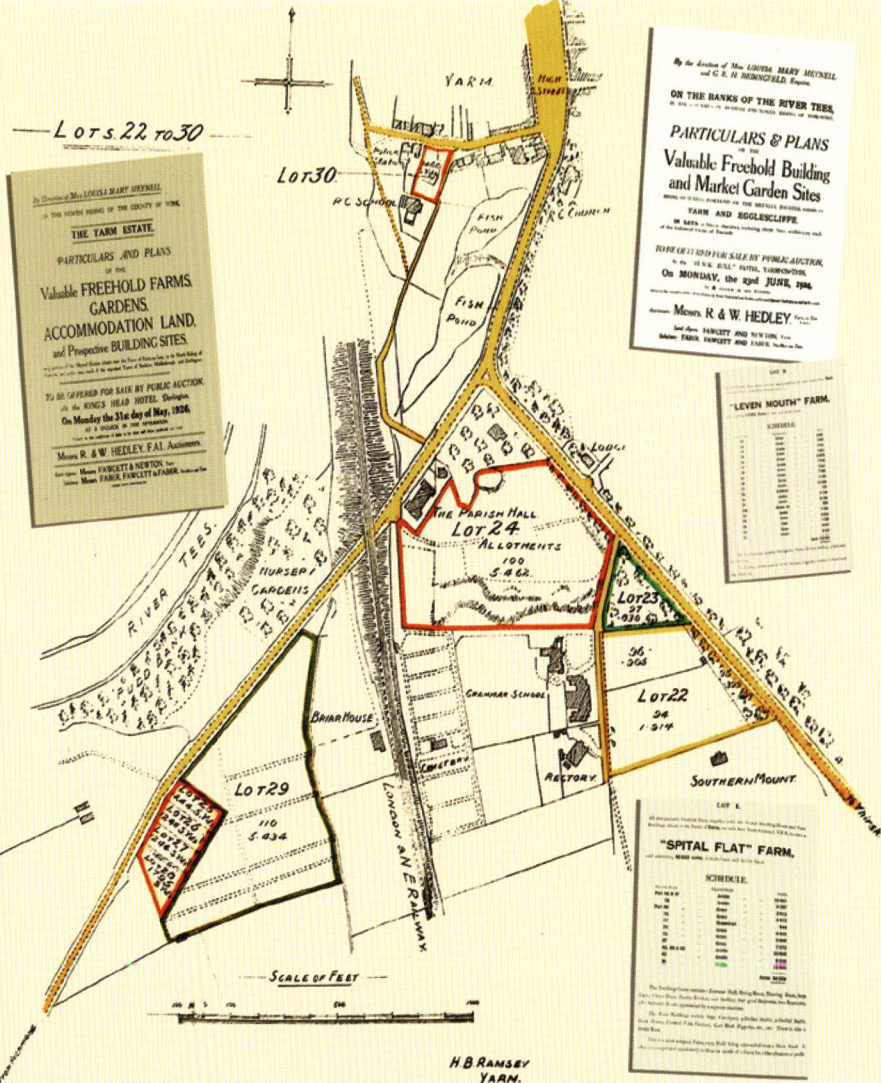

Seen here c1900, Spital Lane, with the Friarage and its grounds behind the wall, was in a poor state. Whilst this area was not part of the Yarm Estate sales, the land which was opposite comprised Lots 22 to 24. In the distance is Rose Hill and Hedley's Garden Nursery.

Selling land for potential development was common between the wars. In 1923 Edgar Meynell who died unmarried, was succeeded by his sister Louisa Mary. She sold the last of the manorial rights to John and Harvey Clapham in 1925 and by 1926 had also sold the manor lands. Catalogues are here for the Yarm Estate sales in June 1924 and May 1926. The auction of 1924 was held in the Black Bull in the High Street whilst that of 1926 was held in the King's Head in Darlington. Louisa Meynell died in 1938

There was some development south of Yarm in the 1930's with housing along Thirsk Road and at Willey Flats.

YARM PROTEST TO COUNTY COUNCIL

Resolution Regarding Need of Improving Dobson's Corner

A resolution was unanimously passed at Tuesday's meeting of Yarm Parish Council expressing regret that no provision had been made in the estimates for the forthcoming financial year for the improvement of a dangerous point at the south end of the town, known as Dobson's Corner. Mr. H. B. Ramsey presided.

This followed on intimation received from the County Surveyor that financial considerations prevented the carrying out in the forthcoming financial year of the improvement of Dobson's Corner suggested by the council.

The resolution passed by the council and forwarded to the County Council went on to say: "As another accident occurred at this point on Saturday, this council feel that unless you can see your way clear to put forward a scheme immediately for the improvement of the corner, they will be justified in appealing to the Ministry of Transport to take action in the matter."

The chairman stated that arrangements had been concluded between Stokesley R.D.C. and Stockton R.D.C., which provided for the availability of the Stockton ambulances for calls in Yarm at a rate of 1s per mile up to 20 miles, and 6d per mile beyond that distance.

The Clerk (Mr. T. Lodge) was instructed to write to Stockton Town Council asking them to remove the now disused gas standards in the parish.

Stokesley R.D.C., it was stated, had intimated their willingness to support the objection which the Yarm Council is to make to the renewal of the Stockton Corporation Transport Department's licence to carry passengers between Stockton and Yarm, at a meeting of the Traffic Commissioners at Stockton on November 18

Popularly known as 'Dobson's Corner', the junction of Spital Lane and Worsall Road was the subject of protest in November 1936 when several serious accidents led to a request from Yarm Parish Council for immediate improvements to be made. Change did come but not for several years due to the coming of war

Spital Corner into Yarm

The road into the southern end of Yarm with the tree lined walls of the Friarage on the right. A few children are fascinated by the camera and the contrast between this somnolent scene and the busy town of today, couldn't be greater.

The Friarage 1888

The Friarage in Yarm is a fine building that has largely survived the ravages of time. Built in 1770 by Edward Meynell on the site of a Dominican Friary founded around 1260, it served as a family home until the mid-20th century, though it was occupied by tenants from 1865. The site included outbuildings such as stables, a malt-house, malt mill, and brewhouse. Edward's son, Thomas, became synonymous with the Stockton and Darlington Railway, which opened in 1825

The Friarage seen from the east with gardens stretching to the river

The Friarage: so many years…

The site has a long history. Excavations in 1928 by Friarage tenant Ralph Hudson, revealed the walls of a large building, glazed tiles, stained glass fragments, and bronze tokens from Edward III's reign. During the monastery days, the site had kitchen gardens, and monks fished on the river. On December 21, 1538, Henry VIII's officials seized the estate, evicting the prior, five priests, six novices, and two servants without pensions. The Crown sold the Dominican Friary on March 20, 1553, to John Sayer. In 1670, the property passed to the Mayes family, who replaced the Friary with the first Friarage in 1717.

In 1770, Edward Meynell inherited the estate and by 1775 had replaced the 1717 building with the current Friarage. Significant funds were spent on rebuilding, with materials brought by boat up the Tees. Formal gardens, including birch and fruit trees, were also established. By 1794, a hot-house existed, and by 1800, the gardens occasionally opened to the public. Secret Mass was held at The Friarage until 1795 when the Penal Laws relaxed, allowing Mass in a first-floor room until a new church was built. The Meynell family let the house to tenants from 1860 to 1957, after which it was used as offices by Head Wrightson and Co. until 1978. It is now part of Yarm School.

1910: the Hurworth gather on the Friarage front lawns

Whit Monday: 10 June 1889..Yarm Gala at The Friarage

WHIT-MONDAY AND TUESDAY,
10TH AND 11TH JUNE, 1889.
YARM GRAND GALA,
Held in the magnificent grounds of the
FRIARAGE, YARM.
SPLENDID COMPANY OF ARTISTES.
ATHLETIC SPORTS
W A T E R P O L O
THE BANDS OF THE 1ST NORTH YORK AND 4TH
DURHAM IN ATTENDANCE.
Excursions from the Hartlepools, South Bank,
Middlesbrough, &c. See Company's bills
Refreshments provided on a large scale, and at
moderate rates.
ROBT. L. WILFORD, Secretary, Yarm.

The highly-popular gala which is held under
the auspices of the Yarm Lodge of Oddfellows
took place, by the kind permission of Mr
Meynell, in the beautiful Friarage Grounds.
The woods and walks are now in their full
summertide splendour, and skirting the banks of
the Tees are exquisitely charming. The varied
sports (which will be continued to-day) were
interspersed with an excellent variety entertainment, in which the following very capable
artistes took part:—The Leopold and Lisbon
troupes; the man monkey, Fargo; the Sisters
Everette, Professor Devereaux, Gilbert and
M'Cann, and the Lindsays. Excursions were
run from various parts of South Durham
and Cleveland, and the weather being fine
there was a large concourse of people.

North Eastern Railways ran special excursion trains to bring people from across the region to the Yarm Gala. Crowds of up to 25,000 attended the two-day event. Special acts and sports events filled the day & in the evening the Friarage woods were lit up as people danced the night away.

The Friarage in the 1920's

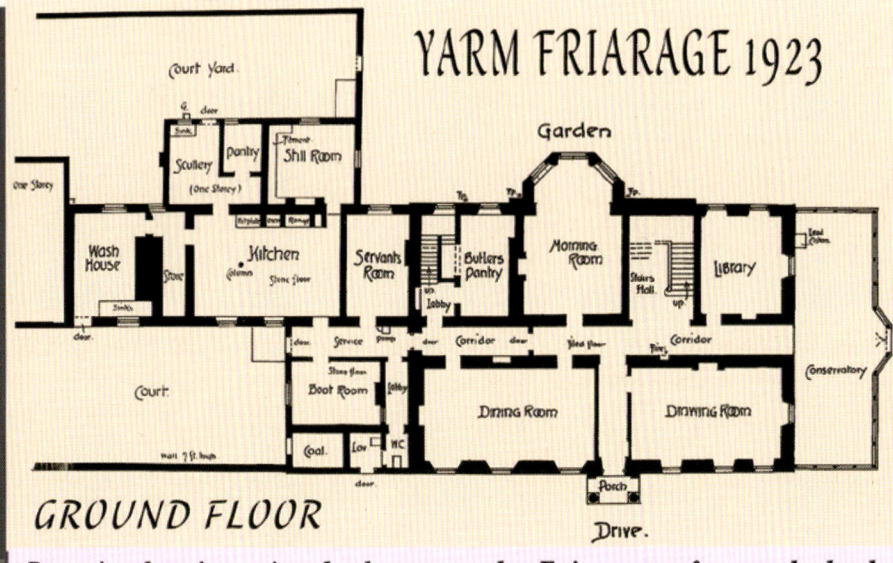

YARM FRIARAGE 1923

GROUND FLOOR

Despite having nine bedrooms, the Friarage often only had a small number of staff - the 1911 census states that a footman, a cook, housemaid and two domestic servants lived at the house, whilst a gardener lived at the Lodge.

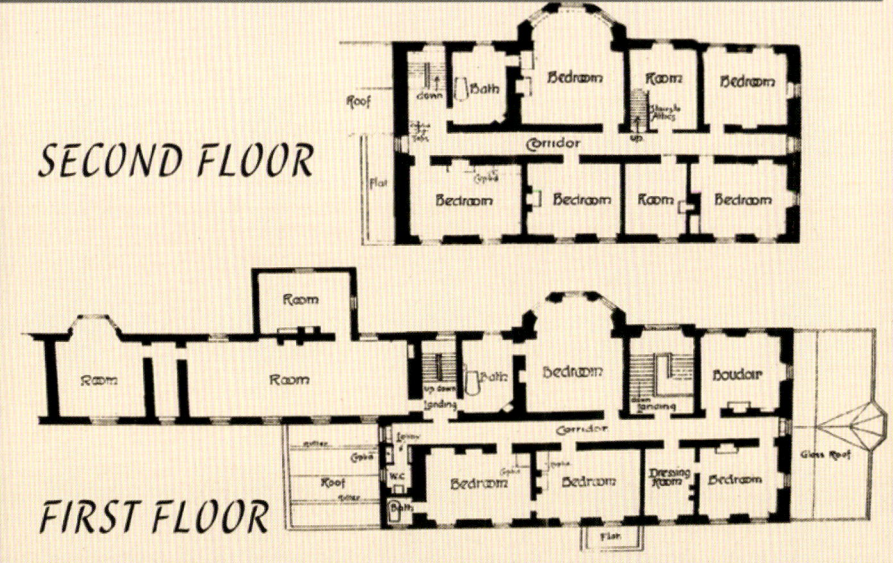

SECOND FLOOR

FIRST FLOOR

The plans of the Friarage are based on the drawings of architect GT Welburn ARIBA

In July 1919, Peace Celebrations were held at Yarm; this group gathered outside the stable-block at the Friarage are waiting to go into the High Street parade.

The Friarage 1926

Until 1822, the road heading south passed very close to the front entrance of the Friarage, crossing over Skytering Beck and into the High Street. Between 1822 and 1825, it was rerouted along the western perimeter of the Friarage grounds to join the Worsall Road, which was also diverted to a new course south of the fishponds that were once part of the Friarage grounds. The inset shows the Hurworth Hunt in front of the Friarage stables in January 1937.

Yarm High Street

Children playing on the cobbles in Yarm High Street c1906, a tranquil scene far removed from Yarm today. The Town Hall, built in 1710 by the Lord of the Manor, the third Viscount Fauconberg dominates the scene. Originally a courthouse, as well as a market, local magistrates sat every two weeks; the steward of the Lord of the Manor also used it for rent audits. An impressive Dutch-style structure it reflects the economic confidence of the time when it was built when Yarm was still able to compete commercially with Stockton.

The familiar cobbles of Yarm High Street, c1907 - a time when street lights have just been installed. Local landmarks include the Town Hall and the chimney stack at Cecil Wren's vinegar factory, visible on the horizon. Although overshadowed economically by Stockton, Yarm was still important as a crossing point on the Tees.

The Green Tree Inn and a view towards the Catholic Church of St Mary and St Romuald, built in 1860 in the grounds of The Friarage by Thomas Meynell opposite the entrance to Bentley Wynd. One regular visitor to Yarm was John Wesley who preached in Yarm on nineteen occasions, from 1748 to 1788 - usually staying with prominent merchant and Methodist, George Merryweather, at No 17 High Street.

Yarm High Street viewed from close to the bridge. Some children and young boys with their bicycles look on - fascinated by the work of the photographer. The Town Hall is in the distance whilst on the immediate left is Bridge House, once the home of Benjamin Flounders, one of the men who attended a promotors meeting at the George and Dragon Inn in 1820 to declare their support for the Stockton and Darlington Railway.

The northern end of Yarm High Street

Yarm Bridge, the viaduct, and Bridge House at the entrance to Yarm High Street are featured here. Originally two houses combined in the 18th century, Bridge House was the residence of Benjamin Flounders, a key figure in launching the Stockton and Darlington Railway, until his death in 1846. The Ketton Ox, one of Yarm's oldest inns, became notorious for cockfighting after it was outlawed. Behind the trees is the former Dragoon Inn, managed by Thomas Brown, celebrated for his bravery at the Battle of Dettingen on June 27, 1743, for which he was knighted before returning to Yarm. Additionally, Eaglescliffe windmill can be seen on the horizon.

Welcome Home....

YARM MAN KILLED AT PAARDEBERG.

The list of killed in the Paardeberg battle contained the names of Private O. O'Shaughnessy, who was a native of Yarm, and only left to join his regiment (the 1st Yorkshire) about two months ago. He is unmarried. Much sympathy is expressed for his mother and brothers and sisters. The Town Hall flag was hoisted half-mast, and at the Parish Church the "Dead March" was played by the organist, Mr Stokoe, after yesterday's services.

PEACE SIGNED.

THE BRITISH TERMS.

MR BALFOUR'S STATEMENT.

THE KING'S MESSAGE.

Peace has been signed and the great Boer war is now over. The news has been received with universal rejoicings. On Monday most of the works were either closed or only partially open, the schools had a holiday, and the joyful news is being celebrated in a more or less quiet and orderly manner throughout Great Britain and the King's dominions beyond the sea. Our soldiers have sustained during the prolonged war the honour and integrity of the Empire. The soldier is the hero of the hour. "Three cheers for those gallant fellows who have been fighting for our country—not forgetting those brave men who have died for England."

Lord Kitchener's despatches are as follows:—

Pretoria, May 31, 5.15 p.m.

It is now settled that the Boer representatives will come here immediately, and also the High Commissioner from Johannesburg.

It is possible that the document will be signed to-night.

I have received from them a statement saying that they accept and are prepared to sign.

Pretoria, May 31, 11.15 p.m.

Negotiations with Boer delegates. The document containing terms of surrender was signed here this evening at 10.30 p.m. by all Boer representatives, as well as by Lord Milner and myself.

A 'Welcome Home' celebration honoured local veterans of the South African (Boer) War (1899-1902), which deeply impacted communities like Yarm. A plaque commemorated volunteers, including Pte Owen O'Shaughnessey, killed in February 1900 at the Battle of Paardeberg.

A view of Bridge Street looking through a viaduct arch to West Street with the River Tees behind the white house.

West Street

Left is the parish church of St Mary Magdalene c1908. It had been rebuilt in 1730 after a fire in 1728 severely damaged the original twelth-century structure.

A view on Bridge Street looking through a viaduct arch to the High Street where an omnibus is approaching Yarm.

Bentley Wynd

THE PRIMITIVE METHODIST CHURCH IN WEST STREET

The Primitive Methodist Church on West Street, opposite Hope House, opened in 1897. Eaglescliffe Windmill, visible on the horizon, was one of three windmills near Yarm. It featured a tall structure with an ogee cap roof and a reefing gallery and was believed to be the last windmill in the area producing stone flour.

CECIL WREN & CO.

LOOKING WEST FROM THE EGGLESCLIFFE MEMORIAL CROSS, TOWARDS THE ROAD TO AISLABY AND YARM BRIDGE.

In 1904 Cecil Wren and Co. bought the old paper mill which stood on a site next to the river on the Egglescliffe side west of Yarm Bridge. The building was converted to a vinegar brewery and as well as brewed malt vinegar, Wren & Co. manufactured a range of pickles and sauces. Note Egglescliffe Windmill close to the brewery on the business card and in the main image.

Fun Days On The River....

For years, Yarm Regatta drew large crowds on summer afternoons along the River Tees, becoming a seasonal highlight. Spectators witnessed thrilling races, such as the Strake Fours by Middlesbrough A.B.C., where J. Livingston Jnr.'s crew surged ahead at the end, winning a gripping contest by half a length. The event featured a prestigious trophy—a five claret jug valued at £10 10s—presented by the Mayor of Middlesbrough.

REGATTA AT YARM.

Last Saturday afternoon the joint regatta of the Tees Amateur Rowing Club (Stockton and Middlesbrough Amateur Boating Club) was held at Yarm. This is the first occasion for some years that Yarm has been honoured by being selected as the scene for aquatic contests of this kind; and the fact is due in a great measure to the peaceful and enjoyable surroundings of the river as it passes the finished town. Saturday afternoon being of a most favourable description there was a considerable attendance of ladies and gentlemen from the two boroughs down the river, who lined the banks on both sides of the stream, and evinced the utmost interest in the proceedings. The regatta was managed by Messrs Jas. F. Smith (Stockton) and J. R. Winpenny (Middlesbrough), while Mr J. Livingston, jnr. (Middlesbrough), discharged the secretarial duties. Mr A. de Lande Long, of Stockton, officiated as starter, and Mr John Livingston, of Middlesbrough, as judge. The course for all the events was from the bend below the Fryerage to the bend below Yarm Bridge.

August 1889... Yarm Regatta

(Illustrated sketch panel)

THE LANDING STAGE

CLOSE QUARTERS

J. Livingston Esq.

A. deL. Long Esq. (Starter) From a photo taken in his rowing days

J. Livingston Jnr. Secretary.

TOO STRONG WITH HIS LEFT

THE FERRY

SKETCHES AT YARM REGATTA.

HUGE CROWDS ALONG THE RIVERSIDE AT YARM

A TEMPORARY BRIDGE ERECTED OVER THE TEES...

... TO PROVIDE ACCESS TO THE OTHER SIDE OF THE RIVER

23 August 1890 Yarm Regatta...

There Was Swimming Too...

Sketches at the Regatta at Yarm.

REGATTA AT YARM.—The joint regatta of the Middlesbrough Amateur Boating Club, the Tees A.B.C. (Stockton), and the Stockton Artisans Rowing Club was held at Yarm last Saturday. There was a large attendance of spectators on the river banks, but the proceedings were exceedingly dull owing to the wretchedly slow manner in which the programme was got through, two important events having to be postponed. Mr J. R. Winpenny (Middlesbrough) and Mr R. Ropner, junr. (Stockton), acted as judges, and Mr W. H. Johnson (Middlesbrough) and Mr Walker (Stockton) were starters.

RIVER TEES POLLUTION.

YARM AND EAGLESCLIFFE COMPLAINTS.

For some months past there has been serious pollution of the River Tees at Yarm and Eaglescliffe, which has aroused general complaints, and a number of these were considered by the Stockton Rural Council on Wednesday, when Mr W. Lawrenson went so far as to remark that " the beautiful river of which we were once so proud is now a huge cesspool."

The popularity of water sports on the River Tees at Yarm also included a swimming club. The Yarm and Egglescliffe swimming Club was formed in February 1910 and in the years leading up to the war the club had as many as 150 members who each paid a subscription of sixpence (5p) a head. Many members actually learnt to swim on the river during this time. The Club held galas and social events and regular swimming sessions in the river. However it is sad to see that even in 1914 there were complaints about the issue of pollution - it's not just a modern day phenomenon.

Winter Sports At Yarm In 1895

ON THE TEES
AT YARM

The frost was exceedingly keen. The Tees above Yarm was frozen over, and skating might be freely indulged in on its glassy surface for a few days.

In the early months of 1895, a very cold winter led to the River Tees freezing over at Yarm. Local people, eager to seize the opportunity to skate, soon took to the river. The freezing temperatures were felt across the country, dropping to their lowest levels in nearly 50 years in early February. Much of the Tees, from Stockton to Worsall, was frozen. In addition to skating, a cricket match was played on the frozen river, as depicted in the image where the church at Egglescliffe is visible on the horizon.

THE BRIDGE THAT FELL DOWN IN 1806

ATLAS WYND

In 1805, a new single-span bridge was built over the Tees. Completed in September 1805, there were differences in height with the Yarm side. A dispute in who would pay to remedy arose. At midnight 12 January 1806, a south abutment collapsed - the bridge would never be used.

THE MUSEUM BOAT

Tom Kelly, a well known 1920's Yarm character, lived on this boat which was moored at the end of Chapel Yard. The boat was known as the 'Museum Boat' as he had a collection of glass cased models of ships and other curios. Entrance was twopence (1p).

YARM WINDMILL

The tower windmill at Yarm was said to be one of the larger windmills in the area. Although the mill is shown here on 24 February 1931 in a state of partial disrepair it was stated as being the 'last of the three old mills at Yarm, over 100 years old, and still standing'.

In Atlas Wynd, children pose near passageways linking the High Street to the river. The skyline features H. & J.C. Hird's chimney, at their skinyard and tannery established in Yarm in 1860. An inset shows a handbill advising precautions against cholera, emphasising a regular and sober lifestyle, including using chloride of lime on walls and diluting it with water to disinfect clothing.

WATER WATER... WATER EVERYWHERE

SAVING HIS BACON

AT THE KETTON OX INN.

WINES

MILK

A CORNER OF THE CHURCHYARD

VENICE AT YARM.

Yarm has been flooded on many occasions. The floods of 1753, 1771 and 1881 were particularly serious. In his entry for 20 November 1771 Ralph Jackson writes that he sent provisions to Yarm which has 'suffered very melancholy by the late Flood, many houses were washed in which several lives were lost; Provisions & Furniture were swept away'. The water flooded to a level of twenty feet in 1771 whilst the flood of 1881 was said to have left a deposit of two feet of sand and silt around the town.

THE INUNDATION AT YARM.

There was less water in the Tees on Friday, and the flood at Yarm, which had on Thursday reached a depth of at least six feet in the High-street and other thoroughfares, disappeared. If, however, there was not a sea of water as on the previous day, there was at least a sea of mud, the streets being in a deplorable condition through a deep sediment. The damage caused by the flood in this old and low lying town has been exceedingly great. The lower storey of almost every house has been inundated, and the furniture and sundry household goods thereby damaged, whilst many shops and their stocks have been very injuriously affected. At the back of the High-street many garden walls have been bodily thrown down, and the trees, bushes and hedges, and likewise many of the tombstones in the churchyard, are covered with straw, hay, and general refuse, which has been washed down. At the top of the town might be seen a boat which had been stranded on the footway when the waters began to subside. The little vessel had been used on Thursday to convey persons from one end of the main thoroughfare—the High-street—to the other. On Friday afternoon the Stockton steam fire engine and the Yarm manual engines were engaged in pumping water out of the vast us cellars which had been flooded, and furniture, &c., was standing about the streets to dry in the sun. The scene was, on the whole, of a very deplorable character. Perhaps there has not, within the memory of the oldest inhabitant, been so injurious a flood in this ancient Tee-side town.—The damage caused by the flood in the Yarm district is considerable, being estimated at £30,000. The town has a strange appearance, all the garden walls being washed down as well as a large part of the pavement.

MARCH 12, 1881.
SERIOUS FLOODS.

YARM INUNDATED.

At Yarm the greatest damage has been sustained in this respect. The water was observed to be rising on Wednesday afternoon, and it continued until Thursday at mid-day. The town lies low, and the water soon made its appearance in the streets. Service at the Parish Church had to be postponed, and later on the inhabitants began to take alarm, as the water made its way into the lower rooms of the dwellings. The work of removing furniture and other property to the upper rooms consequently became general, and few, it may reasonably be inferred, retired to rest. On Thursday morning at day-break there were two or three feet of water in the streets, and from that time until mid-day it increased, until at the Town-hall, the centre of the town, it was eight or nine feet. The inhabitants having taken to the upper portion of their houses, are thus literally imprisoned in their dwellings. To those, however, who had business in the town a small service of boats was brought into operation, and the men who plied them had a rare harvest on Thursday. A man named Hardy was found in a stable in the afternoon, the water at the time being up to his neck, and through fright and the time he had been in the water he has since been exceedingly ill. Another man is stated to be missing. All work has been suspended.

YARM GRAMMAR SCHOOL

Yarm Grammar School was founded in 1590 and was located south of the church in the churchyard (below).

A new building (above) was opened on 5 March 1884 on a site west of the Spital. When North Riding County Council took over the school in 1913 the site was extended, & was extended again in 1935.

The lower images show the Science Laboratory and a class being taught in the Assembly Hall. The inset is Speech Day 8 December 1934 and the presentation to Miss Armstrong of the Chaloner House Cup by the Earl of Feversham. Education continues as the 'new' school of 1884 is now part of Yarm Independent School.

Yarm Fair

Cheese Fair

Yarm October Fair.

THE SHOW of HORSES and the Attendance of DEALERS on the day previous to the GREAT CATTLE, SHEEP, and CHEESE FAIR, held at YARM, on the 19th and 20th of OCTOBER, having exceeded the sanguine expectations of several of the most respectable and extensive Breeders in the Neighbourhood, they have signified their intention to Improve the Fair.

NOTICE IS THEREFORE HEREBY GIVEN, that the SHOW of HORSES will Commence on FRIDAY, the 18th of October, and will be continued Annually to Commence on that Day.

Yarm, September 3rd, 1839. 1839

Horse Fair

YARM OCTOBER FAIR, 1866.—This ANNUAL FAIR will be held for HORSES, on THURSDAY, OCTOBER 18th; for SHEEP and HORSES, on FRIDAY, OCTOBER 19th; and for SHEEP and CHEESE, on SATURDAY, OCTOBER 20th. 1866

YARM FAIR
ANCIENT PROCLAMATION

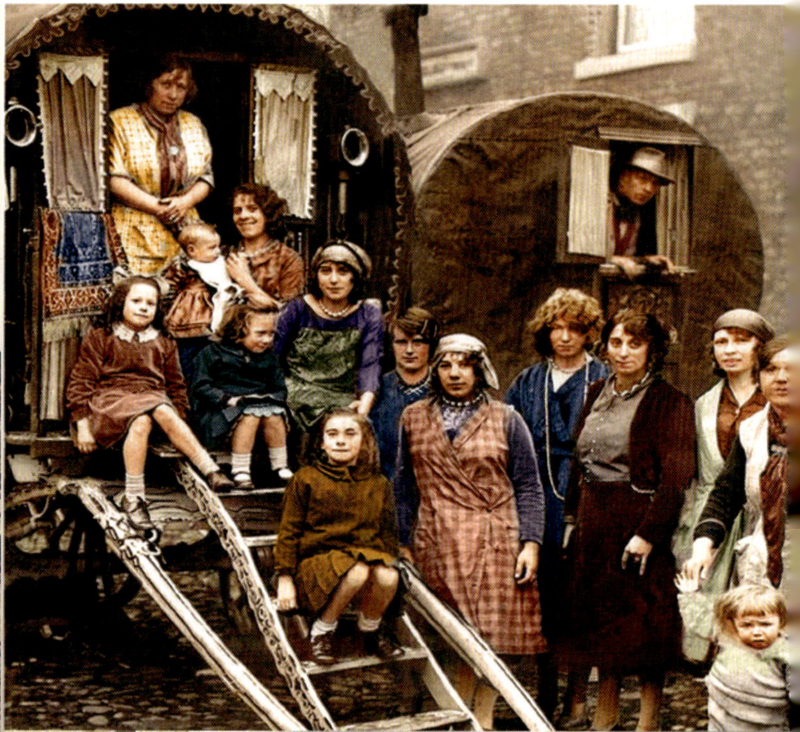

Traditionally, the market days began with horses, followed by cattle, and then sheep and cheese on the third day. The cheese fair alone attracted nearly five hundred carts, making it the largest in the north-east. Livestock sales initially occurred on Yarm's High Street but shifted to the cattle-mart on West Street during World War Two due to increased motor traffic. Since 1945, livestock sales have dwindled, with only a few traditions like the annual 'beating-of-the-bounds' still observed today.

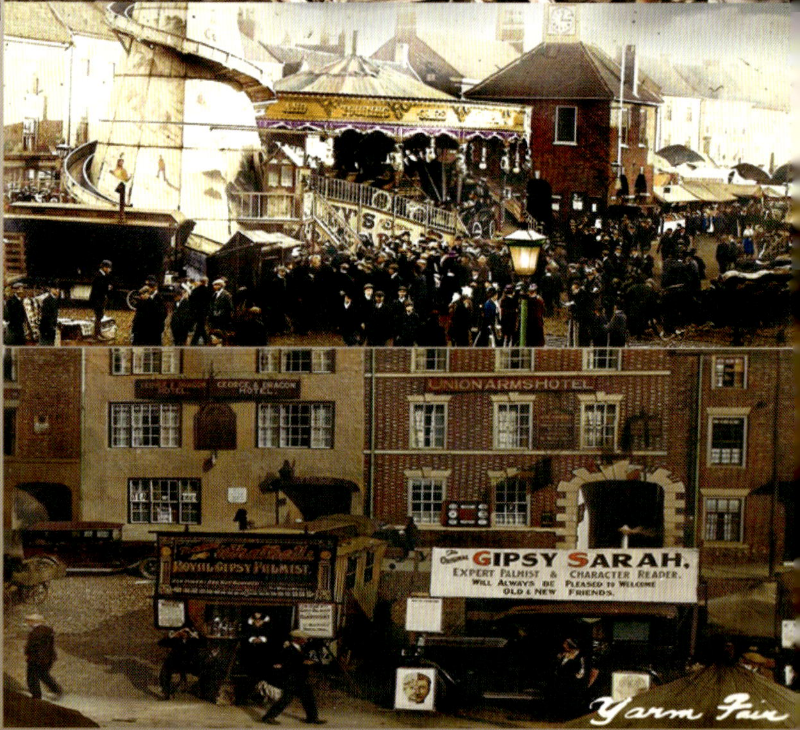

Yarm Fair

All roads lead to Yarm Fair

During Yarm Fair, men travelled from distant places with cattle, horses, cheeses, and various goods for sale. Cattle are seen in the above image, being driven into town from the north, passing the Railway Hotel, with the road to Eaglescliffe (right). Due to space constraints, animals were often kept outside town until market sales. Today, the Railway Hotel is known as the Cleveland Bay public house.

Artist John Atkinson is thought to have painted more pictures of Yarm Fair than anyone else. This 1922 painting captures perfectly the atmosphere of the Horse Fair.

YARM STATION

It's 3:20 PM, and only a few passengers await their train at Yarm station in this view from around 1910, looking north towards Eaglescliffe station. During this period, Yarm had its own goods shed as there was a lot freight traffic.

YARM AND THE RAILWAY

Excursion to Redcar 8 July 1919

L.N.E.R. LUGGAGE From YORK To YARM

Looking south from Yarm Station

This building marks the terminus of the Yarm branch (from Allens West) of the Stockton and Darlington Railway. Located north of the New Inn (later Railway Inn, then Cleveland Bay), coal was transported to here using a horse drawn service - steam locomotives were introduced in 1833.

Early days in railway history

The house, (D13 on the S&D register), was built c1840 for the manager of the coal depot. The branch continued to handle coal traffic until 1870.

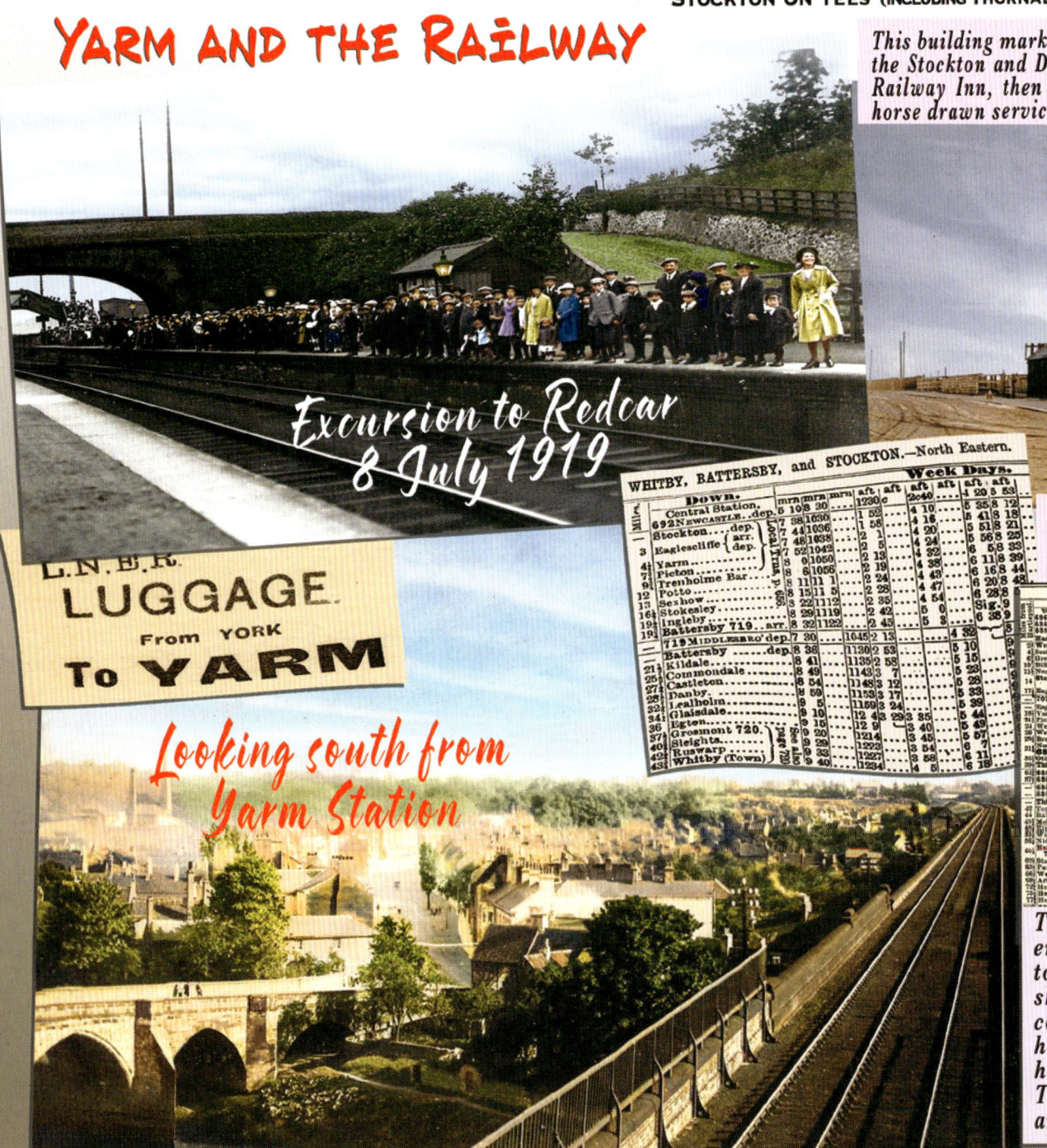

These images capture rail travel at Yarm in the era when North Eastern Railway could take you to almost anywhere in the country. Yarm Station shown here, opened in 1852 when the viaduct was completed. In 1911, 55,615 tickets were issued here - there was also a thriving goods service here for local business and agricultural needs. This station closed to passengers 4 January 1960 and to goods traffic 21 September 1964.

Nelly's Beck

This marvellous photo from 1895 is taken just west of Yarm - many people today will have followed Nelly's Beck. The walk still retains its charm today... Yarm viaduct is visible in the background.

AND BEFORE WE LEAVE YARM...

Aislaby Road (left) & the main route north from Yarm

YARM
1895
Bridge Rents

YARM BRIDGE RENTS.

Until 1956 Yarm Bridge Rents were payable by High Street properties

In the distance is Hird's Skinyard & the Octagnal Methodist Chapel (right)

Egglescliffe...

The village shop (Pear Tree House) that once stood in the north-east corner of the Green at Egglescliffe is shown here. Close to the shop there was a 'boot-maker' who at one time employed several apprentices.

Take a quiet village green.. cottages & trees

Another view of the north-east corner of Egglescliffe Green shows the old cow byre that once stood there.

Village scenes....

Egglescliffe..

...and hidden corners

The village of Egglescliffe is first recorded in the 11th century. There are many theories about the name - Egglescliffe is possibly from 'Ecclesia Church-on-the-Cliffe' whilst it has often been suggested that the name Eaglescliffe occurred when a Victorian sign-writer made a spelling error painting a sign for the new railway station. However note the name 'Eaglescliffe' first appears in the parish registers in 1639. Railway company owners then took the name when they wanted to rename 'Preston Junction' when Eaglescliffe was being developed.

A watercolour of Egglescliffe by:
Alfred Heaton Cooper 1864-1929

... an artist's dream

Egglescliffe: The Church of St John the Baptist

The church at Egglescliffe is built on the site of an earlier Saxon building and with its commanding position over the local area it has been a landmark for many years. Many features of the church offer clues to its age including a stone effigy thought to be of Sir Thomas de Aslackby a knight who died in 1291.

POT AND GLASS EGGLESCLIFFE

1900

1905

1920's

Egglescliffe Rectory

The Rectory was once a three-storey building but was reduced to two by Rector Maltby in 1845

Stoney Bank

Stoney Bank, named after the cobbles once used to surface it, was much steeper in the past & originally descended in a curving line directly to Yarm Bridge. In the late 18th century, the route was straightened, and a cutting was made through the highest part to reduce the gradient. Close-by is a site notable for a skirmish during the Civil War in February 1644.

Highfield

This image from c1890 shows Highfield, a property along the road from Egglescliffe village to the new development at Eaglescliffe Junction. Highfield was one of a number of large houses built in sizeable plots in the late 19th century along the road to Eaglescliffe.

Eaglescliffe Junction

Dunnotar Avenue

Swinburne Road

G.W.R.

Eaglescliffe
JUNCTION

Station Road

Local development was closely linked to the new railway from Leeds, which opened in 1853, connecting with the Stockton and Darlington line near Whiteley Springs Farm and the newly established Eaglescliffe Junction station. Initial growth was slow, centering around property in The Avenue, owned by wealthy businessmen and industrialists from Stockton and Middlesbrough. Rapid expansion occurred in the early 1900s, with the construction of roads like Swinburne Road, depicted here, around 1908.

Woodside Hall

Life at Woodside Hall

1883

THE COMING OF AGE OF MR F. W. APPLETON.

Woodside Hall, the charming residence of Mr R. H. Appleton, presented quite a gay and festive appearance on Saturday afternoon, when the *élite* of Stockton and the surrounding district assembled to celebrate the coming of age of Mr F. W. Appleton, the oldest son of the genial host.

The celebrations were suitably drawn to a close on Wednesday by the employees of the Cleveland Steam Flour Mills being entertained most enjoyably in the extensive and beautiful grounds of Woodside Hall. After various games during the afternoon the guests, numbering upwards of two hundred, did ample justice to a sumptuous repast provided in a spacious marquee.

Eaglescliffe Junction

Woodside Hall

1933

TO GARDENERS.—WANTED, a Young MAN, who thoroughly understands the routine of Gardening; also to assist under glass when required.—Address HEAD GARDENER, Woodside Hall, Preston-on-Tees. *1876*

FESTIVITIES AT WOODSIDE HALL.
PRESENTATION TO MR R. H. APPLETON.

Mr R. H. Appleton, of Woodside Hall, the owner of the Cleveland Flour Mills, South Stockton, having reached his 69th birthday, his employees expressed a desire to present him with a testimonial of their esteem. This having come to the ears of Mrs Appleton, that lady issued invitations to the whole of the workmen to spend an evening at the charming residence of their employer at Preston-on-Tees. The party left South Stockton, upwards of a hundred and fifty in number, by the 3.25 p.m. train on Saturday, and on arriving at Eaglescliffe repaired at once to Woodside Hall, where they were shown up to the gymnasium. Mr J. H. MacDonnell, the manager of the mills, was voted to the chair.—In opening the proceedings Mr MACDONNELL said they had met for a very pleasing duty, and it was due to the kind consideration of Mrs Appleton that they were able to discharge that duty amid those pleasant surroundings.

—The company then adjourned to the beautiful grounds around the mansion, and were served with tea in one of the tennis courts, after which they spent the evening in various amusements.

1881

1884 **VISIT TO MARTON AND WOODSIDE HALLS.** Subsequently the visitors took special train to Ormesby, and visited Marton Hall, apparently being highly delighted with the art treasures it contained. Afterwards the special train conveyed them to Eaglescliffe Junction, whence they proceeded to Woodside Hall, where they were sumptuously entertained by Mr R. H. Appleton, the president. After tea Mr Appleton welcomed in the name of the Association the two foreign visitors present—Mr Palmer, editor of the North American Miller, and Mr Green, of Tasmania.

TO DOMESTIC SERVANTS.—WANTED, at the August term, a strong, active HOUSEMAID, about 20 years of age, where a Parlourmaid is kept. Also, a KITCHENMAID, about 17 years of age.— Apply, first by letter, to Mrs APPLETON, Woodside Hall, Preston-on-Tees. *1876*

Woodside Hall, built in 1876 by Richard Appleton from Stockton, was a striking four-storey building with excellent views of the the River Tees towards Yarm. The conservatory overlooked extensive grounds featuring lawns, exotic plants, trees, statues, fountains, and other water features. Sir John Harrison, Bart., who served as Mayor of Stockton five times, later purchased the hall. In 1935, a donation of the Hall to Stockton Borough Council as a maternity home was not accepted. During World War II, the building was used by I.C.I. In 1945, it became part of Cleveland School. When Teesside High School was formed in 1970, Woodside Hall was demolished.

Map extract reproduced from 1895 Twenty-Five inch series, with the kind permission of the Ordnance Survey

Eaglescliffe Golf Club

ENTERPRISING GOLF "TEAM" AT EAGLESCLIFFE

ALL THAT IS LACKING OUT OF FIRS...

HOLE-IN-ONE

By DORMIE

THE only disappointing feature about the delightful Walter Hagen and Percy Alliss exhibition match at Eaglescliffe last Saturday was the small number of visitors, who only numbered about 1,000. Club officials had counted on at least twice as many coming for this exceptional event, and were at a loss to find a reason why these two star golfers as a bigger gallery ...

HAGEN THE SHOWMAN

AMERICAN RYDER CUP CAPTAIN AT EAGLESCLIFFE

GOLF IN A GALE

(By H.G.S.)

NOT for nothing has Walter Hagen been described as the showman of the links.

When he set out on the first tee on the course at Eaglescliffe golf course to-day, he dominated the scene. For his exhibition match with Percy Alliss, the Ryder Cup player, he made himself an arresting figure in pure white.

| WALTER HAGEN | PETER ALLISS SNR | HG BROWN EAGLESCLIFFE | A WILKINSON HON SEC | A RIEVELEY SEATON CAREW | A HODGKINSON EAGLESCLIFFE |

Eaglescliffe Golf Club was founded in 1914 with 13 hole course at Coatham Stob. The Clubhouse was a wooden structure and the course was laid out using hedges and artifical bunkers. By the late 1920's there were 150 gentlemen and lady members but members were not allowed to play on Sundays! By the late 1920's the Club moved to an 18 hole course in Eaglescliffe, designed by the famous golf architect, James Braid. The course opened in 1930. In 1933 Walter Hagen, USA golf icon and Peter Alliss snr., played there.

Moorhouse Estate

22,000 ACRES TO BE DEVELOPED

HEALTH MINISTRY ASKED TO APPROVE

STRONG OBJECTION

IN THE MID-1930S, HOUSES WERE BUILT ON BOTH SIDES OF THE LANE EXTENDING UP TO MOOR HOUSE FARM, FROM YARM ROAD.

The Moorhouse Farm Estate comprises a double row of houses isolated in the middle of fields. These houses were built in 1936 under the Land Settlement Act to redeploy unemployed miners, steelworkers, and others during the Great Depression. After training in agriculture and small animal husbandry, suitable candidates were rented a house and several acres of land in a cooperative smallholding venture. They raised pigs, produced eggs and vegetables, which were sold through the Stockton Cooperative Society and local markets. A Dutch expert taught cold glasshouse horticulture, enabling the growth of vegetables like tomatoes, cucumbers, and lettuce. The initiative was highly successful, with 4,000 pounds of tomatoes grown and marketed in the first season.

Many men became skilled smallholders easing the issue of unemployment. This unique historical effort aimed to move men from urban areas to the countryside during high unemployment. County Durham fully embraced the scheme, taking 7,000 men off the unemployment register. Moorhouse is one of the 304 estates established under the scheme, standing as a reminder of the ideal behind the project, which ended when World War II brought full employment.

Preston Hall

1826

1908

PIC-NIC AT PRESTON HALL.

Preston Hall has stood on the banks of the River Tees in Preston-on-Tees for nearly two centuries. It was one of several 'country seats' in Cleveland, though relatively new compared to others. Built by lawyer David Burton Fowler, who acquired the land in 1820, the Hall was completed in 1825. Its location was chosen for the fine view across the river bend to Thornaby woods and the Cleveland Hills. The original entrance faced the river to take advantage of this vista, although it was later changed. David Fowler died at ninety-two on January 30, 1828, and the Hall passed to his nephew Marshall Fowler

Preston Hall became the property of local shipbuilder Robert Ropner in 1882 and quickly became a hub for local events. When Ropner Park opened in 1893, the Duke and Duchess of York visited. Ropner made alterations to the Hall, including adding a heavy stone porch and conservatory, shifting the main entrance from the riverfront to face the road from Stockton to Yarm. After Robert Ropner's death, his son Leonard inherited the Hall. Upon Leonard's death in 1937, Ashmore, Benson and Pease took over the building, but plans to develop the estate were denied. In 1953, Stockton Borough Council opened Preston Hall as a museum. Notably, the Stockton to Darlington railway line ran through the grounds until it was diverted through Eaglescliffe in 1852.

Elton Hall

'A modern mansion with a beautiful situation and grounds'
Brewster 1828

Elton Hall, with its eighteenth-century facade, Venetian windows, elegant conservatory, and landscaped grounds, was originally owned by the Shaftos of Whitworth, before it passed to George Sutton, a former mayor of Stockton, in the late eighteenth century. Sutton, frequently visited by Ralph Jackson, enlarged the hall and landscaped the grounds. After his nephew George William Sutton inherited it, further alterations and extensions were made in 1829. George William Sutton's son, John Stapleton Sutton, sold Elton Hall in 1900 to Thomas Appleby. Following Appleby's death, the Hall was demolished in 1910 and replaced in 1912 by the current Edwardian building.

MOST DESIRABLE MANSION TO LET.

TO BE LET, with Possession on the 1st of July next, ELTON HALL, with the Stables, Coach-houses, and other Outbuildings, Lawns, Pleasure Grounds, Plantation, and Grass Land, all now in the occupation of JOHN CASTELL HORNER, Esq., also, THE EXCLUSIVE RIGHT OF SPORTING over 2,500 Acres of Land well stocked with Game.

1912: Plans

Urlay Nook

NAMES OF WORKERS IN IMAGE

BACK ROW	MIDDLE ROW	FRONT ROW	SEATED
McGowan	Slip Hanson	Bob Walls	Alf Henderson
Woods	Ted Metcalfe	Jim Henderson	Alf Savage
Peter Harwood	Ernie Smith	Happy Harwood	Sammy Wallinger
Tom Hutchinson	Everard Ellis	Charles Henderson	
Tom Harwood	Pat Wallinger	Snuffy Johnson	
Tom Bell	Campie Johnson	Kit Ellis	
	Tassy? Cartwright	Ginger	
	Dick Simpson		
	Mark Davison		

A chemical works was established by Robert Wilson at Urlay Nook near Egglescliffe in 1833 to produce sulphuric acid and fertilizers.

The Teesside site had excellent transport links, as it was located along the route of the world's first public railway, which ran from Shildon through Darlington to Stockton.

Several other advantageous factors contributed to the site's favourable location.

These included the availability of essential raw materials, a top-class water supply, and ample energy resources. Coal and water were readily available, as was anhydrite calcium sulphate, which became a key component in the production of sulphate of ammonia fertiliser.

A group of children stand outside the Masham Hotel in East Hartburn. The Masham Hotel, built in the eighteenth century, was modernised in the 1800's.

Hartburn village

Houses on Manor House Terrace

The cows are being walked home in the direction of the Masham Hotel seen in the distance. Despite changes many features of the village have survived.

A group of children gathered outside Hartburn village school - the school had opened in 1877, as a result of the 1870 Elementary Eduaction Act.

Hartburn a small agricultural community, was formerly known as East Hartburn. A pleasant village it became a popular place to live with the wealthier inhabitants of late 19th century Stockton. The tranquillity of village life is evident here.

Norton to Billingham

The historic churches at Norton and Billingham have faced each other across the valley through which Billingham Beck flows, for over a thousand years. These two communities have roots which stretch back to the world of Anglo-Saxon England and before - small communities in which the church has played a pivotal role, perhaps in a way which may seem unfamiliar to some today. Both places have experienced amazing changes but the past can still be found - in colour too - as we record here some memories of times gone by.

MOUNT PLEASANT WINDMILL

In the late eighteenth century, the troubles in France leading up to the French Revolution raised concerns in England about securing grain supplies. As a result, several tower windmills were constructed in the Cleveland area to address this need. Even after the situation in France was resolved, most windmills remained in use. One such windmill was Mount Pleasant Mill, located between Stockton and Norton at the end of Brown Jug Lane. Additionally, Clarence Pottery, known for its brown earthenware, had relocated from near the Kings Arms in Billingham to this area.

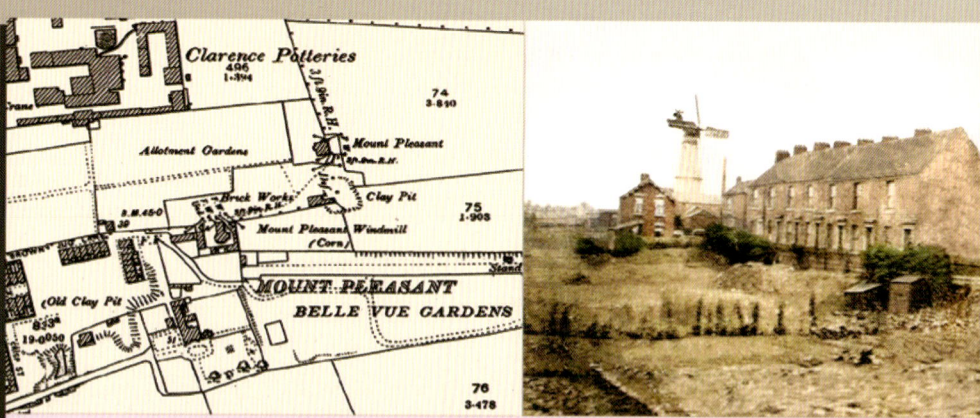

It is not known exactly when Mount Pleasant Mill between Stockton and Norton was built but J.K. Harrison suggests it was pre-1824. The mill was built on high ground close to the Clarence Pottery and Mount Pleasant Farm. It was connected to the turnpike road from Stockton, and Portrack Lane which led to the River Tees and ships which berthed at Portrack. Like the mill at Greatham, this mill was very tall, with four sails and an ogee cap roof. The site later became the Belle Vue Greyhound Stadium and eventually in the 1970's, a housing estate.

Beautiful Norton-on-Tees

The North Ormesby-Middlesbrough tram route followed the road to Norton, making adjacent plots of land attractive for development. This bridge crosses the Billingham Beck Branch Railway with Wesley Place immediate right and Imperial Avenue, beyond left.

SURG.-COLONEL J.W. BLANDFORD

Blandford's Corner named after Surg.-Colonel J.W. Blandford who had his surgery at the corner house. The name came into use through the conductors on the trams, calling out 'Blandford's Corner next stop!' A tram is seen travelling down Norton High Street.

In 1897, Norton on Tees remained much as it had been in earlier times, with the village, its High Street, Green with its pond, features of the locality. The large houses around the Green were still residential, though for some properties this would eventually change.

Norton Green & Darlington Back Lane

This view of Norton Duck Pond c1906 shows West Row, Ragworth Hall and in the distance Darlington Lane. The village water-pump can be seen behind the old Victorian lamp standard

Norton Green to Norton House

High Row in 1931, with Norton House in the distance. There were several large properties around the Green.

Norton House

Norton House, built in 1720 at the eastern end of the Green behind a tree-lined drive, was a three-story building often used as a meeting place by the local hunt. In the early 1800s, it was considered an important house among the social elite, hosting notable guests like Byron, Shelley, Coleridge, and Wordsworth. The house was demolished in April 1936.

The Clock...master of Norton time

This image c1900 shows the eastern side of the buildings which included the Hambletonian Inn (the sign is partially visible). The name of the image is 'The Clock, Norton', a reference to the clock which is above Caskill's shop. High Row is in the distance across the other side of the Green.

St. Mary's Church 1896

...inside the church & the Vicarage

Diamond Jubilee Cross

Interior of St Mary's Church 1896

Norton (the name means 'north settlement') was an important agricultural settlement in Anglo-Saxon times – in fact Stockton was part of the parish of Norton for many years. The village church, St Mary's, pre-Norman in origin, is opposite the Hermitage, a building dating from the eleventh century

Tending the gardens, Norton Vicarage

Opposite Blandford's Corner was the Diamond Jubilee Cross erected in 1897 to celebrate Queen Victoria's sixty years on the throne. These images show the area with the premises of H. Clarke seen behind the cross

Norton Hall Garden Party 1889

Sketches at the British League Garden Party, at Norton Hall.

Tea at Norton Bungalow

NEW BUNGALOW AT NORTON.

Norton Bungalow on the corner of Billingham Road and South Road, opened in May 1900; it was designed by Stockton architect, Arthur Harrison, built by Messrs Craggs & Benson, decorated by M. Baldwin and fitted out by Robinson & Co. The building had a main room 3.25sq.m with a private room for select use. As well as ladies rooms there was a verandah, 2m wide, which ran the whole length of the south and west sides upon which serving tables were laid. Three French doors connected the area to the main room. The whole structure, built on concrete foundations, was tastefully fitted out and surrounded by ornamental gardens with outside cafe facilities too. At a time when outdoor leisure, especially cycling & walking, was becoming very popular the Bungalow was very busy - especially on Sunday afternoons in the summertime

Unfortunately Norton Bungalow didn't last many years and burnt down in 1907 - thought to have been caused by a discarded cigarette. It was rebuilt only to burn down again in 1921.

Junction Road

There is very little development along Junction Road as seen here c1910. This view is close to the turning into Station Road and it's interesting to note the country lane still exists beyond this point.

Rimswell House

Rimswell Manor House, a Victorian mansion in grounds of 62 acres, was home to William Anderson, a Justice of the Peace for North Riding. Born in Newcastle in 1836, Anderson was a Civil Institute of Engineers member, Director at Head Wrightson & Co. Ltd, Governor of Stockton Grammar School and Queen Victoria High School, Alderman of Thornaby, and Thornaby's first Mayor (1892-1894). He co-financed the original Five Lamps feature in Thornaby. Rimswell House was demolished in the late 1950s for post-war housing, but the gatehouse remains. The site is now occupied by the Rimswell Pub and houses on Manor Place, near Bishopton Road West.

STOCKTON WOMEN'S LIBERAL ASSOCIATION GARDEN PARTY AT RIMSWELL.

Ragworth Hall

These images show Ragworth Hall which was on Darlington Lane, on the edge of Norton village. The main image c1920 shows the Hall to the rear with it's well maintained beautiful tree-lined gardens. In 1926 the Hall was purchased by the Church and was later used as a private school. The inset from 23 February 1935 shows the converting of the stable and granary to a church. Despite later becoming rather dilapidated the Hall survived until the 1960's. The area is now covered by housing.

Norton Mill

Winter at Norton Mill

Brighter days at Norton Mill

One of the largest watermills in this area was Norton Mill (mentioned in the Boldon Book in 1183) which stood on high ground west of Billingham Bottoms. An ancient pathway went across the Bottoms from the mill to Chapel Road in Billingham. These views c1900, when the Watson family owned Norton and Wolviston Mills.

Like Wolviston and Billingham Mills however, Norton Mill also fell into decline and by 1924 was no longer in use. Extensively damaged by a bomb in 1940, the remains of the mill disappeared under the present A19 route when it was built in the 1970's. The loss of the mills was complete.

Billingham Bank & the road to Norton 1925

Billingham Bank was widened in October 1929 in response to increased traffic - especially to the new ICI factory. This route across Billingham Bottoms had been used since c1870 - prior to that travellers used the winding 'old toll road' across the Bottoms.

A Turnpike Road Across Billingham Bottoms 1927

This view shows the original turnpike trust road from Norton to Billingham Bank built in 1789 and the new housing development along Hill Road and Bank Road off Billingham Bank. These were 'staff houses' for employees of Synthonia Ammonia and Nitrates, Limited. Four were completed by mid-1926, whilst a further seven were built on Bank Road in 1927 by Lumsdens of Newcastle

From Norton....to Billingham Green

Billingham Green, centre of the village, c1901 with North Row (left), a terrace of labourer's cottages, built c1870. Facing the green, East Row with its School House (1898), 'Thompson' style farmhouse next to Brewery House with its chimney and brewery buildings to the rear. Village and Town End Farms lie beyond. A road divides Parish Green (left) and Common Green where villagers grazed their animals.

Billingham Road c1920, linked Norton to Billingham via Norton Bank shown in this view from the Red Lion Inn; the road followed an ancient track across Billingham Bottoms.

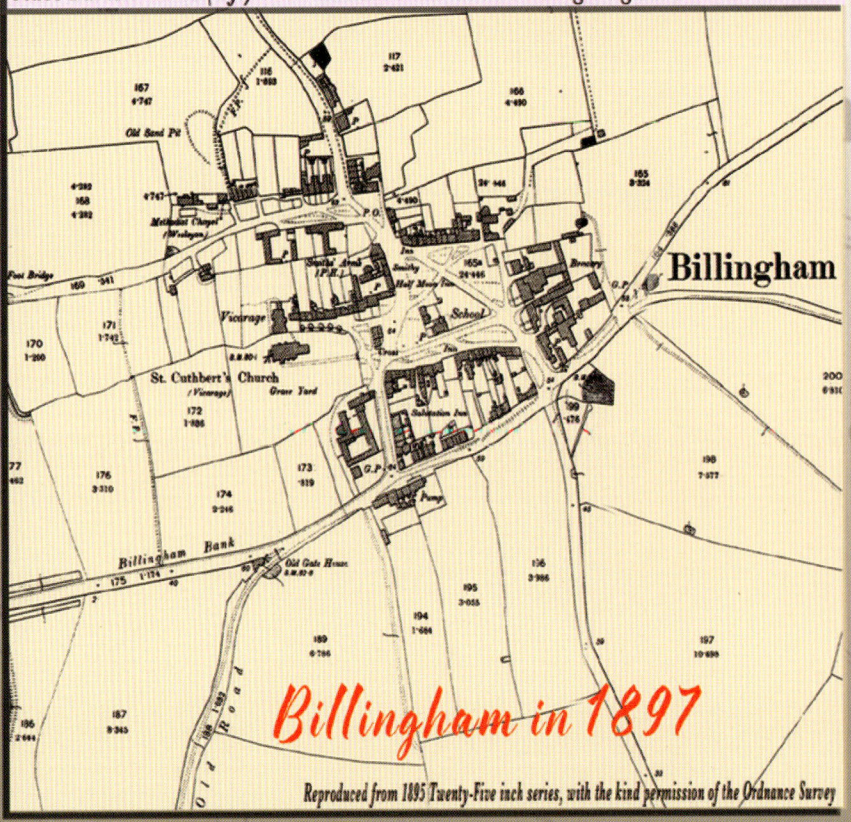

This image, c1894, shows the poor state of the roads – often discussed at Parish Council meetings. In the foreground is Henry Eldon Fletcher's Billingham Cash Trading Stores and the National School extended in 1898 taking in the village pinfold. The village cross and one of the village water pumps are also visible with Brewery House and Village Farm in the distance.

Billingham in 1897

Reproduced from 1895 Twenty-Five inch series, with the kind permission of the Ordnance Survey

The Green Billingham

The Black Horse Hotel shown after its extension c1900 advertises 'Heslop's Noted Stout' from its window. The newly planted trees have wooden guards to prevent damage by livestock. Purchased from Fewsters in Norton they were part of improvements made to the Green in 1904. Six seats and two notice boards were also erected. A group of children are well aware the photograph was being taken.

Since Anglo-Saxon times Billingham Church has been a local landmark. The Rev. Philip Rudd, the incumbent 1852 to 1901, oversaw an extensive rebuilding of the church as well as being closely involved with village life, particularly after the inception of the Parish Council in 1894. The labourer cutting the grass, Bill Handley, later died in the Great War.

East Row was dominated by the 18th-century Brewery House, known locally as Heslop's Brewery. John Heslop and his son built a successful brewing business by 1861, acquiring several pubs, including the Union Inn (later the Station Hotel) and the Black Horse Inn. Brewing in Billingham declined after John Heslop Sr.'s death in 1901, but ales continued to be sold from their Norton brewery for several years. Brewery House was demolished in the 1930s. Beyond Brewery House, Wren's farmhouse is visible, and a path at the corner of East Row and North Row led to farm outbuildings used by Fletcher's for delivery vehicles.

The increased availability of mains water sparked heated debate at Parish Council meetings about the removal of village water pumps. This indecision is evident with this pump still standing in 1906. Also visible is Fletcher's new grocery shop, replacing Billingham Cash Trading Stores, reflecting Henry Eldon Fletcher's success since opening his first shop 18 years earlier. In the distance, a man rides a penny farthing past the Ship Inn.

INNS IN OLD BILLINGHAM c1900

STATION HOTEL

SMITH'S ARMS

BLACK HORSE

The Green Billingham

Billingham

Chiltons Lane

St. Cuthbert's Church

Life in Billingham in 1900 centred around Billingham Green where the church, shops, the blacksmith, carpenter and public houses provided inhabitants with most of their needs. These scenes record a life long gone, in the days before the Great War of 1914 and the coming of industry which would sweep away these memories forever.

SALUTATION INN

HALF MOON INN

THE SHIP INN

Map extract reproduced from 1895 Twenty-Five inch series, with the kind permission of the Ordnance Survey

BILLINGHAM POST OFFICE 1902

Mrs. Rebecca Elstob outside the old Post Office in Church Road c1902 - note the recruiting poster for recruits to fight in the Boer War. Born in 1852 in Grindon, Rebecca Golightly worked as a servant for Joseph Elstob around 1871. She later became his housekeeper in Billingham, and they married in 1887. Joseph became sub-postmaster in September 1899, using part of their living room for the post office. Services were limited, with money orders needing to be cashed in Norton. By 1900, mail arrived twice daily, and Rebecca delivered it on foot around the village and by bike to outlying farms. Joseph was also the church caretaker, ringing the curfew bell each evening at 8 pm in winter and 9 pm in summer.

BILLINGHAM HALL AND NEW DEVELOPMENT 'OVER THE STATION'

BILLINGHAM
HIGH GRANGE FARM

COTSWOLD CRESCENT &
MALVERN ROAD
DEVELOPMENT

STATION RD
ESTATE

BILLINGHAM
STATION

BILLINGHAM HALL

During the 1920's Billingham underwent significant development as the arrival of new industry - in particular Synthetic Ammonia, brought a new workforce and their families to live in the area. New housing estates sprang up particularly near the old village and the railway station. By 1930 building had gone beyond this point as can be seen in this aerial image from May 1930.

Billingham Hall

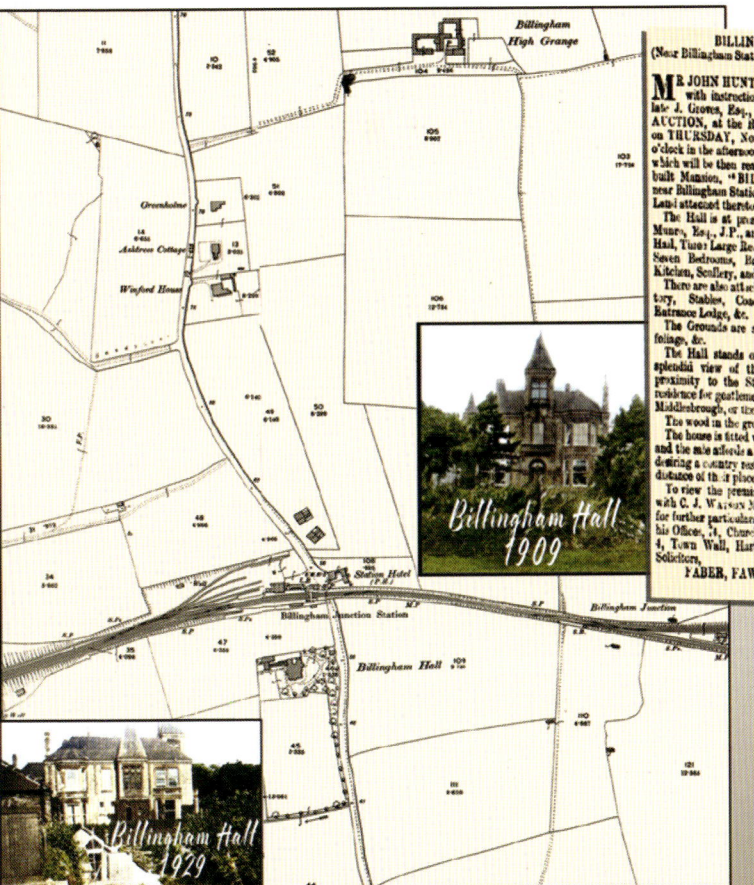

For Sale
1897

Taken on 14 March 1915, this shows the driveway which swept around the house from the road. The south east corner of the house is just off to the right of the picture and there is just a glimpse of the spring gardens. Behind the trees is a three and a half acre field farmed by the Dixons who lived at the Glebe Farm in the village. The Nielsen family were one of the few in Billingham to possess a car before the First World War.

Billingham Hall is Billingham's forgotten landmark. This 1897 map shows details of the grounds as well the general location of the Hall. The two insets show the south aspect of the Hall in 1909 and the west aspect in 1929. Demolished in 1935 to make way for a housing development, very few people alive today actually recall anything about the building. Billingham Hall was located on Station Lane a mile north of the village. It stood in open countryside to the south of Billingham Station. An impressive building, Billingham Hall was situated amidst a one and a half acre site with a sweeping tree lined driveway. Local people could recall many years afterwards the impressive poplar trees which shielded it from the road. Built in the early 1870's, three families lived at Billingham Hall before Charles Nielsen, a shipowner living in Hartlepool, purchased it in 1909.

LEFT: Taken in May 1910 looking east with the south aspect of the house just showing. The background trees on the Billingham to Wolviston road were well known locally and the garden urn marked one of the pathways which went around the house. Many family afternoons were spent in the garden which was maintained by full time gardening staff.

Reproduced from 1895 Twenty-Five inch series, with the kind permission of the Ordnance Survey

Family life at Billingham Hall before the Great War

Gwen's father Charles and brother Luis are standing outside the main entrance to the Hall on 1 June 1909. The previous day, Whit Monday, had seen a family gathering at the Hall with dinner in the evening, followed by musical recitals.

Gwen Nielsen lived at Billingham Hall between 1909 and 1919. A young girl typical of her time, living at home and enjoying a life which embraced a variety of social functions in the village of Billingham and further afield. During the First World War Gwen became a VAD nurse, being stationed at the Army Hospital, Dinsdale. This image, at the south-facing entrance into the Hall, is Gwen with her Uncle Charles, who was visiting with his wife Addie.

Gwen's younger brother Luis in the gardens with the house in the background. Spring weather in 1909 was variable with lots of showery days whilst June continued to be cool. Gwen records long days in her diary being out in the garden whilst many evenings were spent playing billiards – something of a family custom! On other summer evenings the family enjoyed country walks to Sandy Lane and Wolviston or they entertained friends at the Hall.

June 1911 marked Charles and Margaret Nielsen's twenty-fifth wedding anniversary. Celebrations included a garden party at Billingham Hall and a dinner party for eighteen guests. This charming photo, taken on Saturday, June 3, 1911, was described by Gwen (on the right) as a "gramophone party," with the gramophone visible on a table by the front door. The other girls in the image are two cousins staying at the hall.

1914: War comes to Billingham Hall

A rare interior image in 1910; the Hall was described as 'a beautiful place with a lounge and dining room on either side of the front entrance as you went in. Then there was a drawing room, a morning room, library and kitchens.' Upstairs a dressing room as well as seven bedrooms & the East Room – with its magnificent view of the sea and Tees Bay.

Summer at Billingham Hall..

and winter too...

May 1915...a poignant family gathering. Soldier Tom Griffiths and RFC pilot Roger Hay, would both be dead within a few months

1916: Gwen became a VAD nurse

& Luis joined the OTC

1917: Gwen with fiancé Hugh Hay

As normal life returns to Billingham Hall in 1919, Gwen and Hugh are married

WEDDING AT NORTON.

CAPT. H. A. HAY, M.C., AND MISS NIELSEN.

The marriage took place yesterday afternoon at Norton Parish Church, of Capt. Hugh Allport Hay, M.C., West Yorkshire Regt., late attached R.F.C., and Miss Gwendoline Luis Nielsen, daughter of Mr. and Mrs. Charles Nielsen, of Billingham Hall.

The ceremony was performed by the Rev. R. W. Hay, M.A., late Rector of Sarsden, Wilts. (father of the bridegroom), assisted, in the absence from home of the Vicar (Rev. Canon Scott), by the Rev. H. Lee, M.A., curate of the parish. The service was fully choral.

The bride, who was given away by her father, was attired in a charming gown of ivory charmeuse with full court train, the corsage being trimmed with old family Brussels lace (the gift of her mother), and richly embroidered with silk bead, which also formed a deep fringe falling to the hem of the skirt. The train of silk net was edged with Brussels lace, and finished at one corner with a large true lover's knot of net, and ostrich feathers and orange blossom. The only ornament worn by the bride was a diamond and aquamarine brooch, which, with a shower bouquet of choice white flowers, were the gifts of the bridegroom.

The bride was attended by four bridesmaids, the Misses Isabel and Moonie Hay (sisters of the bridegroom), Miss Ethel Fernandez (cousin of the bride), and Miss Nancy Brown, of Norton. They were attired in gowns of yellow Georgette, with pretty cross-over bodices, the skirts being entirely composed of small frills. Their gold lace Dutch caps were finished with heliotrope streamers, and they wore gold and pearl propeller-blade brooches, the gift of the bridegroom, and carried shower bouquets of yellow chrysanthemums, tied with heliotrope ribbons.

The two little train-bearers, Misses Ishiel and Beryl Guthe, also wore frilled yellow Georgette frocks and carried silver purse bags, the gift of the bridegroom.

Lieut. Guy B. Hay, West Yorkshire Regt., brother of the bridegroom, acted as best man.

After the ceremony a reception was held at Billingham Hall, and later in the afternoon the happy couple, who were the recipients of many and beautiful presents, left by motor for the South of England, where the honeymoon will be spent. The bride's going-away dress was of heliotrope crepe-de-chine, with which she wore a grey Georgette hat, the crown being composed of gold and heliotrope brocade.

Wedding Day Scenes at Billingham Hall

Billingham Picture House

Billingham Bank

The old Smiths Arms

BILLINGHAM

IN THE 1920's

The Pinacle & St Cuthbert's

Billingham Hall

Mill Lane

'Chilton House'
Synthetic Offices

Park & Noddings Farm

Development at Haverton Hill...

The opening of the Clarence Railway encouraged development at Haverton Hill and Port Clarence, including a glass works, iron foundry, and forge. In Haverton Hill, the discovery of a large salt bed in 1862 led to the establishment of several salt works, such as Tees Salt Works. Other developments included Pioneer Cement Works (1902) and Haverton Hill Brickworks. Port Clarence became a hub for coal exports from the late 1830s, with Bells Iron Works founded in 1854. Housing expanded, Chilton's Lane connected to Haverton Hill, and a new road to Cowpen Bewley was built in 1914. During World War One, the need for wartime ship replacements led to the creation of Furness shipyards at a deep-water bend in the river. Despite the challenging 85-acre swampy site, the first ship keel was laid in May 1918, followed by the first launch a year later. This image shows a steam crane in action during the yard's construction, with St. John's Church (1865) and its vicarage, visible in the distance.

Furness Ship Building Co. - digging out the fitting-out basin

A major part of the construction was the fitting-out basin shown here and this image from 1919 provides evidence of the work involved.

We couldn't have done it without you...

All part of the war effort

The role of women workers in their contribution to the war effort during World War One cannot be overestimated. There was a significant presence during the digging out of the Furness Shipyard in 1917-1919 and as these images show, the women took the place of male workers with great success.

Working together...

Furness Offices

Building a new town

St John's Church

The Furness Offices, shown here in the 1920's, stood at the entrance of the yard, a monument to the status that the shipyard enjoyed at this time.

The Furness Estate

With such an increasing population there was a need for new housing. The Furness Estate, shown here under construction 20 May 1919 was built on the area close to ancient Belasis Hall and Middle Belasis Farm. Consisting of 564 houses this estate was known as 'Belasis Garden City'. Like those later to be built at Billingham, the houses were of a high quality and the development was regarded as a model of its kind.

Once it was called Samphire Batts...

Originally the Stockton and Darlington Railway had intended to use Haverton Hill as a shipping point for coal but abandoned this in favour of Middlesbrough. When the Clarence Railway took over the scheme they extended the line to Samphire Batts – renamed Port Clarence, a point where deep water allowed access to shipping. It was on 30 January 1834 that the first cargo of coal was shipped, carried by the vessel the 'Willing Mind' of Scarborough. This drawing shows the coal drops in use.

..most people recall it as Bell's Iron & Steel Works

The coming of industry meant the end for several farms & buildings as Billingham changed forever...

Synthetic Ammonia and Nitrates Ltd. arrives

Billingham Mill, seen here left, in a somewhat dilapidated state c1900, has been demolished for so long that today few people remember it. There is mention of Billingham Mill as far back as 1368 and 1380 when villagers were told by the Halmote Court they had to grind their corn there. Although there seems to have been some decline in the value of the mill it belonged to a Captain Eden by 1649. The buildings shown here were constructed of narrow two inch bricks and date from 1700-1720 suggesting an increase in importance again.

Older residents of Billingham recalled Billingham Mill being an area of rural tranquillity, popular for wildfowling. The Mill was linked to the village by Mill Lane, which became a footpath continuing across the mill race to Portrack. Locally the mill was known as 'Moons Mill', though the mill was last worked by the Moon family c1903-1906. It then became a house for the hind employed at nearby Brook House Farm. The lower view shows two men standing next to Billingham Beck beyond the fork with the mill race with the mill visible behind them. Both the mill and the farm were demolished in the early 1930's due to the expansion of ICI.

BILLINGHAM MILL

BROOK HOUSE FARM

Brook House Farm, over two hundred acres in size, farmed by the Robinson family for over sixty years, was close to the mill & Mill Lane, which went to Billingham.

Billingham Mill & Brook House were lost to the coming of industry, swept away after hundreds of years...

TIBBERSLY FARM

John Forster and his wife Elizabeth, seen here c1908, had moved to Tibbersly Farm from Norton in the early 1890's. John was born in Shildon c1848, becoming an engineer before he moved to Tibbersly Farm. He was to remain there for almost thirty years before the farm was taken over by the Brunner Mond factory. Well known locally, John Forster was very active in Parish Council affairs in the years leading up to the First World War.

Both Billingham Grange and Tibbersly Farm were reached from the village via Chilton's Lane, though Tibbersly at just over 100 acres, was only half the size of Billingham Grange. Tibbersly farm land ran down to the river and some local people could still recall famous people coming to Stockton races which had been held there between 1839 and 1846.

John Forster was a well known local figure, a 'gentleman farmer' - the 1901 census shows that in addition to the Forster family four farm servants were also living and working here - more than most farms had at this time. This image shows the eighteenth century farmhouse in 1914 with its well-kept garden enjoyed by John and his two sons and daughter.

Billingham Grange and Tibbersly Farm both became part of the Synthonia Ammonia Nitrates factory although it was not until the 1920's that farmer John Forster had to leave his farm.

BILLINGHAM GRANGE

TIBBERSLY FARM

Billingham Grange Farm (extract above from a sketch in 1880) became part of the Synthonia Ammonia Nitrates site in 1920 as the farmhouse was the first company offices. The eighteenth century farmhouse was on Chilton's Lane (Marsh Lane until the 1860's). The farm was just over two hundred acres and farmed for many years by the Chilton family, a member of which owned Middlesbrough Farm when it was sold in 1828 to the consortium who built the town of Middlesbrough. The last person to farm Billingham Grange was John Emmet before the land was taken over by the Ministry of Munitions in 1917. The farmhouse, the centre of operations in the early years, remained familiar to workers as ICI First Aid centre. It was part of the factory for over 60 years before eventually being demolished in 1982.

CHILTON'S LANE

NEW NITRATE WORKS.

Enterprise Involves Closing of Public Road.

Stockton Rural District Council to close up Chilton's-lane, which leads from Billingham village to Haverton Hill.

IN 1920 CHILTON'S LANE WAS CLOSED & REPLACED BY NEW ROAD

Chilton's Lane connected Billingham Grange and Tibbersly Farm with Billingham village and Haveron Hill.
In 1916 a Nitrogen Products Committee was set up by the Ministry of Munitions to consider producing nitrates in the UK, reducing the dependence on nitrates from Chile. In 1917 when Brunner Mond were asked by the Ministry of Munitions to help locate a site for a nitrites factory they chose a site east of Billingham - based on availability of raw materials, a local labour force, basic transport infrastructure and most important, electricity from the Newcastle Electricity Company's new power station nearby. Construction began in 1918 only to be halted when the First World War ended later that year.

A SUITABLE SITE FOR A FACTORY?

BILLINGHAM GRANGE

MINISTRY OF MUNITIONS
BY DIRECTION OF THE DISPOSAL BOARD
(Lands, Buildings, and Factories Section.)
SALE BY PRIVATE TREATY

H.M. NITRATE FACTORY
BILLINGHAM
STOCKTON-ON-TEES

To be DISPOSED of by Private Treaty in ONE LOT, subject to certain conditions. The following is a brief description :—

Situation.— Billingham, on the N.E. bank of the Tees, opposite Middlesbrough, about two miles from Haverton Hill and Billingham. (N.E.R.) Goods and Passenger Stations.

Area of Land.— The total area of the site is about 266 acres held under D.O.R.A. The land has been developed with railways, roads, drains, sewers, &c., at the expense of the Ministry, and these improvements are included in the sale.

Construction. — Two permanent buildings only are complete, viz:—The workshops and stores erected of brick, concrete blocks with steel and corrugated iron roofs. A number of buildings are foundation high only, and the remainder consist of timber huts in weather-board.
The floor area of the building is:—

Old Farm Buildings (used as offices and stores) ...	8,607 ft. sup.
New Buildings (permanent) ...	39,920 ft. sup.
Temporary Wood Buildings ...	111,282 ft. sup.
	159,809 ft. sup.

There is on the ground a large quantity of plant for an Atmospheric Nitrogen Factory.

Lighting and Power.— Electric from Public Supply. An important agreement has been entered into for the supply of current.

Water.— Public Supply and from River Tees.

Sidings.— The Private Sidings laid down in the Factory are connected with a siding of private ownership which is a branch of the Billingham Beck Line and a small rental is payable for this privilege.

River.— River Tees is about a quarter of a mile.

A Statement of conditions and all other particulars may be obtained from Sir Howard Frank, K.C.B., &c., at Whitehall Court, London, S.W.1.

MINISTRY OF MUNITIONS OF WAR.
MUNITIONS INVENTIONS DEPARTMENT.

NITROGEN PRODUCTS COMMITTEE.

FINAL REPORT.

Presented to Parliament by Command of His Majesty.

PUBLISHED BY HIS MAJESTY'S STATIONERY OFFICE.
To be purchased through any Bookseller or directly from
H.M. STATIONERY OFFICE at the following addresses:
IMPERIAL HOUSE, KINGSWAY, LONDON, W.C.2, and 28, ABINGDON STREET, LONDON, S.W.1;
37, PETER STREET, MANCHESTER; 1, ST. ANDREW'S CRESCENT, CARDIFF;
23, FORTH STREET, EDINBURGH;
or from E. PONSONBY, LTD., 116, GRAFTON STREET, DUBLIN.
1919.
Price 4s. Net.

With construction by the Ministry of Munitions halted the factory was advertised for sale in The Times in November 1919. In April 1920 the same newspaper carried an article confirming the sale to Brunner Mond to be developed as a subsidiary company, Synthonia Ammonia and Nitrates Limited. The production of ammonia nitrates and other by-products would be their eventual aim but first a great deal of development was necessary. Billingham Grange farmhouse was used as offices by the Ministry of Munitions constructors - the insets are the Nitrogen Products Committee Report and the sale advert in The Times, both from 1919.

FROM FARMLAND TO ONE OF THE WORLD'S LARGEST CHEMICAL FACTORIES

The raw edge of industrialisation...

NEW INDUSTRY FOR TEES-SIDE.
£5,000,000 TO BE SPENT ON WORKS AT BILLINGHAM.

NITRATES FROM THE AIR.

A tough challenge...

The Grange, seen here in the summer of 1921, was the main office for seven years. In this view from the front garden, complete with fruit trees, an employee can be seen walking from the wooden huts which acted as administration offices, along to the farmhouse.

New housing for workers was crucial; this is the end of Mill Lane in July 1922 with farmland and the fencing around the new factory site visible. The chimneys of Middlesbrough and Brook House Farm can be seen in the distance.

An Executive Committee was established in November 1920 with George Pollitt as Chief Executive. A major force in the project, he urged that 'housing, laboratories, new roads, railway access... be hurried forward.' By early 1921 contracts for housing in Mill Lane and the Roscoe Rd/ Crescent Ave area were issued and work on the plant also started. However in May 1921 Brunner cut their financial support because of industrial unrest and trade depression. The building and project was kept alive on a minimum budget by Pollitt but with major changes, including the committee having to be content with plans for a temporary 'scratch plant'.

Amos Cowap famously called the site 'a good imitation of a prairie' and guests were invited along for rough shooting. D. L. White, shown here, was employed by the Ministry to look after the site whilst its future was being decided and he poses here close to the farm house whilst out shooting.

The meadows were a blaze of poppies and marguerites...

BIG LABORATORIES & 250 HOUSES TO BE BUILT AT BILLINGHAM.

Mr J. T. Gaunt presided over the monthly meeting of Stockton Rural District Council on Wednesday morning.

Plans were passed on behalf of Synthetic Nitrates Ltd. for three blocks of laboratories on the works at Billingham, for several streets, and for the erection of 78 semi-detached houses and 172 houses in blocks of four on the north side of Billingham

Research was crucial to development. Plans for three blocks of laboratories passed in March 1921 were operational in 1922. Dr Kenneth Warne, who began work in the new Research Buildings in January 1922 as a laboratory boy, recalled to me they were built about half a mile away from the Grange standing back from Chilton's Lane behind a large meadow, which during the summer became 'a blaze of poppies and marguerites.' The meadow, seen here, later became the site of the first main Synthonia Ammonia and Nitrates offices.

We ran it from here....

The men leading the development at Billingham were based here; George Pollitt was downstairs on the left, Amos Cowap on the right, whilst Herbert Humphrey and Philip Dickens were both upstairs. Chemist Roland Slade awaiting a laboratory had a small room at the back of the house. Philip Dickens had the Grange kitchen as his secretarial office!

The latest in high tech offices..

The factory site had been sold with some temporary wooden buildings. This multi view shows an example of these - the Traffic Department HQ in the winter and summer of 1922 along with some of the personnel who worked in them. Working here in this rural area must have brought its own challenges and it is a tribute to those employed in the early days that these were met in such a positive and enterprising way.

Construction days..

This remarkable aerial view c1924 looks across the Grange site towards Tibbersly Farm and Newport in the distance. With a little vision the area can be pictured as it would have previously been when it was fields down to the river. Chilton's Lane runs mid picture and across the field from Tibbersly Farm is the truncated eastern end of what would soon become New Road, with fields where Cassel Works would later be built.

Middlesbrough

Newport

R. Tees

Billingham Beck

site of Stockton Racecourse at Tibbersly Farm 1839-1846

Tibbersly Farm

Chilton's Lane

Billingham Grange

Haverton Hill

Billingham

Belasis Halt

This is the construction of the boiler plant which was completed in early 1923 and was then providing steam very soon afterwards.

Constructing the framework for the ammonia plant

The sulphate plant takes shape

Creating an industrial marvel

Railway lines were built to transport materials on-site, linking to the local LNER line. This autumn 1922 scene shows the construction of the Sulphate Silo in the foreground with the Sulphate Plant and catalysed gas holder visible. Steam rises from the crane, with men visible working on the steel framework of the silo.

A view to the Gas Plant from the water cooling pool. The site is in its early days of construction here with the Sulphate Plant visible but only half built

Men unloading from a rail wagon at the stores close to the railway line from Billingham to Haverton Hill.

Another view of the stores taken from the western perimeter of the site at this time, December 1922.

SYNTHETIC AMMONIA & NITRATES,
LIMITED.
BILLINGHAM,
STOCKTON-ON-TEES.

One of the early laboratories where Dr Ken Warne worked. The original Scratch Plant was renamed No 2 Unit but plans to be operational in January 1923 were halted by further labour problems, but Pollitt was undeterred and on Christmas Eve 1923 Roland Slade reported to the Executive Committee that the 'first traces of ammonia had appeared at 11.30pm on December 22nd.'

Where history was made...

1924: 'up and running'

With No 2 Unit operational there was no time to stand still. By January 1924 the sulphate plant was operational and by 1925 'systematic development of the site with plants 'capable of indefinite expansion' was being planned'. Within five years the factory would be acclaimed as one of the world's biggest with an output of two thousand tons of nitrate per day. No 3 Unit was operational by early 1928 and Nos. 4 and 5 Units were to follow. This view c1925 looks north to the Haverton Road with another phase of construction underway next to the boiler plant.

They came from far and wide to see ICI at work...

GEORGE BERNARD SHAW

ICI WORKERS

THE PRINCE OF WALES

KING GEORGE VI & QUEEN ELIZABETH

RAMSEY MCDONALD

EX-PREMIER'S DECLARATION

National Defence As Peace Influence

STRIKING SPEECH

New Industry "Like A Fairy Tale"

Oh what a difference.....from a village to a town

1926

Chilton's Lane 1926

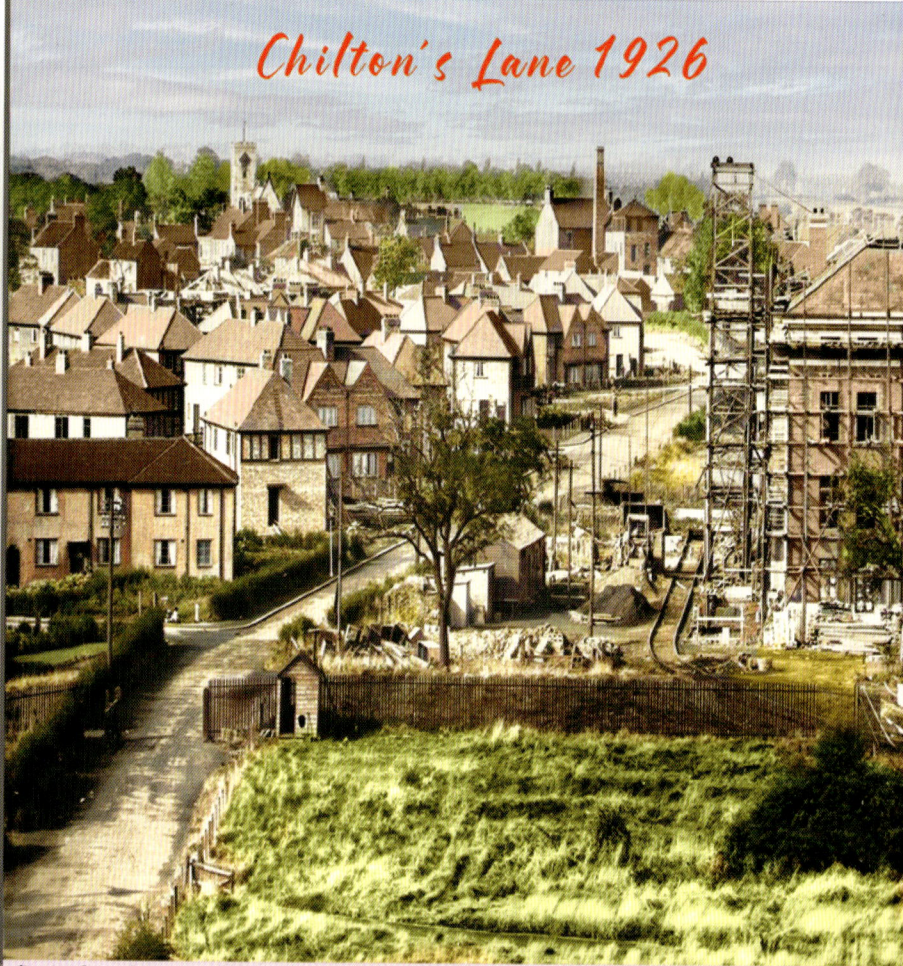

This is an excellent view from the church tower looking across Billingham in 1926. It clearly shows the ongoing construction of the factory, particularly the new main offices which are in the middle of the image. The old village green can also be seen with the open farmland and hedgerows behind it. The road to the left of Brewery House chimney is Belasis Lane. In the far distance Teesmouth can be seen.

BELOW: a similar view in the late 1930's. Most of the agricultural land has been swallowed up by the factory and the huge housing estates that were still being built. Even the green itself has changed. In the north east corner replacing old cottages the new Methodist Church is visible - Brewery House once the dominant building on East Row has been demolished.

1938

Several projects ancillary to the design and erection of plants were ongoing in the mid 1920's. A major scheme was the construction of the main office in Chilton's Lane on a piece of land in front of the Research Buildings. Work was begun by Lumsdens of Newcastle in 1926. The offices were fully occupied by May 1927. As well as offering improved office facilities for staff the new building in the opinion of many, reflected the status now achieved by the company. This view looks towards the village with the church and Brewery House visible. In the far distance the development at Billingham Station is just visible whilst new housing adjacent to Chilton's Lane is in the foreground

Developments at Billingham..

The Billingham Picture House costing £10,000 and accommodating seven hundred people was opened on 8 October 1928. The programme for the grand opening was the popular comedy 'The Kid Brother' with Harold Lloyd

Billingham underwent rapid development from 1920 - initially centred around Mill Lane with new retail units close to the new housing estates - even a cinema.

In May 1930 a new Co-operative stores building was opened on the site of Town End Farm - it was a prototype of today's shopping centres with eight different shops ranging from a butcher to a barber. It also had a Public Hall seating six hundred and fifty people and music bands such as the Venus Dance Band appeared regularly.

Newcastle Electric Supply Company who were building the North Tees Power Station on the north bank of the Tees, built their 'Garden City', a small estate of 73 houses on the top of Billingham Bank close to Old Road. This housed approximately three hundred people and was the start of a substantial post war development in the area.

Building over the station

Central Avenue

Billingham Station 1905

Malvern Avenue

Villagers regarded Billingham Station as a community boundary so when development spread north of the station it was the start of a whole new settlement which would lead to the modern town of today. The population of Billingham in 1931 was 17,972, an increase of 10,000 in ten years with the result that there was a massive expansion in the building of housing schemes initiated by both the council and private enterprise. Between 1925 and 1933, over 1,600 houses were built in the Central Avenue area and north of Billingham Station. Central Avenue itself was hailed as an example of excellent town planning.

Malvern Avenue was one of the roads built on the 'Cotswold Estate' as it was known. There was a lack of school places too so plans were passed in January 1935 for a new school north of the station. The Tudor-style Pentland School which opened June 1938 under its new headmistress Miss Sarah Roxby, was described as one of the most modern schools in the county, with nine classrooms for the 384 pupils who were to attend.

BILLINGHAM SCHEME

MINISTRY PASSES PLANS FOR NEW SCHOOL

URGENT SCHEME

PLANS for a large new school at Billingham have been passed by the Board of Education, the "Herald" is officially informed. It will be situated at the north-eastern side of Billingham Station, where rapid housing development is taking place.

BILLINGHAM HIGH GRANGE FARM

A lot of the land which the new housing and the post-war Town Centre would be built on belonged to Billingham High Grange Farm.

THE DIXONS PLOUGHING CHAMPIONS

Farming before the Second World War was labour intensive, hugely dependent on men and horses. A series of images record the working life of Britain's foremost ploughing family, the Dixon's who lived at Glebe Farm, Billingham. John Dixon started the tradition winning 78 championships. His son Tom followed this on by winning two hundred and sixty three ploughing championships before retiring in 1932. Tom's sons, John and Leslie (seen here), won many ploughing contests, becoming the third generation to become champions. The tower of Billingham Hall can be seen behind the fence and trees.

1924 & 1925

Winning Certificates

The ploughing team...

Skelton Agricultural Society.

Ploughing & Hedging Competitions
WEDNESDAY, 9th FEBRUARY, 1908.

Best Opening by any make of Plough.

SPECIAL

NORTH RIDING WAR AGRICULTURAL EXECUTIVE COMMITTEE.
Wensleydale District Technical Development Sub-Committee.

Ploughing and Hedge-Cutting Competitions
MANOR FARM, NEWTON-LE-WILLOWS, BEDALE.
SATURDAY, 18th DECEMBER, 1943.

FIRST PRIZE.

CLASS 6. _____

Awarded to _____

STOCKTON-ON-TEES
AGRICULTURAL & HORTICULTURAL
SOCIETY.
Championship Sheep Dog Trials.
SECOND PRIZE Cl. 6 (Sheaf Throwing)
WHIT-MONDAY,
MAY 29th, 1950.

Awarded to _____

A Celebration Across The Years Of The Dixon's Agricultural Expertise...

Until the 1920's Wolviston Road was a country lane with little development apart from three houses called Greenholme, Ashtree Cottage and Winford House. A small group of houses were built at the top of Sandy Lane in 1929 – these are shown here behind the farm workers. This field too would soon give way to a housing development as Billingham developed ever northwards. The workers include John Dixon sitting down.

A way of life lost in time...

Most of the land farmed by the Dixons was some distance from the village so the lunch basket with its jug of tea was used often! The workers (and the dog) are having lunch close to Billingham Hall, a horse standing watching them. It's remarkable how farm workers wore a tie and waistcoat to work in the fields. Tom Dixon's watch chain is visible and next to him sits his eldest son John.

Sandy Lane Billingham 1930's...

the Dixons - in the shadow of a scene from Thomas Hardy or Laurie Lee...

The inevitability of change...

Wolviston Grange Farm - the Swan Hotel is in the distance

Wolviston Grange Farm, Billingham

The Swan Hotel

The development north of Billingham Station continued to gather momentum in the 1930's as more housing was built. Grosvenor Road which was part of the Monkseaton Estate, built just before World War Two was typical of the new housing to be found in these areas. The nearby Swan Hotel public house which opened in the late 1930's after the transfer of the licence from the White Swan in Wolviston, was an example of developers not only building houses but also the associated facilities which were to be expected as part of a new 'modern' lifestyle in these new communities. The coming of war would bring a halt to development but it was coming and this would see change on an unprecedented scale in the history of Billingham - change would continue for over fifty years creating the world we know today.

Wolviston Road & entrance to The Grove c1938

Grosvenor Road c1938

Wolviston Road c1938

The Monkseaton Estate was west of the A19, which was much smaller than it is today. The coming of war meant that it would be autumn 1946 before building began again.

Wolviston 1904.. an unchanging world?

1900: WEDDING AT RED LION INN

The Village of Wolviston occupies a pleasant situation on the Stockton and Sunderland turnpike road, about five miles north-by-east from the former place. An annual festival is held here on the first Sunday after Lammas Day; and on the following day, a horticultural show takes place; races and shows of various kinds follow; and, in the evening, balls take place at the public-houses.

The Chapel, dedicated to St. Mary Magdalen, stands near the centre of the village, and consists of nave, chancel, and square tower: the latter was erected in 1830, at which time the chapel was enlarged. It now contains 320 sittings, and in consequence of a grant from the society for promoting the enlargement and building of churches and chapels, 130 of that number are free and unappropriated. An organ, purchased by subscription, was opened in 1854. The chapelry of Wolviston was severed from the mother church in 1577; from which year the register is dated. The emoluments of the living are derived from glebe lands belonging to it, and amount to about £180 per annum. The living, which is not in charge nor certificated, is in the patronage of the dean and chapter of Durham, and incumbency of the Rev. L. C. Clarke, B.A., who was appointed in 1832.

WHITE SWAN HOTEL

Public Notices
WOLVISTON RACES
SATURDAY FIRST
AT 2.15.

SPLENDID ENTRIES FOR ALL RACES.

DON'T BE PUT OFF—
COME TO WOLVISTON ON
SATURDAY
AND ENJOY A GOOD DAY'S RACING
IN THE COUNTRY.

GOOD BUS SERVICES FROM ALL PARTS.

H. LOFTHOUSE
(Late Edwin Lofthouse, F.G.I.)

HIGH STREET, WOLVISTON, - STOCKTON-ON-TEES.

High-Class Grocer & Provision Merchant, Draper, - Gentlemen's Outfitter, and Boot & Shoe Dealer.

Goods delivered Daily to all Parts of the District.

TRY OUR SPECIAL COFFEE. Roasted Daily on the premises.

We are Sole Agents in this District for—
CARTER'S TESTED FARM ROOT AND GARDEN SEEDS.

Best English
Meat only...
Reliable for Freshness and Quality all the year round.

A POSTCARD TO
J. B. BERRY,
Will ensure a Call for a Trial Order.
Pickled Ox Tongues, Brisket and Silversides always ready. Large supply of Beef, Mutton, Veal, Lamb and Pork from Monday Morning to Saturday night. Constant deliveries.

HIGH STREET ——— WOLVISTON.

Still Here!
S. PINKNEY,
Shoeing & General Smith,
Wolviston.

All kinds of Farmer's and Garden Tools, Cartridges Cycles and Accessories.

Best Quality Machine, Tractor & Motor Oils.

Wolviston High Street

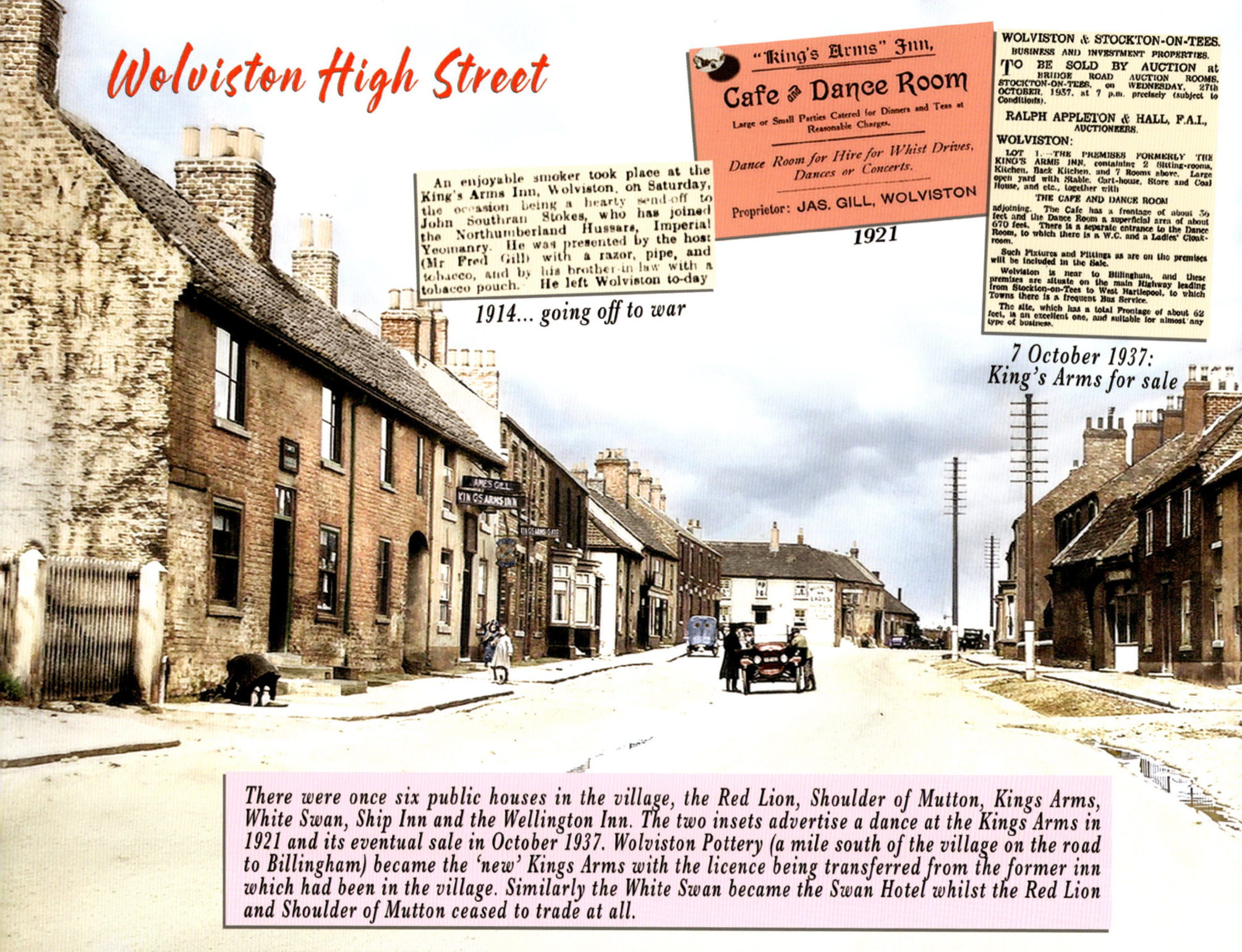

An enjoyable smoker took place at the King's Arms Inn, Wolviston, on Saturday, the occasion being a hearty send-off to John Southran Stokes, who has joined the Northumberland Hussars, Imperial Yeomanry. He was presented by the host (Mr Fred Gill) with a razor, pipe, and tobacco, and by his brother-in-law with a tobacco pouch. He left Wolviston to-day

1914... going off to war

7 October 1937: King's Arms for sale

There were once six public houses in the village, the Red Lion, Shoulder of Mutton, Kings Arms, White Swan, Ship Inn and the Wellington Inn. The two insets advertise a dance at the Kings Arms in 1921 and its eventual sale in October 1937. Wolviston Pottery (a mile south of the village on the road to Billingham) became the 'new' Kings Arms with the licence being transferred from the former inn which had been in the village. Similarly the White Swan became the Swan Hotel whilst the Red Lion and Shoulder of Mutton ceased to trade at all.

Last orders at the White Swan Hotel....

The 'new' Swan Hotel 1938

A LANDLORD AT EIGHTY

HE BELIEVES IN BEER

OLD TRADITIONS

Mine host of the White Swan, Wolviston, is one of the oldest landlords in the country.

In his 80th year, Mr John T. Skeen will view with regret the passing of the White Swan, the licence of which is to be transferred to a proposed new hotel to be erected north of Billingham railway station.

For 38 years he has been the licensee of the White Swan, where he has carried out the role of host in the grand old manner.

It is still the tradition in Wolviston for villagers to assemble in the cheery atmosphere of the hostelry of an evening and exchange a fund of anecdote and reminiscence with Mr Skeen over a foaming tankard of ale and a pipe of tobacco.

Mr J. T. Skeen.

Mr Skeen is a strong believer in the tonic value of the commodity he retails.

John Skeen was the final landlord amd host at Wolviston's White Swan Hotel, having been there since 1897. It was announced in February 1935 that the licence would be transferred to a proposed new hotel in the rapidly developing residential area north of Billingham railway station. The new premises would be the Swan Hotel on a site east of the Wolviston Road opposite the new Monkseaton Estate development. Skeen was very much a traditional landlord and the White Swan embodied his approach with its mock tudor exterior and traditional interior bars.

Wolviston & District Agricultural Society, 1921.

President:

R. B. WEBSTER, Esq., Wolviston Hall, Wolviston.

Vice-Presidents:

H. DOBSON, Esq., High Grange,
T. B. BAINBRIDGE, Esq., "Alncliff

Hon. Veterinary Surgeon: Capt. H. HICKS

Committee:

Chairman: H. DOBSON, Junr.,

Mr. J. H. Atkinson.   Mr. A. J
 ,, T. Bainbridge.   ,, A. Lo
 ,, C. Bainbridge.   ,, T. Ma
 ,, G. Dresser.   ,, J. Pay
 ,, A. Darling.   ,, W. Pal
                                ,, R. Ston
                                ,, J. Scots
                                ,, H. Scots
                                ,, Swin
                                    Staint

JUDGES.

Horses and Agriculture.
Mr. W. CLARK, Ferryhill.
Mr. T. PETCH, Great Ayton, York

Cattle and Sheep.
Mr. W. FELL, Stressholme.
Mr. J. RENNI Dowsfield.

Dairy Pr
Mrs. J. FARROW
Mrs. LOCKIE

Racin
Mr. A. SWINBANK, Breeon Hill.
Mr. J. T. WATSON, Greatham,

Starter
Mr. W. TIDYMAN

ars. E. W. FLET
on, Treasurer: J

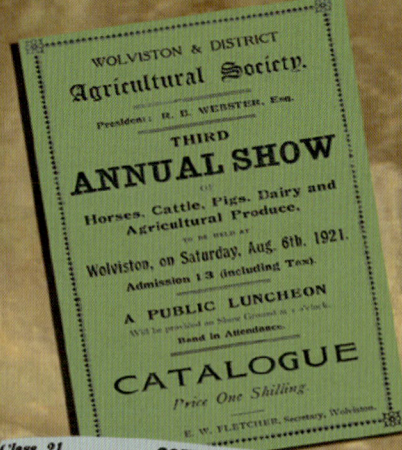

Hang the washing out on the Green

Durham Road

Village Life In Wolviston

Wolviston Mill

WOLVISTON
in the early 1900's

T. JOHNSON,

Joiner and Cartwright,

High Street,

WOLVISTON.

ESTIMATES GIVEN.

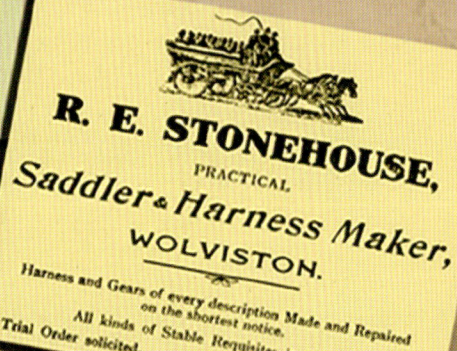

R. E. STONEHOUSE,

PRACTICAL

Saddler & Harness Maker,

WOLVISTON.

Harness and Gears of every description Made and Repaired
on the shortest notice.
All kinds of Stable Requisites in Stock.
A Trial Order solicited.

Satisfaction Guara

The Village Blacksmith

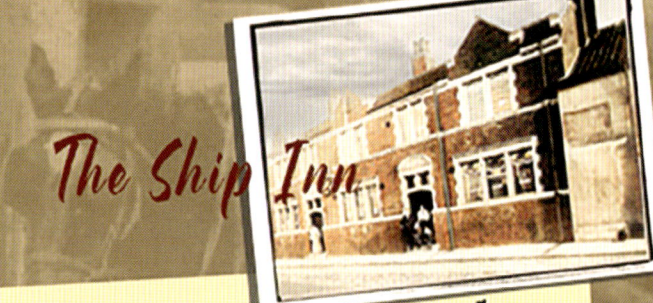

The Ship Inn

The Wellington Inn

Geo. Swales,

DURHAM ROAD,

WOLVISTON.

— FIRST-CLASS —

Horseshoer & General Blacksmith

*Work of every kind done on the
shortest notice.*

WOLVISTON ....THE VILLAGE SCHOOL

January 29th Monday
Wolviston Board School opened
Today by George Lishman, Certificated
1877

Wolviston Board School opened in January 1877, replacing
Wolviston Parochial School which closed in December 1876.
The Headteacher, George Lishman, was obliged to keep a
School Log Book; these extracts make interesting reading ....

LOG BOOK.

Aug: 7th 1883 — Wombwell's Menagerie is in front of the School this afternoon. The master having given two lessons to the very few children present, dismissed them.

Oct 20th 1896 — The Prince of Wales who is visiting Wynyard drives through Wolviston this morning to the Shooting. Many boys away bush beating in consequence

Oct 21 1903 — Today the children had an opportunity of seeing the King, who passed through Wolviston during play-time

Standing outside Wolviston School House c1905

Feb 11 1895 — Intense frost. Thermometer 4° below zero! School decimated. only 45 in Mixed dept. 12 Infants. Exam & Inspectors next month. We are working as hard as possible & do the best we can which is not much for the children are absent mostly

VICTORIAN 1897 CELEBRATION

June 18 1897 — Broke up for a week's Holiday, the occasion being the celebration of Her Majesty's Diamond Jubilee on Tuesday next, June 22nd 1897.

The School House c1907

Wolviston Green

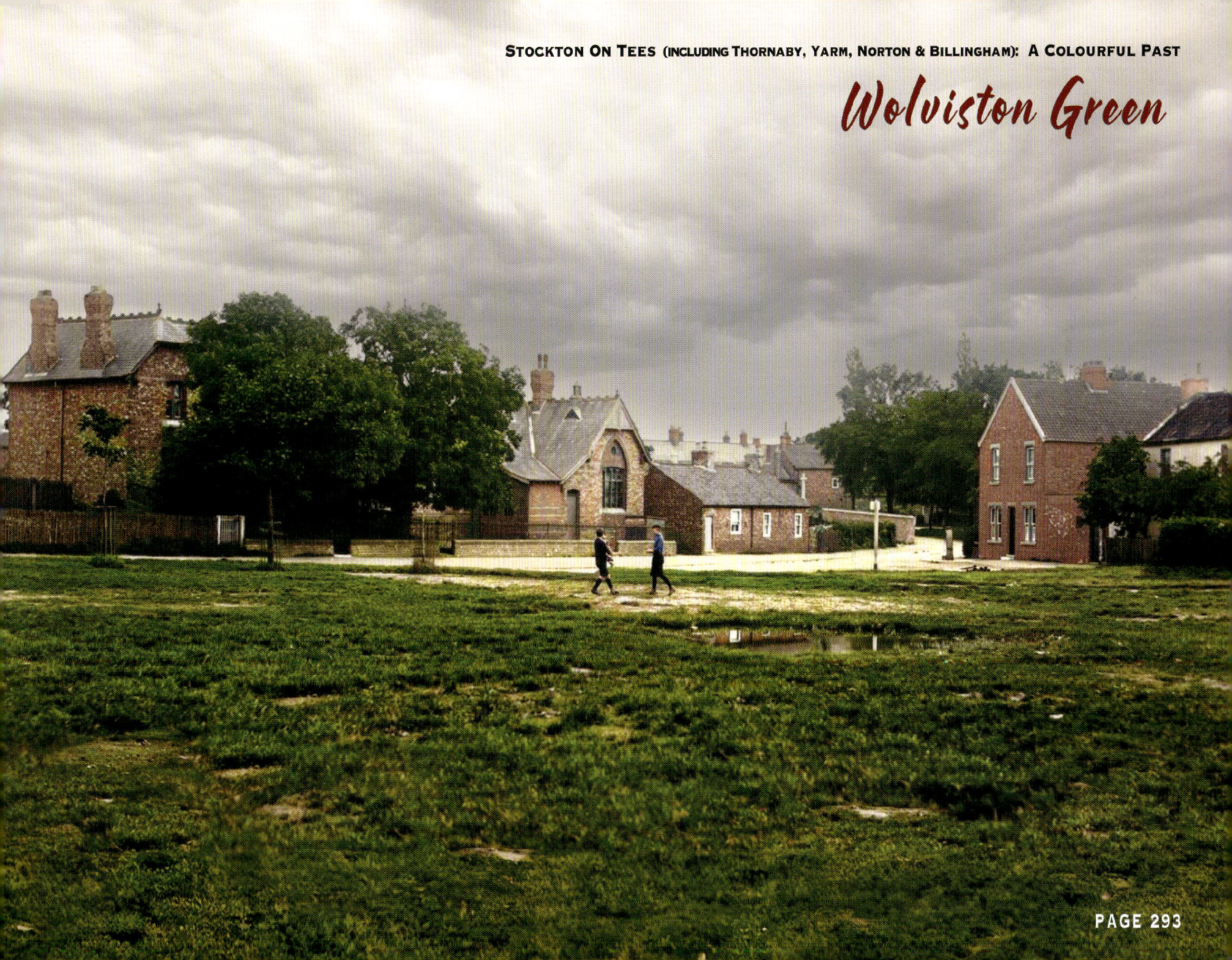

Wolviston Rectory

WOLVISTON PREPARATORY SCHOOL

PREPARATORY SCHOOL.—Boys 7-14 prepared for Public School. Fees £90; two September vacancies at £75 p.a. Small classes. Weekly reports.— Rev. M. Brack, Wolviston, Stockton-on-Tees.

The Reverend Martin Brack was the longest serving rector in the Stockton Deanery. Born in Stockton in 1866, he was educated in Stockton, London and then Cavendish College Cambridge. Brack became Rector at Wolviston in 1906 and having accepted the living he remained until his retirement in 1950. He also became Private Chaplain to Lord Londonderry at Wynyard Hall. He met a range of people in this role including future Prime Minister Harold Macmillan, Felix Brunner & Alfred Mond (who discussed the future ICI company at the Rectory) and he also met Joachim von Ribbentrop during his visit to Wynyard Hall in 1936. In the 1920's Brack who had married in 1911 and had five children, Christopher, Honor, Mary, John & Peter, opened a Preparatory School to supplement his income. The Revd. Brack, who was close to the Webster family at Wolviston Hall, remained active in village affairs after his retirement until his death in 1953 aged 87.

RECTORY DINING ROOM

RECTORY STUDY - WITH A SHERATON TABLE

ANOTHER VIEW OF WOLVISTON RECTORY 1925

Wolviston Church

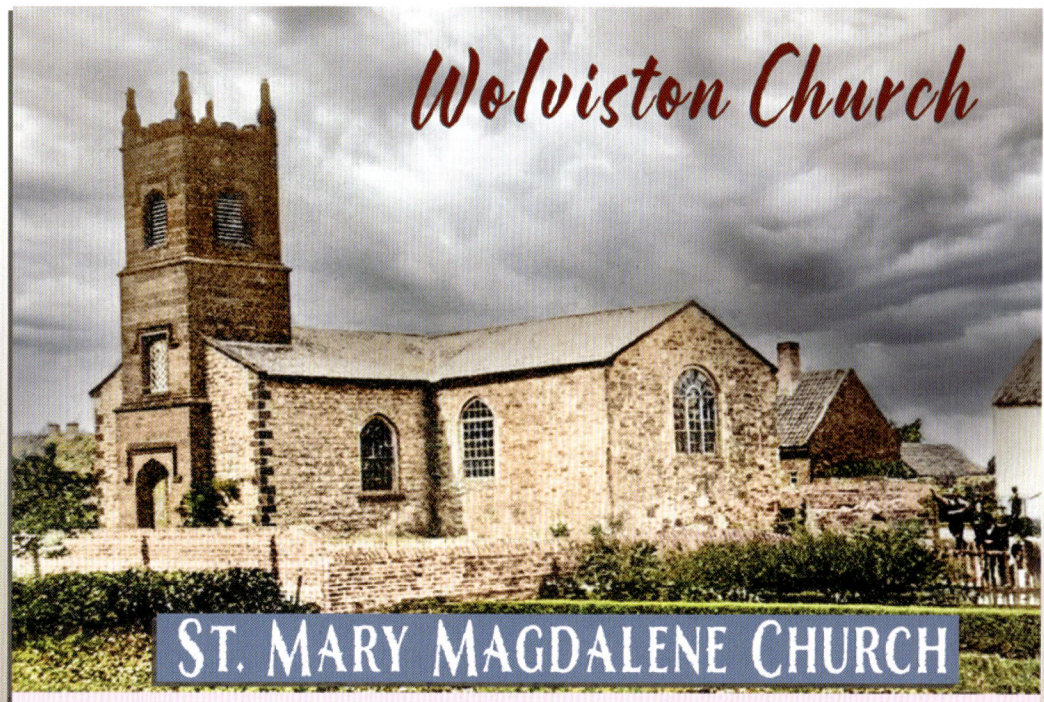

ST. MARY MAGDALENE CHURCH

St Mary Magdalene Church was used until 1876 when it was decided to move to a new church, moving from the site in North Kevyll Street to the site used today for the Church of St Peter. The former church was demolished in 1878. The new church was on a larger site and also had a burial ground.

HONOR BRACK IN THE RECTORY GARDEN 1928

THE CHURCH OF ST. PETER

Wolviston Hall

The gardens at Wolviston Hall

1930: Entrance to Wolviston Hall

Agnes Webster (Hall owner) & Rev Martin Brack & family

PRISONER OF WAR POST
KRIEGSGEFANGENENPOST

Written in German

Army Form No. W.3494 (Revised)

Russian Zone

ADRESSE

An Frau Ella Walzer

Empfangsort Dresden N 23

Strasse Reketzlaer Str. 58

Land Deutschland

Absender Gren. Wolfgang Walzer

Gefangenennummer 262456

Lager-Bezeichnung Wolviston Hall
No. 139 P.O.W. Camp, Billingham

Great Britain

Wolviston Hall: POW camp

1888 For sale

Telegrams WOLVISTON
STATION BILLINGHAM JUNC
TELEP. 29 WOLVISTON

Wolviston Hall
nr Stockton-on-Tees.

January 28/36.

Wolviston Hall

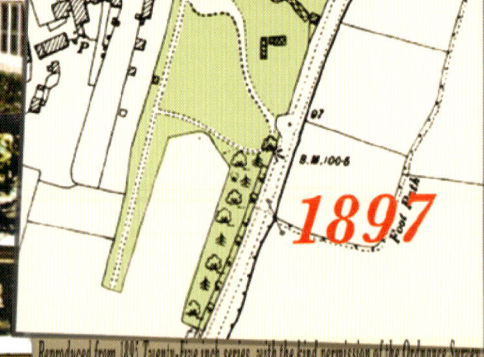

1897

Reproduced from 1895 Twenty-five inch series, with the kind permission of the Ordnance Survey.

The entrance hall and stairs

Wolviston Hall, built by the Appleby family c1826 was originally called Rose Villa. In 1865, Captain William J. Young bought it and lived there with his wife Mary until her death in 1876. After Captain Young's death in 1885, the Hall was sold in 1888 to shipowner Ernest J. Webster and his wife Agnes. They became popular community figures and lived there until 1943, when Agnes died. The Hall then became a POW camp for German and Italian soldiers. In 1945, the new owners, the Linton family, converted it into flats. In 1965 the Hall was demolished and housing was built on the site.

Cowpen Lane c1930

The Billingham Junction to Port Clarence railway crosses Cowpen Lane...
the recently built Synthetic Ammonia and Nitrates factory is in the distance

COWPEN BEWLEY

c1906

Map Reproduced from 1897 Ordnance Survey map 25 inch se
with kind permission of the Ordnance Survey

WINSTON CHURCHILL VISITS HAVERTON HILL 31 JULY 1940

During World War Two, Prime Minister Winston Churchill made a visit to Haverton Hill. A crowd quickly gathered to greet him as he stood on the ledge of his car and addressed the people. He went to Furness Shipyard as part of a tour which took in Hartlepool too.

31 JULY 1940 CHURCHILL VISITS FURNESS SHIPYARD HAVERTON HILL

Bibliography

BOOKS:

Bradshaw's Railway Guide 1910
Graves Rev. J., *History of Cleveland (Jollie 1808)*
Harrison J.W.H. *Eight Centuries of Milling in North East Yorkshire (North York Moors Nat. Pk 2001)*
Harrison, J.W.H., *A Survey of the Lower Tees Marshes (publisher unknown: 1916)*
Heavisides M. var.: *In and Around Picturesque Norton on Tees, History of First Public Railway, History of Stockton (Heavisides 1906, 1912, 1917)*
Hempstead C.A., *Cleveland Iron and Steel Industry (British Steel 1979)*
Horton M., *Story of Cleveland (Cleveland County Libraries 1979)*
McDougall C.A. *The Stockton and Darlington Railway 1821-1863 (Durham County Council 1975)*
McLaurin S. *Thornaby on Tees In The Past (Stockton LHG 2005)*
Menzies P. var.: *Around Stockton, Around Cleveland, Around Billingham, (History Press 2008, 2009, 2011), Billingham Vol 1 & Vol 2 (Countryside 1985 & 1986)*
Nicholas K. *The Social Effects of Unemployment on Teesside 1919-1930 (Manchester University Press 1986)*
Ord J.W., *History and Antiquities of Cleveland (London 1846, reprinted Shotton 1982)*
Owens F.G. *Winds of Change (Stockton B.C.)*
Parkes V.E. *Billingham - The First Ten Years (ICI 1957)*
Race M. *Yarm of Yesteryear (Strickland & Holt 1981)*
Richmond T. *Local Records of Stockton & Neighbourhood (Robinson 1868)*
Tomlin D.M., *Past Industry along the Tees (A.A. Sotheran, 1980)*
Wall J. *First in the World - The Stockton and Darlington Railway (Sutton Pub. 2001)*
Waterson E., and Meadows P., *Lost Houses of Yorkshire and the North Riding (Raines 1990)*
Wilkinson L., *The Kipper Patrol (Pneuma Springs) 2009*
Woodhouse R., *Stockton A Pictorial History (Phillimore 1989)*

OTHER SOURCES:

Ancestry website, ancestry.co.uk, Births, Marriages and Deaths Index, Census Records 1841-1901
Beamish Museum - various images 1917-1925
Billingham Express, various eds. 1952-1966, available on microfiche at Middlesbrough Reference Library
Billingham Press, various eds. 1946-1952, available on microfiche at Middlesbrough Reference Library
British Newspaper Library Archive: Newcastle Courant & Stockton Herald (Public Domain), & permission to use a source from the York Herald, November 1838
Cleveland and Teesside Local History Society: History of Stockton in maps (Middlesbrough 1982)
Evening Gazette Teesside, various eds.1870-1968, on microfiche at Middlesbrough Reference Library
Evening Gazette Teesside, various eds.1867-1990 Evening Gazette,
Historic England Aerial Photograph Billingham May 1930, used under licence
Jeffrys Thomas, Map of North Yorkshire 1771
Lantern magazine April 1895 Middlesbrough Reference Library
Northern Review various editions 1886-1894 Middlesbrough Reference Library
Ordnance Survey, 6 inch & 25 inch series, 1857, 1893, 1897, 1916)
Sallabank George, sources relating to Eaglescliffe Golf Club
Smallwood Album US742, held at Teesside Archives
Stockton and Teesside Herald, various eds. 1857-1940, Evening Gazette & microfiche at Middlesbrough Reference Library
The Times, Online Archive 1785-1985, (Times Newspapers, 2008)
The Diaries of Ralph Jackson 1749-1790 - consulted 1982-1992 at Middlesbrough Reference Library.
Various oral interviews conducted 1978 and 2008, typed up as statements of individual memories
Various source materials made available at Middlesbrough Reference Library, Teesside Archives, Dorman Museum & Stockton Library & Museum Services
Various Trade Directories for County Durham and North Yorkshire, 1828 to 1939